T0319715

Institutionalist Method and Value

For Dale

Institutionalist Method and Value

Essays in Honour of Paul Dale Bush

Volume 1

Edited by

Sasan Fayazmanesh
California State University, Fresno, USA

and

Marc R. Tool
California State University, Sacramento, USA

Edward Elgar
Cheltenham, UK • Northampton, MA, USA

© S. Fayazmanesh and M. Tool 1998

All rights reserved. No part of this publication may be reproduced, stored in a
retrieval system or transmitted in any form or by any means, electronic,
mechanical or photocopying, recording, or otherwise without the prior
permission of the publisher.

Published by
Edward Elgar Publishing Limited
8 Lansdown Place
Cheltenham
Glos GL50 2HU
UK

Edward Elgar Publishing, Inc.
6 Market Street
Northampton
Massachusetts 01060
USA

A catalogue record for this book
is available from the British Library

Library of Congress Cataloguing in Publication Data

Institutionalist method and value: essays in honour of Paul Dale Bush
    / edited by Sasan Fayazmanesh, Marc R. Tool.
    ISBN 1 85898 561 7 (v. 1) — ISBN 1 85898 562 5 (v. 2)
    1. Institutional economics.   I. Bush, Paul Dale.
    II. Fayazmanesh, Sasan, 1950–   .   III. Tool, Marc R.
    H899.5.I583   1998
    330—DC21   97–46640
                                                             CIP

ISBN 1 85898 561 7

Printed and bound in Great Britain by
Biddles Ltd, Guildford and King's Lynn

Contents

List of Contributors

Dopfer, Kurt, *Department of Economics, University of St. Gallen, CH-9010, St. Gallen, Switzerland*

Fayazmanesh, Sasan, *Department of Economics, California State University, Fresno, CA 93740, USA*

Hodgson, Geoffrey M., *Lecturer in Economics, Judge Institute of Management Studies, University of Cambridge, Cambridge, CB2 1AG, United Kingdom*

Jennings, Ann L., *Department of Economics and Business, Lafayette College, Easton, PA 18042, USA*

Kilpinen, Erkki, *Department of Philosophy, University of Helsinki, Helsinki, Finland*

Miller, Edythe S., *Professor Emeritus of Economics, 580 Front Range Road, Littleton, CO 80120, USA*

O'Hara, Phillip Anthony, *Department of Economics, Curtin University of Technology, Perth, 6001, Australia*

Samuels, Warren J., *Department of Economics, Michigan State University, East Lansing, MI 48823, USA*

Tool, Marc R., *Professor Emeritus of Economics, 5708 McAdoo Avenue, Sacramento, CA 95819, USA*

Waller, William, *Department of Economics, Hobart & William Smith Colleges, Geneva, NY 14456, USA*

Preface

In the spring of 1995, Professor Paul Dale Bush informed the Department of Economics at California State University, Fresno, that he would retire from active teaching in June 1996. The news did not come as a surprise; after all, Dale Bush had been teaching in the department for over thirty years. There was, however, a general sense of disappointment. Bush's contributions to the department and to the university at large were multifaceted and irreplaceable. He was an outstanding scholar who had published many articles, notes and book reviews. His work, especially in the field of institutional economics, was widely cited in the United States and around the world. He participated in numerous professional conferences, and served on the editorial board of the *Journal of Economic Issues*. He also served as the President of the Association for Institutionalist Thought (AFIT) and the Association for Evolutionary Economics (AFEE). Such scholarship did not go without notice in our department. Even those of us who did not consider ourselves institutional economists, and therefore did not fully comprehend Bush's theoretical work, could not but admire his active scholarship.

When it came to teaching, Bush was exemplary. Over the years, he taught just about every course listed in the university catalogue under 'Economics'. His encyclopaedic knowledge of economic theory and policy, history of economic thought, methodology, philosophy of science, general history, and even such subjects as the history of art and music, would impress even the most unimpressionable minds in his classrooms. Bush's intellect was the magnet that attracted some of the finest students on our campus to the Department of Economics. Many of these students, in turn, have become scholars in their own rights.

Our general sense of loss following Bush's decision to retire, however, was not due solely to foregoing the company of an active scholar and an exemplary teacher. Many of us were also concerned about losing our everyday contact with a colleague who possessed those characteristics that create and sustain a collegial and supportive environment. He is an individual who, in addition to his fine scholarly contributions, was always available as an adviser offering reasoned counsel in times of need. He is a selfless individual willing to devote much time and effort to helping others. Above all, he is a person who sets and observes high ethical standards for himself and his institution. He urges colleagues and students to share and defend that sense of scholarly commitment and integrity that is the *sine qua non* of meaningful collegial life for both faculty and students.

In appreciation of Bush's contributions as a scholar, a teacher, and a selfless colleague and friend, the Department of Economics decided to honour him with a festschrift volume. For this, we asked the assistance of Professor Emeritus Marc R. Tool, California State University, Sacramento, a noted institutional economist and one of Bush's close friends and colleagues. Tool generously agreed to participate in the project; he accepted the role of co-editor for this two volume work.

In the fall of 1995, a letter of invitation was sent to many of Bush's colleagues, friends and former students, requesting contributions of essays toward a festschrift volume. The response was immediate and overwhelming. We received far more proposals than we expected; indeed, far more than we had space to accommodate in a single volume. The problem of selecting from so many fine proposals was in part resolved when Edward Elgar kindly proposed publishing the festschrift in two volumes. The result is the present work.

We would like to acknowledge and thank a number of individuals who made this work possible. First, we are grateful to all individuals who submitted abstracts and essays; we extend our sincere regrets to those whose work could not be included.

We also thank Provost and Vice President for Academic Affairs Alexander Gonzalez and Dr Peter Klassen, the former Dean of the School of Social Sciences at California State University, Fresno, for their generous support of this project.

As the co-editor of this project, I would personally like to acknowledge the support and the encouragement of the members of the Department of Economics, particularly Professors James Cypher, Donald Leet and Linda Shaffer, and Ms Shirley Pennell. Above all, however, I am indebted to my co-editor, Marc R. Tool. Without his help, his relentless devotion to the project, his keen insight and expertise, his efficiency, his calmness and flexibility, none of this would have been possible.

Sasan Fayazmanesh
Fresno, California, USA

June 1997

1. The Contribution of Paul Dale Bush to Academic Freedom and Institutional Economics[1]

Phillip Anthony O'Hara and Marc R. Tool

INTRODUCTION

Paul Dale Bush, Professor of Economics, California State University, Fresno, has been for over three decades an imaginative and important contributor to the neoinstitutionalist economic literature in the United States. He works in the philosophic tradition of American pragmatic instrumentalism and the analytical tradition of Veblenian institutional economics. He has clarified the normative theoretical content of neoinstitutional economics and creatively extended its explanatory reach and relevance in contemporary debates and policy applications. He has, as well, been an articulate spokesman, an activist leader and an untiring participant in the development and maintenance of open inquiry and collegial governance in higher education in California. These volumes are a tribute to this influential career.

This paper seeks to examine in some detail Bush's major contributions to academic life and to neoinstitutional economics. The first section, after some introductory biographical commentary, considers his courageous support of academic freedom and governance. The second section investigates his contributions to neoinstitutional economics, especially in the area of social value theory. The third section explores and extends the principles of institutional change. The fourth section examines his contributions to systematizing the logical structure of neoinstitutional economics. The concluding section suggests some areas of research that can be undertaken in the future on the basis of these seminal contributions.

Paul Dale Bush ('Dale' to his friends and colleagues) was born on 26 February 1933 in St Louis, Missouri into a middle-class family. His father is Paul Elbert Bush, a retired federal official; his mother is Juanita LaDonne Bush. He has a younger sister, LaDonne, an attorney in Denver. He married Barbara Bush (nee Hill), a social science major and teacher, in 1955. They have a daughter, Katherine. Until his teen years, the Bush family moved often as his father's assignments dictated. From 1947 on he lived and was educated in Denver. The previous decade had required continuing and sometimes dramatic personal adjustments to new environs, social pressures and political uncertainties. Maturation was sometimes painful and sometimes hilarious, as it is for most perceptive and sensitive people.

Bush completed his BA in Social Science at the University of Denver in 1954. At DU he was taught by an extraordinarily able group of scholars, including J. Fagg Foster (economics), John Livingston (political science) and Francis Myers (philosophy). He continued with a Master's Degree programme in economics at DU, writing a thesis on 'The Concept of Balance in the Theory of Collective Bargaining' (1957) under Foster, himself a major contributor to neoinstitutional thought. The Foster influence was dramatic and continuing. Bush completed his PhD in Economics at Claremont Graduate School under the supervision of Paul Sultan. His doctoral thesis, entitled 'Marginalism and Institutionalism in Labour Economics' (1964), examined the methodology of marginalism in the light of the institutionalist critique. At the time, he thought that the two traditions might be fruitfully integrated in labour theory; he shortly abandoned that view as illusory.

Three years before he completed his PhD (1961), he was appointed as an Assistant Professor at Fresno State College that later became California State University, Fresno. He reached the rank of Full Professor in 1972 at age 39. His primary teaching areas were in institutional economics, ecological economics, microeconomics and macroeconomics. Happily his own Economics Department was generally supportive; it lived up to its billing to offer 'a well developed and balanced curriculum encompassing the major schools of modern economic thought, including neoclassical, Marxian, and American institutionalist schools'. It perceived its role as to foster study into how a society is, or can be, organized 'to produce the goods and services that sustain and enhance the life process of the community' (California State University, Fresno 1995, p. 243).

During the 1960s, an era of turbulence on many campuses, Bush actively represented academic personnel and students as a faculty counsel on issues of academic freedom and political rights. In the mid-1960s Bush joined other institutionalists in the new Association for Evolutionary Economics (AFEE) to challenge the hegemony of neoclassical economics and contribute to the further development of an alternative paradigm in economics. In 1969 he was elected Statewide President of the Association of California State College Professors (ACSCP) and fought for the establishment of collective bargaining rights for the faculties of the California State University system. In this role, he sought to promote academic freedom, due process and collegial governance.

Bush began his post-doctoral scholarly writing in the late 1960s with a paper on 'The Normative Implications of Positive Analysis' that was presented at meetings of the Western Economic Association (Bush 1968a). The paper develops a theme common to all of Bush's subsequent academic work: social values and philosophical preconceptions are inherent in all of economic inquiry and discourse. In the late 1970s and early 1980s, Bush extended these insights in scholarly papers by exploring and augmenting Foster's principles of institutional adjustment. Bush's contributions include, for example, the normative and analytical distinction between progressive and regressive institutional change, the creation (with Louis Junker) of the 'principle of ceremonial encapsulation' (Bush 1986), and the axiomatic formulation of the logical structure of the Veblen–Ayres–Foster paradigm (Bush 1983) in which he derived, among other concepts, the 'index of ceremonial dominance'. With all, Bush formalizes and facilitates the application of the institutionalist dichotomy between instrumental and ceremonial judgments and conduct to enhance explanations of processes and consequences of institutional change. He synthesized these ideas in a paper entitled 'The Theory of Institutional Change', which appeared in 1987. Most of his scholarly writing in the 1990s has been addressed to further clarification and refinement of the pragmatic instrumentalist model of inquiry. These and other contributions are considered more fully below.

In the 1980s, after many years of active participation in and contributions to the Association for Institutional Thought (AFIT) and the AFEE, he was elected President of each, AFIT in 1982 and AFEE in 1990. He served as Editor of the *Review of Institutional Thought* (1981–86) and joined the Editorial Board of the *Journal of Economic Issues* (1982–85). During the 1990s he helped to establish linkages with the European Association for Evolutionary Political Economy and extended his contacts with scholars in other countries. His lecture tour in Europe in 1991 helped to expand transnational interest in institutional and evolutionary approaches to economic inquiry. An exploration of the substance of these contributions follows.

ACADEMIC FREEDOM AND GOVERNANCE

Under the influence of the enlightened American pragmatic and neoinstitutionalist traditions, and of his teacher, J. Fagg Foster, Bush championed the cause of academic freedom. In the 1950s, and into the 1960s in the United States, the 'fear of ideas and the suppression of free speech had become a shameful standard of normalcy in the community at large' (Bush 1992, p. 1). In a way similar to that of Foster, who sought to defend intellectual freedom against McCarthyism, Bush vigorously and systematically defended colleagues against the narrow views of certain academic bureaucrats when they denied academic freedom and due process to academics.

Bush represented professors and students in grievance and disciplinary action hearings at Fresno State between 1968 and 1977. He acted as faculty counsel for many who were dismissed from their academic posts because the

President and/or the administration of the college objected to their academic views, ethnicity or religion. For instance, in 1968 he represented Professor Robert Mezey, a famous poet, author of *The Lovemaker* and winner of the Lamont Poetry Award. Mezey proposed the decriminalization of marijuana, an end to the war in Vietnam, and an end to racist practices on campus. His public comments on marijuana were used to justify the non-renewal of his employment contract on the grounds of 'unprofessional conduct'; as one administrator put it, 'professors should not question laws publicly'. Bush argued that this action violated academic freedom, freedom of speech, and due process, and that a university administration that does so reduces the quality of education through demanding conformity rather than academic excellence (Bush 1968b). In this case, access to a great poet was denied to students at Fresno.

Bush was asked to provide counsel to many others, including Dr Joseph Toney, an African American Professor of Chemistry, who actively supported racial equality, and to Marvin X, an African American instructor in Black Studies, who was discriminated against for being a Muslim (Seib 1979, pp. 44–7). In his official capacity as President of ACSCP, the major state-wide faculty organization, he helped defend faculty throughout the (then) twenty campuses of the California State University System against myriad attacks on academic freedom and due process, and participated in the formulation of legal theories upon which law suits could be filed on their behalf. Bush also proposed a plan of action for a viable system of collective bargaining in the California State College System (Bush 1969a), and another to assist severely handicapped students (Bush 1973a). In all these cases, he worked for a more democratic and collegial system of academic governance for the California State College System. He sought to change the system so that it would nurture the life of the mind, surmount serious obstacles to scholarly inquiry, and promote the growth of knowledge – social, physical and artistic.

Academic freedom has been defined as:

> the liberty to develop knowledge and communicate it within an institution of learning without interference from administrative officials, political and ecclesiastical authorities, or any others . . . The need for such freedom stems from the traditional functions of university: to increase, preserve, evaluate, and impart knowledge. Freedom to pursue truth wherever the evidence may lead is necessary if the teacher–scholar is to make new discoveries and offer new judgments. (Raichle 1994, p. 55)

Bush understood how critical academic freedom is to the intellectual growth and health of the community generally. In attempting to preserve academic freedom, he and his like-minded colleagues in the state universities were up against a conservative Board of Trustees that denied due process, democratic decision-making, and scholarly openness. As President of ACSCP, Bush argued the case that the state college system was in a serious crisis (Bush

1969b), and that progressive institutional change was necessary to promote free inquiry and association within these universities.

Bush became a member of the Academic Freedom Committee of the United Professors of California (a successor organization to the ACSCP) in the early 1970s. In that and related capacities, he wrote position papers exploring the future of academic governance and the costs of denying academic freedom. His pragmatic perspective included the proposition that academic tenure is critical to academic freedom and, in accordance with the first Amendment of the Constitution (United Sates Supreme Court 1967), that academic freedom is a non-negotiable right. He argued that technical details of the institutional practices designed to ensure tenure rights may need to be included in collective bargaining procedures, even if the rights themselves are in principle non-negotiable (Bush 1973b). To underscore the economic waste attendant to the academic tyrannies perpetrated on the faculties by administrators, he calculated that the purely monetary costs to the state of denying academic freedom had been very high – $33,000 (approximately $86,000 in 1997 dollars) per action (Bush 1979a). This amounted to a substantial sum of taxpayer dollars, given the numerous academic freedom and due process cases generated during this period.

Bush believes that academic freedom requires democratic *academic* governance in universities. Unilateral governance by business leaders and/or individuals with unlimited powers, impairs intellectual freedom, as Veblen (1918) observed much earlier in his *The Higher Learning in America*. Academic freedom implies and requires the academic responsibility of scholarly integrity. Such integrity precludes plagiarism and the conscious falsification of research data and conclusions. If this concept of responsibility is broadened by university administrators to preclude professorial challenges to the arbitrary and capricious administration of the universities by professional administrators, or to intellectually grounded criticisms of public laws and values, academic freedom is impaired and the quality and integrity of the learning process are compromised.

SOCIAL VALUE THEORY

Normative Inquiry

Academic freedom is inextricably linked to the expression of values and normative perspectives, a subject that has permeated all of Bush's writings, and that of neoinstitutionalists generally. He rejects the neoclassical proposition that economics should be value free and hence presumably 'positive', as against value permeated and 'normative'. Scientific inquiry requires language structures and analytical tenets that are value laden. Scholars cannot avoid the use of normative criteria in choosing among alternatives. Facts do not exist autonomously from values. Selection, placement and use of facts, as purposive acts, require recourse to criteria of choice. Many scholars, especially . economists, have deeply ingrained ideologies that impinge on their view of the world and their policy recommendations. For example, the philosophy of methodological individualism, underlying neoclassical economics, assumes that individuals, as utility maximizers, do and should engage in choices and action. But neoclassicists do not analytically incorporate social and cultural influences as determinants of individuals' rational choices. This noncausal, noncultural view of rationality conditions the methodological individualist's theories and policy proposals (Bush 1981a, 1981b). Assuming that economic processes are reducible to the atomistic actions of individuals leads the neoclassical economist to advocate 'free market' policies and to ignore or underplay the role of institutional conditioning and habit (for example, regarding social class, gender and race).

Methodological collectivists, such as neoinstitutionalists, come to quite different conclusions on the basis of their own assumptions and perspectives (Bush 1968a). Bush's belief in methodological collectivism is shared with many other heterodox economists, including feminists, neo-Marxists, social economists and most Post Keynesians. Bush says ' "methodological collectivism" or "holism" . . . is the hypothesis that individual valuations are conditioned by cultural processes and that [an] understanding of these processes requires a direct inspection of the social valuations involved' (1981–82, p. 15).

Bush believes that economics is an inherently controversial field of study because of the different valuations, assumptions, paradigms, concepts and languages of the various schools of thought. Along with many other political economists, Bush rejects the dualistic view of economic methodology, whether it be based on the dualisms of fact–value, theory–practice, means–ends, science–ethics and/or objective–subjective. In his evolutionary view of economic institutions, one necessarily sees the system as a whole in dynamic motion through historical time, and recognizes that it is important to observe and appraise values and behaviours as part of the process of socioeconomic adjustment and change. Consideration of preconceptions of economic agents and economists is an indispensable part of institutional inquiry.

Bush subscribes, as noted, to the pragmatic instrumentalist movement in philosophy that originated with Charles Sanders Peirce, William James and John Dewey. Important to this perspective is a critique of 'eternal verities', the notion that there are first principles, essences or theoretical foundations which are anterior and impervious to inquiry, history and change. Neoinstitutionalists do not rely on antecedent foundationalist principles, because they contend that all elements of scientific inquiry must be subject to ongoing reexamination, change and reformulation. Pragmatic institutionalists eschew the notion that there are objective laws to be discovered and applied, and which are independent of scholarly inquiry. Instead, they believe that the scholar is part of the very culture he or she is scrutinizing and cannot be seen as an autonomous agent abstracted from the field of inquiry. They recognize the importance of indeterminacy, context and the processual character of inquiry in a holistic study of institutions (Bush 1991, 1993).

Instrumental Value Theory

One of the major aspects of Veblen–Dewey-based institutionalism, to which Bush and other neoinstitutionalists have contributed, is the normative theory of the instrumental and ceremonial functions of institutions (ICFI). The basic construct explains that all institutions, as prescribed patterns that correlate behaviour, encompass two different kinds of warrant for conduct observed: one is ceremonial or invidious warrant; the other is instrumental warrant. The former is rooted in noncausal affirmations of power and status; the latter is rooted in causal comprehension of events and consequences.

As Bush explains:

> [P]atterns of behaviour correlated by ceremonial values are observed to be those social practices that manifest the use of power and coercion in the conduct of human affairs: social practices that require invidious distinctions and status relationships to justify their existence. On the other hand, patterns of behaviour correlated by instrumental values are manifest in those problem-solving activities upon which the life processes of the community depend. They are subject to change and modification as the instrumental character of the problems change . . . or as the scientific processes produce better technology with which to address these problems. (1983, p. 37)

The holistic version of ICFI incorporates a processual view of political economy that encourages or appraises economies on the basis of the *degree* to which the following three attributes are present: (1) integrated community, (2) instrumentally warranted knowledge, and (3) participatory democracy throughout the socioeconomy (O'Hara 1995). Integrated community is the basis of economic progress in the sense that cooperative human relations between and among members of a society are the pivotal element of development. Cooperation does not mean the absence of dissent, or hegemonic agreement on the essentials of life and livelihood. Rather, this form of cooperation requires reflective and intellectual openness, a relative decline in individualism as an ideology, and a decline in discrimination based on class, gender and ethnicity. This is the highest aim of economic progress designed to reduce exploitation, oppression and social divisions.

Instrumentally warranted knowledge is the second element of instrumental value theory. This relates to the acquisition of the most instrumentally dominant form of evidentially warranted skills, information, knowledge and communication networks available in society that enable people to form durable and effectual institutional relationships of production, distribution, exchange and reproduction. Central to the generation of warranted knowledge is a public commitment (facility and funding) to the provision of continuing and noninvidious access to educational experience that encourages and equips each person to develop the capacity to think critically and coherently over the whole range of evidential experience. Thinking critically and coherently about the social order means generating and mastering instrumental capabilities for cognitive perception, causal comprehension, creative insights, analytical capabilities, coherent communication and participatory involvement. It requires as well the erosion of ceremonial and invidious emulation, conspicuous consumption, socialized pressures of nationalism and chauvinism, and the political dominance of the pecuniary culture. A community's generation and expansion of instrumentally warranted scientific knowledge, social and physical, is dependent upon the developmental and reflective intellects of its members.

The third element of instrumental value theory is participatory democracy. Self-rule is inextricably linked to community because it is the expression of community and involvement of individuals in decision-making in the home, workplace and polity. It is closely linked to warranted knowledge because democracy itself promotes the growth of knowledge, enhancement of social skills, communal cooperation and participatory decision-making. Research has shown, for example in the Mondragon Group of Companies in Spain, that worker control and ownership can provide an incentive for higher productivity and product quality (Booth, forthcoming). This occurs because group cooperation can enhance the quality of life and capabilities of individuals in an integrated system of production, distribution, exchange and reproduction. A similar case is made by Bush for democratic governance in universities (Bush 1969b, 1970). Hickerson explains that freedom involves the active involvement of people in organizing social practices, modifying the rules and changing customs. But this 'involvement [needs to] be founded on reliable knowledge' (1984, p. 437); without a critical scrutiny and understanding of the prevailing institutional fabric, participation may be superficial and ineffectual.

In this holistic version of instrumentalism, then, the dominant theme is individuals collectively creating and modifying the rules, laws, customs and accepted practices using warranted knowledge of social and political realities in the pursuit of a relatively noninvidious set of objectives. Only a system dominated by internalized collective freedom, where the population understands the close connections of the socioeconomy with biospheric structures and processes, and where they are included in the decision-making relations, can the continuity of the life process as a whole be sustained and enhanced in the long term (Junker 1982).

THEORY OF INSTITUTIONAL CHANGE

Bush has made important theoretical contributions to and applications of instrumental social value theory in the analysis of institutional change. Following are the primary contributions considered here: (1) He extends the theory of institutional adjustment by identifying and exploring two 'analytically distinct' phases; ceremonial encapsulation as phase one; 'progressive' institutional change as phase two (Bush 1986, pp. 30–37). (2) He enhances two of Foster's three principles of institutional adjustment – recognized interdependence and minimal dislocation (pp. 37–41). (3) He provides an axiomatic formulation of the logical structure of the theory of social value and institutional change (Bush 1983). This third contribution is explored in the next section.

Ceremonial Encapsulation

The concept of 'ceremonial encapsulation' provides an important addition to the theory of instrumental value. The idea was developed separately, but at about the same time in the late 1970s, by Louis Junker and by Bush. When they discovered their parallel analyses, they planned jointly to write a paper on the topic. Sadly, this effort was prevented by the untimely death of Junker in 1981. Bush's development of the concept began in 1977, was extended in 1979, and refined in a persuasive essay in the *Review of Institutional Thought* in 1986.

Bush affirms the institutionalist premise that the dynamic force in social change is the expansion of the fund of warranted knowledge. It creates conditions that foster the recognition of a difference between what is and what ought to be. Perceptions of the need for institutional modifications emerge. What Bush and Junker recognized, however, is that, in the 'initial phase', ceremonial encapsulation occurs. This principle states that 'the new knowledge will be incorporated into the institutional structure only to the extent that it can be made ceremonially adequate: that is, only to the extent that its incorporation can be accomplished without upsetting the existing degree of ceremonial dominance embedded in the value structure of the community' (Bush 1986, p. 30). It must not be permitted to upset existing status and power relations; Veblen's 'vested interests' will be sustained initially.

To understand this principle we need to recognize that there are certain hegemonic, or culturally dominant, structures of power embedded within existing institutions (Waller 1987). These power structures are maintained by the vested interests on the basis of wealth acquisition and political dominion; they are rationalized by the invidious use of class, gender, ethnicity, and ideologically dominant beliefs and values. The ruling groups gain a lion's share of national income and wealth through control of the dominant institutions, through the hierarchical forces of socialization and through the manipulation of information and ideology. This ensures that the population does not question, or at least can rarely challenge, the structures of control. Ceremonial encapsulation simply means that changes in the fund of knowledge must pass through these structures of control. The dominant power structures 'encapsulate' or sequester the knowledge so long as its use poses a threat to the continuity of their existing patterns of control. New additions to the fund of knowledge may propose to modify institutions, but so long as the balance of ceremonially dominant behaviours exceeds or forestalls instrumentally dominant behaviours, the status quo remains, power centres prevail and ceremonial encapsulation continues.

Bush distinguishes analytically between three main types of ceremonial encapsulation (Bush 1986). First there is the 'past-binding type', in which innovations must not be permitted to change the status quo of hegemonic power centres, corporate hierarchies, ceremonial sex-roles, status rosters, racist stereotypes or distributive income shares. For example, a new production method may be designed for the technical specifications of male (not female) workers, for upper-class family control of managerial functions, and for the assurance of continuity of existing controls. Ceremonial adequacy is provided for traditional patterns of power and status.

Another example is the conservative economists' opposition to, and ultimate encapsulation of, Keynes's revolutionary theory of income and employment (Bush 1979b). Innovative elements in Keynes's general theory included recognition of fundamental macroeconomic uncertainty, the significance of maintaining aggregate effective demand, and a continuing need for public management of macro phenomena. Given the uncertainties, firms use conventions and habitual techniques to determine their propensity to invest; they respond to the prevailing business climate about the future. Investment will be forthcoming at a rapid rate if expectations of the future are positive (that is, if the marginal efficiency of capital exceeds the rate of interest) and at a low rate if expectations are negative. The business cycle and levels of effective demand are affected by the general business environment, rather than simply by microeconomic factors. Thus, for Keynes, the government must assume responsibilities for fiscal and monetary policies seeking fuller employment and rising income. Any such governmental role threatens private centres of power and undercuts traditional orthodox economic analysis (for example, Say's law) about the unfettered functioning of markets. Accordingly, this 'radical' theory was emasculated through creation of the 'neoclassical synthesis' which ensured that the old classical themes of flexible markets and aggregate equilibrium tendencies would remain dominant. The revolutionary nature of Keynes's theory was toned down and largely negated by orthodox rational expectations analysis.

The second type of ceremonial encapsulation is 'future-binding' encapsulation, in which powerful elites decide the future of society. 'Future-binding' ceremonial encapsulation does not involve a resistance to technological innovation, but rather the active effort to develop, control and choose among alternative technological paths through time; that is, it involves the selection [by megacorps] among alternative 'futures'. The future must conform to present requirements of continuing dominion, to the prevailing patterns of ceremonial dominance in the community. (Bush 1986, p. 34)

But if these innovations, for example, significantly pollute the environment, promote structural unemployment (without retraining schemes) and/or enhance the centralization of industry, can this be called a 'forward-looking' strategy proffered by the vested interests? The perpetuation of market power is put at centre stage, at the expense of social costs. The livelihood of the community at large is impaired, not enhanced, by such innovations.

In these first two types of encapsulation, progressive institutional change may ultimately occur as real innovations force changes in the institutions that provide power, privilege and unproductive use of resources. But the vested interests will do all they can to sustain their dominance and privileged access to money and real income.

The third form of ceremonial encapsulation is the 'Lysenko type', in which ceremonial patterns of behaviour actually displace instrumental patterns of behaviour, creating *regressive institutional change*. Instrumental patterns are actually reduced. This is the most insidious and backward form of ceremonial encapsulation. In this case, changes occur which have little rationality, except protecting hegemonic institutions or dominant groups. This type takes its name from the Soviet doctrine of the 1930s and 1940s in which Lysenko's pseudo-science claimed that genetic biology in agriculture is overridden by environmental determinants. Soviet biological science was sidetracked for a generation. Other examples include Nazi racial theories and genetic experiments on humans and the supply-side economics doctrine of the Reagan administration that assured that lower tax rates would increase total tax revenue.

In sum, powerful groups and classes, then, will often utilize instrumental values and behaviours to further their own ends. They need access to knowledge, information, technology and skills for the establishment and maintenance of their sphere of control; but their use must not abridge the continuity of this control.

Limitations on the availability of warranted knowledge is an important constraint on institutional change generally. For any culture, this stock of knowledge is a major component of collective social wealth (Veblen 1899, pp. 152–4; O'Hara 1995). It includes, broadly, the available skills, language, networks and industrial arts that are embedded in institutions. It is a product of the community, largely inherited from the past. Changes in the stock are minor

compared with the total stock of social wealth. In any case, it is often possible
to divert, privatize or exploit social wealth for private purposes of gaining and
retaining power (pecuniary and political). Ceremonial encapsulation is a
familiar route for the pursuit and retention of such control.

However it is a probability, but not a certainty, that at some point the
community's awareness and understanding of the significance of advancements
in warranted knowledge will increase to the point where ceremonial
encapsulation (the 'initial phase') will erode and new knowledge will be
instrumentally incorporated, launching the 'second phase' of 'progressive'
institutional adjustments. Bush states that ' "progressive" institutional change
occurs when, for a given state of the arts and sciences . . . instrumentally
warranted patterns of behaviour displace ceremonially warranted patterns of
behaviour'. This induces a 'change in the value structure of the community'
(Bush 1986, p. 31). New knowledge is embodied and embedded in instrumental
patterns of behaviour. Ceremonial dominance of those with status and power
is eroded with reference to this given enhancement of knowledge.

Progressive institutional change, therefore, occurs where the social wealth
as warranted knowledge is directed to projects which will enhance well-being
and be available to all members of society. The growth of the dynamic stock of
social wealth will be severely curtailed if the vested interests deny academic
freedom and therewith forestall the creation and use of warranted knowledge.

Principles of Institutional Change

If, as noted, these three principles of ceremonial encapsulation (past-binding,
future-binding, regressive) represent the chief ceremonial limits to progressive
institutional change, Foster's theory of institutional adjustment, discussed
below, identifies the main non-ceremonial limits to progressive social change.
The principles emanate from the basic institutionalist perspective of holism or
interdependency (Wilber and Harrison 1978; Wilber, forthcoming) according
to which institutions are interconnected in varying degrees. A change in one
structure will typically impact on other structures as linkages permit or direct.
Such linkages are a manifestation of Veblen and Myrdal's principle of circular
and cumulative change.

Foster formulated three principles of institutional adjustment: technological
determination, recognized interdependence and minimal dislocation (1981a).
The first of these, the principle of technological determination, that Bush
captions the 'technological dynamic' (Bush 1987, pp. 1089–90), refers simply
to the emerging fund of technological, social and physical knowledge
(characterized above as collective social wealth) that currently obtains. It
extends and/or delimits what institutional options can realistically be considered
in the search for solutions to real problems confronted and experienced. It does
not mean that technologies 'determine' institutional structure; technological

inquiries provide warranted knowledge on which to ground, and with which to justify, institutional change. The technological continuum provides an institutionally sited fund of human knowledge that sets boundaries and parameters for social inquiry and policy making. Foster argued that 'social problems can be solved only by adjusting the institutional structures involved in the problem so as to bring them into instrumentally efficient correlation with the technological aspects of the problems'. Such correlation means that 'the instrumental functions of the institutions in question be carried on at a level of efficiency tolerable to the members of the institution in view of the possibilities indicated by those same technological factors' (Foster 1981a, p. 932). The community at large cannot 'unknow' what communal warranted knowledge discloses, for example that chemical pollution of drinking water is a health threat. Adjusting institutions to constrain/preclude the contaminating use of such substances must take that fact into account. The growth of warranted physical knowledge as technology often is the source of institutional problems, but it does not *determine* the character of structural changes needed. It does identify what *kinds* of institutional change will resolve the problem where resolution means increased instrumental efficiency.

The second principle, 'recognized interdependence' simply adds that, for instituted changes in structure to be effectively implemented, the altered patterns of behaviour proposed must be known and internalized to a considerable degree by those participating in the change (Foster 1981a, p. 933). As proposed change is specified, economic agents must consciously recognize and understand the implications of altered expected behaviours and be aware of the wider impact on, and interaction with, their non-problematic behavioural patterns. The more agents have such knowledge and recognition of the interdependencies, the more institutional change will be orderly and evolve as intended. As Bush puts it, 'the transition from a state of "ceremonial encapsulation" to "progressive" institutional change depends upon the ability of those whose behaviour will be affected to understand and accept the changes in behaviour that the "progressive" change entails' (Bush 1986, p. 39). Accordingly, if agents are ignorant of the nature of the interactions, or lack information in varying degrees of its implications, their ability to participate in and support such change will be limited. Institutions evolve in many different directions, depending on the nature and extent of information and the speed of adjustment of values and behaviour (Bush and Tool, forthcoming).

The third principle, minimal dislocation, is also related to circular and cumulative causation. It states that: 'All institutional modifications must be capable of being incorporated into the remainder of the institutional structure ... It discloses the limits of adjustment in terms of rate and in terms of degree and area' (Foster 1981a, p. 934). Evolutionary change is possible so long as anticipated changes are capable of being instrumentally linked to the wider socioeconomy. Revolutionary changes, though also possible, are less likely to ensure this constructive linkage.

The holistic perspective of neoinstitutional economics, as an evolutionary approach, is ideally suited for the analysis of public and private change, because changes in one area can be designed to connect to other areas in a way that minimizes ceremonial or invidious outcomes. This principle of minimal dislocation cautions against introducing changes that significantly disrupt instrumental functions being satisfactorily performed elsewhere in the socioeconomy. But as Bush explains, ' "Progressive" institutional change will always involve the dislocation of ceremonially warranted patterns of behaviour which are attached to well-established vested interests'. Such change 'may very well be associated with a certain amount of social unpleasantness as the vested interests are dislodged from positions of status and power' (1986, p. 40). Disruptions, dislocations, behaviour modifications should be kept to that minimum adjustment that will accomplish the restoration or expansion of instrumental activities that were suppressed, abandoned or are awaiting incorporation. Adjusting institutional structure resolves problems of non- and malperformance of instrumental functions.

An historical example of a failure adequately to understand and employ the principles of recognized interdependence and minimal dislocation may be observed in recent changes in the former Soviet bloc. The revolutions in economic and social life that were experienced in Russia and Eastern Europe during the early 1990s were designed to change the system from a planned to a market economy in a very short space of time. Using a 'cold turkey' strategy, the theory behind the policy was that, in the short run, there would be some degree of economic turbulence, but that in a few years the advantages of flexible markets would start to show themselves in higher productivity and income. Instead, however, many of these economies have experienced a systemic collapse of confidence in their institutions. Changes which occur too fast, relative to the habits of the economic agents, often result in maximal dislocation because agents have not internalized the interdependencies associated with the new market relations (the principle of recognized interdependence), and the institutional changes have occurred too fast for the continuity of the economic process to be re-established (the principle of minimal dislocation) (Tool 1995, pp. 197–211).

The breakdown of the former Soviet bloc is in large measure a consequence of the breakdown of institutions. The result has been socioeconomic instability and a lack of confidence of economic agents in the system. Inextricably linked to this situation is the contradiction of the dis-embedded economy: capitalism requires relatively flexible markets, yet if markets become too flexible they threaten the very survival of the institutions which provide the structured stability necessary for sustained production and distribution. The market system, therefore, has a dual movement: flexible markets emerge; in addition, considerable 'institution building' in the form of accords between labour and capital, industry and finance, nation and world, men and women, and different ethnic groups must also occur. A dynamic form of relative balance between 'flexibility' and 'institutional building' has been historically necessary for capitalism to continue to be reproduced in a viable form (Stanfield 1995). These processes may be fruitfully analysed employing the principles of ceremonial encapsulation, technological determination, recognized interdependence and minimal dislocation.

LOGICAL STRUCTURE OF NEOINSTITUTIONALISM

Bush's contributions to the neoinstitutionalist theory of social value and the principles of institutional change, discussed above, firmly enhance the explanatory capabilities of neoinstitutional economics. These contributions are also very much in the mainstream of neoinstitutionalism as developed in the tradition of Veblen, Dewey, Ayres and Foster. In one area, however, Bush has challenged neoinstitutionalists seriously to extend their historically dominant modes of expression and analysis by considering his development of a formal model of the logical structure of neoinstitutional economics. While most institutionalists have been content to generate pattern models, and have eschewed deductivistic approaches because of their seeming affinity with neoclassical economics, Bush explores the potentially powerful analytical and predictive properties of a deductivistic model of the neoinstitutionalists' paradigm. He argues that a cogently drawn, deductively formulated, model can be compatible with pattern models. His overriding concerns are to fashion a fresh logical format with which to explain and express neoinstitutional theory and to facilitate a 'more precise statement of testable empirical hypotheses and a clearer delineation of policy issues' (Bush 1983, p. 36). Regrettably, only a general characterization of his axiomatic, set-theoretic approach can be provided; his graph-theoretic formulations and demonstrations are too extensive to be presented here.

Bush constructs 'an axiomatic system based on the rich theoretical and empirical implications of the Veblen–Ayres–Foster paradigm. The "artificial" language used to express the structural logic of the model is taken from the mathematical field of "graph theory"' (Bush 1983, p. 36). The basic structure comprises ten axioms and eight theorems deduced from the axiom set. Proofs are provided for the theorems introduced. The explicit subject and substance of this axiomatic system is the now familiar theory of institutional change embodying the institutionalists' dichotomy between instrumental and ceremonial or invidious warrant for behaviour. This dichotomy has long been 'the primary theoretical construct by which institutional structures and the changes in them are analysed' (Bush 1983, p. 39; Waller 1982, pp. 757–72).

The subject matter, then, is traditional, but the axiomatic treatment of that subject matter is not.

An introduction to the logical structure of this axiomatic model is provided by the following abbreviated presentation (in quotations and paraphrasing; with symbols deleted) of the constituent axioms and theorems (Bush 1983, pp. 35–66):

'*Axiom #1*: An "institution" is defined as a set of socially prescribed patterns of correlated behaviour.' These patterns contain two subsets: behaviours and values that correlate behaviours (p. 39).

'*Axiom #2*: The set of all values contains two disjoint subsets: ceremonially warranted values and instrumentally warranted values.' The value structure is dichotomous. Ceremonial values reflect the logic of 'sufficient reason'; instrumental values require a logic of 'efficient causes' (p. 39).

'*Axiom #3*: The set of all behaviours is formed by two subsets and their intersection.' The subsets are ceremonial behaviour and instrumental behaviour. The intersection of these subsets is behaviour that has both ceremonial and instrumental significance. Thus, behaviour is dialectical in nature (pp. 39–40).

'*Axiom #4*': For every behaviour there is an associated value. 'All behaviour is rationalized according to the value structure of the institution. This "linking" of a value with each behaviour . . . determines whether [it] plays a ceremonial or instrumental role' (p. 40).

'*Axiom #5*': Values correlate behaviour. 'Correlate' means both 'ordering and coordinating of behaviour' and the 'determination of the dominance relationship between behaviours correlated'. Correlations can be either ceremonial or instrumental (p. 40).

'*Theorem #1*': Given Axioms 1 to 5, 'the set of all possible behaviour patterns may be specified' and 'be partitioned into . . . the set of ceremonially warranted patterns of behaviour and the set of instrumentally warranted behaviour patterns'. Elements of the subsets are specified (pp. 40–42).

'*Axiom #6*: The institutional structure is defined as a set of ceremonial and instrumental patterns of behaviour . . . Institutional structure is neither purely ceremonial nor purely instrumental' (p. 46).

'*Theorem #2*': Given Axioms 1 to 6, 'the minimal institutional structure must take the form of one or the other of the two sets of behavioural patterns'. Ceremonial patterns are connected to instrumental patterns. Indeed, some ceremonial patterns encapsulate instrumental behaviour and give 'the appearance of experiential warrant to ceremonial practices' (pp. 46–7).

'*Theorem #3*: The "index of ceremonial dominance" describes the value structure of the institution to the extent that it indicates the degree of dominance of ceremonial patterns of behaviour over instrumental patterns of behaviour. It is, perhaps, *the pivotal concept of the model*' (pp. 50–51, emphasis added).

'*Axiom #7*: Dominance relations are transitive within the ceremonial and instrumental subsets of behavioural patterns. Transivity within ceremonial patterns reflects hierarchies based on invidious distinctions. Within instrumental patterns, transivity reflects causal sequences' (p. 51).

'*Theorem #4*: Ceremonial patterns dominate instrumental patterns of behaviour within the institutional structure' (p. 51).

'*Axiom #8*: The society's fund of knowledge is embedded in the behavioural patterns of its institutions. The knowledge fund is "encapsulated" within ceremonially warranted patterns of behaviour and "embedded" in instrumentally warranted patterns of behaviour' (pp. 51–2).

'*Axiom #9*: A change in the fund of knowledge will be partly "encapsulated" within ceremonial patterns of behaviour and partly "embodied" in instrumental patterns of behaviour. The distribution of knowledge will be governed by the index of ceremonial dominance prevailing in the institution' (p. 52).

'*Theorem #5*: For a given index of ceremonial dominance, an increase in the fund of knowledge will always result in less than the maximum feasible increase in instrumental behaviour' (p. 53).

'*Corollary to Theorem #5*: [T]he lower the index of ceremonial dominance the higher [will be] the level of technological innovation generated by an increase in the fund of knowledge' (p. 55).

'*Theorem #6*: A structural change may occur without changing the index of ceremonial dominance [but it] is *strictly confined to ceremonial patterns of behaviour.*' However, 'changes in dominance relations among patterns of instrumental behaviour are strictly the function of changes in either the fund of knowledge or the index of ceremonial dominance or both' (pp. 54–5).

'*Axiom #10*: A "progressive" institutional change occurs when there is a decrease in the index of ceremonial dominance' (p. 56).

'*Theorem #7*: For a given fund of knowledge, the necessary condition for technological innovation is a decrease in the index of ceremonial dominance, and the sufficient condition is that the increase in instrumental behaviour results in a displacement of ceremonial behaviour' (p. 56).

'*Theorem #8*: If a progressive institutional change occurs simultaneously with a change in the knowledge fund . . . the resulting technological innovation will be greater than that which occurs under conditions of the ceremonial encapsulation phase of institutional adjustment' (p. 58).

'*Corollary to Theorem #8*: The index of ceremonial dominance [may decline] not as a result of a "displacement" of ceremonial behaviour patterns by instrumental behaviour patterns, but by [the] "adding on" of instrumental patterns to the previously existing behaviour set' (p. 59).

Elsewhere, O'Hara (1997) has developed extensive applications and illustrations of Bush's formal axiomatic and digraph model, encompassing the distinction between instrumental and ceremonial functions of institutions (ICFI), in (a) the generation of a microeconomic analysis of structures of labour organization (pp. 109–15) and (b) in 'a macroeconomic measure of socioeconomic progress based on the holistic view of ICFI' (pp. 115–26).

In the former, he contrasts the status of labour, in the ICFI sense, under (a) Fordist (assembly-line, Taylorism), (b) post-Fordist (flexible assignments, quality circles), and (c) worker-control (Mondragon model) systems of labour organization. The index of ceremonial dominance evidently is lowest in the worker-control setting. In the latter, he develops an 'Index of Community, Warranted Knowledge and Participation (ICWP) . . . for assessing the macroeconomic functioning of the system, region, or industry on the basis of the degree to which community integration, warranted knowledge, and participatory democracy dominate over invidious distinctions such as status competition, differential privileges, and master–servant relationships' (p. 104). ICWP augments existing measures of macroeconomic performance such as the per capita GDP, the Index in the Human Development Report (1996), and the Daly–Cobb Index of Sustainable Economic Welfare (1994) by bringing the Veblenian dichotomy (as reflected in the index of ceremonial dominance) into fundamental deliberations over the general conditions of social, political and economic well-being. In our view, Bush's axiomatic model provides both an accessible and a significant analytical approach to normative social inquiry.

CONCLUSION

The purpose of this paper has been to review Bush's main contributions to academic life and to neoinstitutional scholarship. More than anything else, he was and is (a) a courageous and capable faculty leader seeking to create and sustain a vigorous and collegial learning environment; and (b) a committed and highly competent scholar successfully creating, refining and extending fundamental principles of neoinstitutionalist methodologies and analyses of social and economic change.

In the 1960s he served ably as counsel to faculty and students, and contributed significantly to the promotion of academic freedom and collegial governance on State University campuses in California. In the 1970s he continued this counselling responsibility and accelerated his participation in meetings of institutionalists. In the 1980s, he greatly expanded his writing and publications on methodological issues and the theory of institutional change. In the 1990s, he has continued to write and publish on the philosophical methods and principles of neoinstitutional economics.

His major contributions to the intellectual tradition of institutional and neoinstitutional economics include his revitalization and employment of the Deweyian theory of knowledge and social value, his refinement and extension of the theory of institutional adjustment, his creation (with Junker) of the theory of ceremonial encapsulation and its applications, and his formulation of a deductivistic structural logic, and an axiomatic ordering, of the neoinstitutionalist paradigm. These are path-breaking contributions that should stimulate much additional research and writing, especially, we would recommend, in four areas.

First, it is desirable to continue work begun by Bush on the nature and forms of ceremonial encapsulation, on the particulars of the theory of institutional adjustment, on the index of ceremonial dominance and the distinction between regressive and progressive change, and on the formal structuring of the neoinstitutionalist paradigm.

Second, it is important to enhance the empirical analysis and application of these principles and theories. For example, the index of ceremonial dominance could be applied variously to the institutions of the family, the sphere of corporate production, the financial system, the loci of political power, the economic role of the state, and national and global market structures. There is a need for the development and use of new and modified tools of empirical analysis.

Third, it is important to apply Bush's principles more extensively in the area of macroeconomics, especially as measures of economic performance and institutional change over time. Areas that would benefit from such analysis include long-term determinants of economic growth, business cycles, systemic change and distributional outcomes, and various derivative policy applications.

Fourth, and more generally, Bush's constructs may be used to explore the nature and form of the collective social wealth in greater detail in pursuit of a better theoretical and empirical understanding of the lingual and causal linkages among and between the growth of warranted knowledge, advancing technology and emergent institutions.

Fagg Foster, Bush's mentor at the University of Denver, believed that 'the central function of higher education is the extension and dissemination of knowledge and understanding' (Foster 1981b, p. 970). Bush has made major contributions to the extension and dissemination of knowledge, and he has actively supported the creation and maintenance of the conditions for inquiry that make such knowledge growth and dissemination possible.

NOTE

1. We wish to thank Paul D. Bush for providing requested information and Sasan Fayazmanesh for editorial assistance.

REFERENCES

Booth, Douglas (forthcoming), 'Mondragon Experiment' in Phillip Anthony O'Hara (ed.), *Encyclopaedia of Political Economy*, London: Routledge.

Bush, Paul Dale (1968a), 'The Normative Implications of Positive Analysis', paper presented at meetings of the Western Economic Association Conference, Corvallis, Oregon, August.

_____(1968b), 'Free Speech and the Mezey Case' in George P. Rice and Nancy G. McDermid (eds), *1968 Yearbook of the Committee on Freedom of Speech*, Speech Association of America, pp. 49–62.

_____(1969a), 'A Proposed Pattern of Collective Bargaining for The California State College System', presented to the Executive Committee of the State Council of the Association of California State College Professors, February. With the assistance of Kenneth Russell, Alexander Vavoulis and Eugene Zumwalt.

_____(1969b), 'The Current Crisis in The California State College System: A Challenge to the Faculty', a position paper prepared for the Association of California State College Professors, State Council Meetings, March.

_____(1969c), 'The Variety of Marginalist Methodologies: A Critical Appraisal', paper presented at meetings of the Western Economics Association, Long Beach, California, August.

_____(1970), 'Where Should Authority Reside?', *The ACSCP Voice of the Faculties*, January–February, pp. 11-3.

_____(1973a), 'An Interdisciplinary Study of the Rehabilitation of the Severely Handicapped for Professional Careers', May. With the assistance of Philip H. Stephens.

_____(1973b), 'Academic Freedom and Faculty Responsibility Under Conditions of Collective Bargaining', paper presented to the Task Force on 'Academic Freedom and Faculty Responsibility' for the Academic Freedom Committee of the United Professors of California.

_____(1977), 'A Veblen–Ayres Model of Institutional Change: A Provisional Formulation', paper presented at meetings of the Western Economics Association, Anaheim, California, June.

_____(1979a), 'The Cost to California Taxpayers of the Denial of Academic Freedom and Due Process to Faculty in The California State University and College System', mimeo.

_____(1979b), 'The Ceremonial Encapsulation of Capital Formation in the American Economy', paper presented at meetings of the Western Social Science Association, Lake Tahoe, Nevada, April.

_____(1980), 'Analysing the Energy Problem: Pecuniary Logic versus Institutional Analysis', paper presented at meetings of the Western Social Science Association, Albuquerque, New Mexico, April.

_____(1981a), 'A Radical Individualist's Critique of American Institutionalism', *American Journal of Economics and Sociology*, **40** (2), April, pp. 139–47.

_____(1981b), 'Radical Individualism's Philosophical Dualisms as Apologetic Constructs', *American Journal of Economics and Sociology*, **40** (3), July, pp. 287–98.

_____(1981–82), 'The Normative Implications of Institutional Analysis', *Economic Forum*, **12** (2), pp. 9–29.

_____(1983), 'An Exploration of the Structural Characteristics of a Veblen–Ayres–Foster Defined Institutional Domain', *Journal of Economic Issues*, **17** (1), March, pp. 35–66.

_____(1986), 'On the Concept of Ceremonial Encapsulation', *Review of Institutional Thought*, **3**, December, pp. 25–45.

_____(1987), 'The Theory of Institutional Change', *Journal of Economic Issues*, **21** (3), September, pp. 1075–116. Reprinted in Marc R. Tool (1988) (ed.), *Evolutionary Economics, I: Foundations of Institutional Thought*, Armonk, NY: M.E. Sharpe, pp. 125–66. Also reprinted in Geoffrey M. Hodgson (1993) (ed.), *The Economics of Institutions*, Aldershot, UK: Edward Elgar Publishing.

_____(1989), 'The Concept of "Progressive" Institutional Change and its Implications for Economic Policy Formation', *Journal of Economic Issues*, **23** (2), June, pp. 455–64.

_____(1991), 'Reflections on the 25th Anniversary of AFEE: Current Philosophical and Methodological Issues in Institutional Economics', *Journal of Economic Issues*, **25** (2), June, pp. 321–46.

_____(1992), 'Comments on J. Fagg Foster: Teacher and Scholar', paper presented at the J. Fagg Foster Award Ceremony, University of Denver, April.

_____(1993), 'The Methodology of Institutional Economics: A Pragmatic Instrumentalist Perspective' in Marc R. Tool (ed.), *Institutional Economics: Theory, Method, Policy*, Boston: Kluwer Academic Publishers, pp. 59–107.

_____(1994a), 'The Pragmatic Instrumentalist Perspective on the Theory of Institutional Change', *Journal of Economic Issues*, **28** (2), June, pp. 647–57.

_____(1994b), 'The Theory of Social Change' in Geoffrey M. Hodgson, Warren J. Samuels and Marc R. Tool (eds), *The Elgar Companion to Institutional and Evolutionary Economics*, Aldershot, UK: Edward Elgar Publishing, pp. 291–6.

_____(1997), 'Answers to Biographical Questions Posed by P.A. O'Hara', 26 pp.

_____(forthcoming), 'Ceremonial Encapsulation' in Phillip Anthony O'Hara (ed.), *Encyclopaedia of Political Economy*, London: Routledge.

_____and Marc R. Tool (forthcoming), 'The Evolutionary Principles of American Neoinstitutional Economics' in Kurt Dopfer (ed.), *The Evolutionary Principles of Economics*, Boston: Kluwer Academic Publishers.

California State University Fresno (1995), Handbook 1995.

Daly, Herman E. and John B. Cobb (1994), *For the Common Good: Redirecting the Economy Toward Community, the Environment, and a Sustainable Future*, 2nd edn, Boston: Beacon Press.

Foster, J. Fagg (1981a), 'Syllabus for Problems of Modern Society: The Theory of Institutional Adjustment', *Journal of Economic Issues*, **15** (4), December, pp. 929–35.

_____(1981b), 'Freedom and License in Higher Education', *Journal of Economic Issues*, **15** (4), December, pp. 969–73.

Hickerson, Steven R. (1984), 'Complexity and the Meaning of Freedom: An Instrumentalist View', *American Journal of Economics and Sociology*, **43** (4), October, pp. 435–42.

Human Development Report (1996), Published (annually) for the United Nations Development Programme. Oxford: Oxford University Press.

Junker, Louis (1982), 'The Ceremonial–Instrumental Dichotomy in Institutional Analysis: The Nature, Scope and Radical Implications of the Conflicting Systems', *American Journal of Economics and Sociology*, **41** (2), April, pp. 141–50.

O'Hara, Phillip Anthony (1995), 'Thorstein Veblen's Theory of Collective, Social Wealth', Working paper #95.01, School of Economics and Finance, Curtain University, Perth, Australia.

O'Hara, Phillip Anthony (1997), 'A New Measure of Macroeconomic Performance and Institutional Change: The Index of Community, Warranted Knowledge, and Participation', *Journal of Economic Issues*, **31** (1), March, pp. 103–28.

Raichle, Donald R. (1994), 'Academic Freedom', *Collier's Encyclopaedia*, vol. I, New York: P.F. Collier, pp. 55–6.

Seib, Kenneth A. (1979), *The Slow Death of Fresno State*, Palo Alto: Ramparts Press.

Stanfield, James Ronald (1995), *Economics, Power and Culture: Essays in the Development of Radical Institutionalism*, New York: St. Martin's Press.

Tool, Marc R. (1995), *Pricing, Valuation, and Systems: Essays in Neoinstitutional Economics*, Aldershot, UK: Edward Elgar Publishing.

United States Supreme Court (1967), *Keyishian vs. Board of Regents* (New York), 87 S.Ct 675; *US Reporter* 385 US 589.

Veblen, Thorstein B. (1899), *The Theory of the Leisure Class*, (1970), London: Unwin Books.

_____(1918), *The Higher Learning in America*, (1965), New York: Augustus M. Kelley.

Waller, William T. (1982), 'The Evolution of the Veblenian Dichotomy: Veblen, Hamilton, Ayres and Foster', *Journal of Economic Issues*, **16** (3), September, pp. 757–72.

_____(1987), 'Ceremonial Encapsulation and Corporate Cultural Hegemony', *Journal of Economic Issues*, **21** (1), March, pp. 321–8.

Wilber, Charles (forthcoming), 'Holistic Method' in Phillip Anthony O'Hara (ed.), *Encyclopaedia of Political Economy*, London: Routledge.

Wilber, Charles and Robert S. Harrison (1978), 'The Methodological Basis of Institutional Economics: Pattern Models, Storytelling and Holism', *Journal of Economic Issues*, **12** (1), March, pp. 61–90.

2. The Pragmatic Foundations of the Institutionalistic Method: Veblen's Preconceptions and their Relation to Peirce and Dewey[1]

Erkki Kilpinen

Human nature will have to be restated in terms of habit.

Thorstein Veblen

Thorstein Veblen's intellectual relation to his philosophical forerunners and colleagues, the classical American pragmatists, Charles Peirce, William James, John Dewey and G.H. Mead, has been one of the hoary topics in Veblen scholarship.[2] In this paper I attempt to pursue this line further, and to bring to light some new features of this philosophical tradition. These features, in turn, have an uncanny similarity to many of the central ideas in the methodological parts of Veblen's literary output.[3] It turns out that a thorough pragmatistic reading of Veblen's own presuppositions throws new light on those aspects of his thought and also on his historical position as a classical theorist.

In those methodological writings one finds Veblen, time and again, criticizing all contemporary movements in economic theory, for one and the same basic fault: their hedonistic passivity. It is this hedonistic passivity which comes into the open when one juxtaposes Veblen's teachings with those of classical pragmatism. At an often-quoted point in *The Theory of the Leisure Class*, Veblen avers that 'as a matter of necessity, man is an agent – a centre of unfolding impulsive, "teleological" activity' (1899, p. 9). As it stands, this phrase is ambiguous and innocuous. At first sight it might seem that any social theorist would claim more or less the same thing. Perhaps most of them would, but not in quite the same sense as Veblen and the pragmatists do. This peculiar sense is what the present paper attempts to tease out.

THE MEANING AND RELEVANCE OF PRAGMATISM

The question about the meaning of pragmatism is not made any easier by the fact that today there are so-called 'neo-pragmatists', for whom this word seems to mean a licence to no-holds-barred relativism, and whose views have gained wide currency at some quarters. As for these latter-day converts, I think there are good reasons to agree with Christopher Norris to the effect that, 'the first generation of American pragmatists – James, Dewey and Peirce – would scarcely have acknowledged any kinship with the doctrine now offered in their name' (Norris 1992, p. 64).[4] The aptness of this evaluation is based on the fact that the neo-pragmatists, whatever their other merits, are no great champions of social criticism and social research, unlike the original pragmatists (Norris 1992, p. 130). Of course, opinions may, and do, differ as to whether 'the promise of pragmatism' (Diggins 1994) has remained unfulfilled or not, but its character as a social philosophy, a philosophy committed to social criticism and social reconstruction, as John Dewey put it, should never be forgotten.

This side of pragmatism has recently been aptly treated in historical analyses such as those by Campbell (1992) and Feffer (1993). The only point where one wishes to disagree with them somewhat, and to enlarge their view, is the impact of Charles S. Peirce, pragmatism's founding father, on the later development of this philosophy. It is true that he did not actively participate in social reconstruction and social research, as did the other pragmatists. However, he gave the original impetus which has its effect also on the more socially oriented thought of later pragmatism, and it is his conception of the relation between human thought and action (or, rather, activity) which constitutes the rational kernel of all pragmatist thought. I submit that this same view is to a large extent shared also by Veblen.

What follows is an attempt at a brief summary rather than a detailed recapitulation of the pragmatistic conception of action or activity.

'The whole function of thought is to produce habits of action,' Peirce said in his famous 1878 article, 'How to Make Our Ideas Clear?' (1878, pp. 256–7). In so saying, he laid the foundations of the pragmatistic conception of action at the same time as he laid the foundations of pragmatism itself, in his six-piece series of articles, 'Illustrations of the Logic of Science' (1877–78). Various changes took place throughout Peirce's philosophical career, but one thing which did not change was this principle. By the term 'thought', Peirce did not mean mental representations taken one by one; the Cartesian doctrine about clear and distinct ideas was his main target of criticism. In its stead he offered a conception of an ever-ongoing semiotic process of sign interpretation, where there is no beginning or end, neither any first premiss nor a last conclusion. 'There is no exception to the law that every thought-sign is translated or interpreted in a subsequent one, unless it be that all thought comes to an abrupt and final end in death,' Peirce claims (1868, pp. 169–70). It is this, in principle endless, series of mental representations and interpretations which is actualized in human action in and against the outer world. 'A court cannot be imagined without a sheriff,' Peirce sometimes puts it (1902a, p. 93); that is, 'thinking implies existential action [physical action in the outer world], though it does not consist in that' (1909, pp. 222–3). From these two principles it follows that for Peirce human action is not a collection of separate individual actions, but an endless process of activity, or 'continuous permutation of action', to paraphrase the title of a first-class volume on this topic (Strauss 1993). Now and then this continuous action is punctuated by doubtful or critical moments when the activity is hindered and does not lead to its expected outcome in the outer world. This is what is known by Peirce's famous cycle of *belief* and *doubt*.

What this theory accomplishes, in the words of one of its later commentators, is that it 'reverses the order of naturalness, as the modern concept of inertia reversed the natural state from rest to motion', as Israel Scheffler says (1974, p. 59). It is not action *per se* which needs an explanation, according to this pragmatistic view. Action is *supposed* right from the beginning, as the conception of movement (instead of rest) is supposed in modern mechanics. What stands in the need of explanation is non-activity, or passivity, as well as *a change in* (the direction of, intensity of, and so on) the activity (Short 1989).

Recent Dewey scholarship has established a direct historical continuity between Peirce and John Dewey at this point. 'Dewey takes over this pattern of inquiry virtually intact, but he interprets it more liberally than Peirce intended,' says R.W. Sleeper in his commendable explication of Dewey's philosophy (1986, p. 49).[5] Hans Joas, the eminent Mead scholar, has for his part shown how George Herbert Mead joins forces with Dewey in their common project for socially oriented pragmatism.[6] In his *Human Nature and Conduct* (1922), Dewey draws some radical conclusions for social theory from those pragmatistic premises: 'The idea of a thing wholly inert in the sense of absolutely passive is expelled from physics and has taken refuge in the psychology of current economics. In truth man acts anyway, he can't help acting. In every fundamental sense it is false that a man requires a motive to make him do something' (Dewey 1922, p. 119). Dewey's words about the psychology of current economics have a sensitizing effect on Veblen scholars who recognize here a central theme of his. Is there also a common background for these two parallel and critical viewpoints on the action–theoretical presuppositions of economics?

THE FACT OF THE MATTER OF HABIT

Above we met Peirce pointing out how the whole function of thought is to produce habits of action – that is, not merely actions as such. In pragmatism the concept of 'habit' carries a heavier burden than it does in mainstream social science. In the latter tradition, 'habit' is usually understood as 'routine', as opposed to 'reflective action' (Camic 1986; Ault and Ekelund 1988; Waller 1988). Not so in pragmatism. Peirce went to great pains to point out that habit should not be taken as 'mere slothful repetition of what has been done' (1898c, p. 143). On the contrary, it is 'deliberately formed, self-analysing – self-analysing because formed by the aid of analysis of the exercises that nourished it' (Peirce 1906, pp. 334–42) – that is to say: a *conscious and reflective phenomenon*. Habitual action is for Peirce 'the final, logical interpretant' of a representation, toward which sign-interpretation tends (1906, pp. 342–3). His semiotic[7] critique attacked Cartesianism, not only for its doctrine of clear and distinct ideas, but also for its mind–body dichotomy (compare also Halton 1995; Strauss 1993). The concept of habit is there to bring body and mind together. Thus for Peirce, mental, intellectual and *logical* phenomena are also to be understood in terms of habit: 'That particular habit of mind which governs this or that inference . . . is called a *guiding principle* of inference' (1877, pp. 227–8, original emphasis). Accordingly, in Peirce's usage habit does not designate merely the sum of preceding separate actions,[8] but also the general principle according to which that summation takes place. That principle, in its turn, is also an object of human reflection, not merely separate actions seriatim. For a pragmatist habit is not one aspect among others in human behaviour; it is the most important, constitutive feature. Activity deprived of habit cannot be anything more than 'erratic activity that in some way must get superseded by a habit', as Peirce puts it (1905, p. 279). These same points are again repeated by Dewey, who maintains, also in a logical context, that 'habit is a way or manner of action, not a particular act or deed' (Dewey 1938, p. 13), and explains elsewhere its social scientific import as follows:

> The reason why a baby can know little and an experienced adult know much when confronting the same things is not because the latter has a 'mind' which the former has not, but because one has already formed habits which the other has still to acquire. The scientific man and the philosopher like the carpenter, the physician and politician know with their habits, not with their 'consciousness'. The latter is eventual, not a source. (Dewey 1922, pp. 182–3)

Two further points need to be made on the basis of this pragmatistic, reflective understanding of habit. In the first place, it enables us to tell who is a genuine pragmatist and who is not. Here we can rely on Peirce, who from various viewpoints has commented on the similarities and differences between himself and the other pragmatists.[9] There are differences, he notes, but also genuine similarities: 'Among such truths – all of them old, of course, yet acknowledged by few – I reckon their [the pragmatists'] denial of necessitarianism; their rejection of any "consciousness" different from a visceral or other external sensation; their acknowledgment that there are, in a

Pragmatistical sense, Real habits (which Really *would* produce effects, under circumstances that may not happen to get actualized, and are thus Real generals)' (Peirce 1908, pp. 331–2; original emphasis).

Now, it is an old hat in Veblen scholarship that he makes frequent use of the habit-concept, and his usage has been interpreted before. Here, I submit yet another interpretation: Veblen understands this concept also in its pragmatistic, reflective sense, not merely in the garden variety way! The best evidence to support this assertion is given in his *The Instinct of Workmanship* (1914) where he not only speaks, throughout the volume, about 'habits of life' and 'habits of thought', but also at one point pauses to explain their exact relation:

> Habitual occupation with workmanlike conceptions . . . carries with it habitual thinking in the terms in which the *logic of workmanship* runs. The facts of observation are conceived as facts of workmanship, and the logic of workmanship becomes the logic of events. Their apprehension in these terms is easy, since it draws into action the faculties of apperception and *reflection* that are already alert and facile *through habitual use* . . . In latter day psychological jargon, human knowledge is of a 'pragmatic' character. (Veblen 1914, pp. 53–4, emphasis added. See also pp. 29, 38, 51 and 176–7)

In a moment I shall return to this logic of workmanship and its further implications. Before that, I would like to draw together those ingredients of the pragmatistic conception of habitual action met so far. (1) We recall Dewey's words to the effect that 'in truth man acts anyway, he can't help acting' (1922, p. 119). Now and then, however, he or she is prevented from acting. In the words of G.H. Mead: 'Reflective thinking arises in testing the means which are presented for carrying out some hypothetical way of continuing an action which has been checked. Lying back of curiosity there is always some activity, some action, that is for the time being checked' (Mead 1938, p. 79). This is a version of the classical Peircean doubt/belief model, according to which action is an ongoing process, but temporarily stopped by some disturbance; a model where habitual action and conscious reflection take turns. (2) However, they not only take turns, they also *overlap and interact*, according to the pragmatistic interpretation. Naturally, human consciousness attempts to anticipate those recurrent doubtful or critical situations, and to prepare for them. This, says Peirce, 'is in the last analysis . . . my whole motive in reasoning; to plan my reasoning so that I evidently shall avoid disappointment and surprise' (1902b, p. 103). (3) On top of this, for pragmatism human reflection is not merely self-reflection of the consciousness; the sensory-motor proficiency of the human agent is also an essential object of reflection. John Dewey provides a very eloquent expression for this:

How delicate, prompt, sure and varied are the movements of a violin player or an engraver! How unerringly they phrase every shade of emotion and every turn of idea! Mechanism is indispensable. If each act has to be consciously searched for at the moment and intentionally performed, execution is painful and the product is clumsy and halting. Nevertheless the difference between the artist and the mere technician is unmistakable. The artist is a masterful technician . . . This fact alone should save us from opposing life and mechanism, thereby reducing the latter to unintelligent automatism and the former to an aimless splurge. (Dewey 1922, pp. 70–71; see also pp. 64–5)

Here we have a nice illustration of the idea met above as formulated by Peirce, namely, the idea of a deliberately formed and self-analysing habit, 'self-analysing, because formed by the aid of analysis of the exercises that nourished it', as his saying went. In the pragmatistic conception of action, intellectual sagacity and psycho-motor proficiency meet and support each other. One might put their relation as rationality with habituality being empty, while habituality without rationality is blind.[10] Veblen scholars need not be reminded of the similarity between this notion and his idea of workmanship, and I attempt to elucidate the similarity further.

THE QUESTION OF ABDUCTION

In what is perhaps the most detailed discussion of Veblen's relation to his philosophical predecessor and sometime mentor, Peirce, Alan Dyer tells us that 'Peirce's creative logic of inquiry is found intact in Veblen's philosophy of science . . . [To] understand Veblen's philosophy of science one must first look to Peirce' (Dyer 1986, pp. 35, 36).[11] Referring to Veblen's debuting 1884 article, 'Kant's Theory of Judgment', Dyer maintains that Peirce's conceptual process of abduction, though not the concept, recurs in Veblen's methodological thought (Dyer 1986, pp. 31–3).

Abduction refers to Peirce's peculiar way of understanding scientific reasoning, where, he says, not two but *three* basic modes of inference are to be distinguished, namely induction, deduction and abduction. The last mode refers to the creation of possible explanatory hypotheses for unanticipated empirical findings, hypotheses which then are to be tested by the other modes of inference. According to this theory, the generation of hypotheses is a creatively imaginative and, at the same time, a *logical* process.[12]

Indeed, 'the question of pragmatism is the question of abduction', as Peirce said when he for once had a chance to exhibit his brain-child, pragmatism, to a wider audience, in his 1903 Harvard lectures (1903b, pp. 121–3). By this he meant that abductive inference plays an inalienable role, not only in scientific methodology, but in human rationality as a whole. 'Not the smallest advance can be made in knowledge beyond the stage of vacant staring, without making an abduction at every step,' he avers elsewhere (1901, p. 900). However, this understanding of scientific creativity also reflects a deeper and more general conception of human creativity.[13]

In the first place, for Peirce abduction is not merely a peculiar mode of inference. By it he also wants to highlight the essential continuity between logic and instinctive action. It might sound paradoxical, he notes, to talk about instinctive logic, but the paradox is merely apparent. 'Think of a man whose business it is to lend out money. The accuracy of his cool reason is what he relies upon; and yet he is not guided by a theory of reasoning, but much rather upon an intense love of money which stimulates his faculties of reasoning. That is what I call his *logica utens*' (Peirce 1902c, p. 33).[14]

Veblen, we know, never uses the term 'abduction', but he goes to pains to show how human rationality and human instinctive behaviour are continuous, not two psychologically separate phenomena. '[A]ll instinctive action is intelligent in some degree . . . It aims to achieve some ends and involves some degree of intelligent faculty,' he tells in his *The Instinct of Workmanship* (1914, pp. 30–32; see also *passim*). Above we met another formulation from the same work, namely 'the logic of workmanship' (pp. 54, 61, and so on). It turns out that we have every reason to take quite literally this expression of Veblen's, it is approximately the same thing as Peirce's *logica utens*. The latter is, as Peirce says, 'like the analytical mechanics resident in the billiard player's nerves' (1898a, p. 343), an admixture of intelligent and sensory-motor features, joined together by habit. The logic of workmanship runs in terms of habitual thinking, which in turn reflects habitual ways of doing things, Veblen claims (1914, pp. 52–7, *et passim*).

With this conception of 'instinctive logic', the idea of an overlap between instinct and reason, Peirce and Veblen radically part company with mainstream traditions in the social sciences. 'It is indeed proved that intelligence and instinct always vary in inverse ratio to each other,' argues Émile Durkheim, for example, in his classic *Division of Labour in Society* (1964, p. 323; see also pp. 346–7). He seems to follow to the letter John Stuart Mill (1843), who also emphatically denies that inference or reasoning might have anything to do with 'operations performed by mere instinct . . . or animal impulse' (Mill 1843, p. 317n). For Peirce and Veblen no such thing is proved as Durkheim claims, such an idea is a remnant of pre-Darwinian thinking. However, this disagreement notwithstanding, both Peirce and Veblen still share Mill's conclusion to the effect that 'the Logic of Science is the Universal Logic, applicable to all inquiries in which man can engage . . . The logic of science is also that of business and life' (Mill 1843, pp. 314–18). The disagreement is about the genesis and *modus operandi* of the logic of science, or of business and life, but not about its domain of application.

A new question arises here. There is, indeed, uncanny similarity between those conclusions reached by Peirce and Veblen in their mature methodological

thought. How is this similarity to be explained? Were those seeds sown by
Peirce in 1881 by themselves so fertile that Veblen came to agree with him
even 30 years later, or have they meanwhile received some reinforcing
impulses? One possible source of reinforcement is John Dewey's philosophy
of psychology. In the next section I take up the connection between Veblen and
Dewey at this point.

THE UNCONDUCIVE REFLEX-ARC

Veblen's repeated attacks on the hedonistic conception of psychology, a
conception prevalent in all economic theories, according to him, are famous in
Veblen literature. In his opinion this conception is a metaphysical relic that
needs to be replaced by more up to date ideas congruent with the findings of
recent biological and anthropological research.

In this endeavour Veblen has a precedent in John Dewey and his discussion
about the status of physiological psychology and the so-called reflex arc in
psychological explanation. In his landmark article (1896) Dewey purports to
show the obsolescence of the old metaphysical conception of psychology, as he
calls it, but at the same time also to criticize those features of the then new
physiological psychology that he finds misconceived. In Dewey's opinion
physiological psychology hitherto has made only sham progress *vis-à-vis* the
previous 'soul-theory', in describing and explaining the functioning of the
sensory-motor apparatus:

> [T]he ordinary conception of the reflex arc theory, instead of being a case of plain
> science, is a survival of the metaphysical dualism, first formulated by Plato, according
> to which the sensation is an ambiguous dweller on the border land of soul and body,
> the idea (or central process) is purely psychical and the act (or movement) purely
> physical. Thus the reflex arc formulation is neither physical (or physiological) nor
> psychological; it is a mixed materialistic–spiritualistic assumption. (Dewey 1896, p.
> 104)

This is what stymies progress in psychology, Dewey maintains. What is needed,
he adds, is that the sensory stimulus, central connections, and the motor
response shall not be taken as separate entities or occurrences connected by
causal relations, but rather as organic parts or 'divisions of labour within a
larger coordination' (Dewey 1896, p. 97f.). Stimulus and response take place
inside, not outside that coordination, or an 'act', that is Dewey's other name for
the basic behavioural unit. They are to be explained in terms of the act, not the
other way round. Stimulus means a disturbance of an ongoing coordination,
response is the 'reconstitution' of that coordination; together they make up a
rupture within a flow of action. Stimulus takes place in relation to the ongoing
conduct of the subject, not 'ex abrupto', Dewey says (1896, p. 100).

Veblen, in the concluding part of his trilogy of articles, 'The Preconceptions of Economic Science' (1899–1900), obviously takes up and generalizes Dewey's theory while offering his most detailed alternative for the psychological presuppositions of economics. The purposeful life-activity of the living thing comes first; its causal interaction with the outer world comes second, in terms of the former. Neither Dewey nor Veblen wants to deny that the stimulus works causally, but for them it is not the starting point for its analysis. The behaviour of the living thing has a history preceding the occurrence of the stimulus. Veblen's conclusion is similar, not to say the same as Dewey's. 'The constitution of the organism, as well as its attitude at the moment of impact, in great part decides what will serve as stimulus, as well as what the manner and direction of the response will be,' he says (Veblen 1919, p. 155). He goes on to explain the standpoint of the new, biological psychology as opposed to its metaphysical predecessor (both terms are also Veblen's), as follows:

> The causal sequence in the 'reflex arc' is, no doubt, continuous; but the continuity is not, as formerly, conceived in terms of spiritual substance transmitting a shock: it is conceived in terms of the life activity of the organism. Human conduct, taken as a reaction of such an organism under stimulus [involves], of course, a very close-knit causal sequence between the impact and the response, but at the same time [imputes] to the organism a habit of life and a [self-direction] and selective attention in meeting the complex of forces that make up its environment. (Veblen 1919, pp. 155–6)[15]

But what have stimulus and response to do with economics in the first place? Economics deals with conscious rational action; stimulus and response with unconscious behavioural conditioning. To find out how Veblen has ended up with these concepts, we have to take a look at his critical methodological conception in its entirety.

VEBLEN'S CRITIQUE OF ECONOMIC REASON: WRONGS

In the remainder of this paper I discuss Veblen's critique of economic preconceptions from the pragmatistic point of view. I take the pragmatistic conception of reflective habitual action for my working hypothesis, and proceed with the assumption that it is more or less this conception that Veblen has in mind as an alternative, while he criticizes the psychological and philosophical preconceptions of economics. I also suggest that Veblen's train of thought makes better sense when understood from this, rather than from other comparable viewpoints. Not being an economist, I leave the economic validity of his conclusions for others to evaluate, and approach him as a social theorist.

First and foremost, I am interested in Veblen as a member of the founding generation of classical social theory, so that it is his contribution to what might be called the critique of economic reason that is pertinent here.

Let us accordingly begin together with Veblen and his famous critical question, 'Why is Economics not an Evolutionary Science?' (1919). The main reason why economics has not reached the state of an evolutionary, or, as we might say today, paradigmatic[16] science, is given within the suggestion that Veblen offers for improving this state of affairs. It is as laconical as provocative: 'Economic action must be the subject matter of the science if the science is to fall into line as an evolutionary science' (Veblen 1919, p. 72; see also p. 78).

Now, what else have economists been doing, if not studying economic action? 'Political Economy or Economics is a study of man's actions in the ordinary business of life,' are the opening words of Alfred Marshall's celebrated *Principles of Economics* (1890), for example. Veblen of course knows all this. His point, then, is not that economists had forgotten about action, but that they have a wrong understanding about it; they conceptualize it in an inconsequential way. In his own words, 'In all the received formulations of economic theory, whether at the hands of English economists or those of the Continent, the human material is conceived in hedonistic terms, that is to say, in terms of a passive and substantially inert and immutably given human nature' (Veblen 1919, p. 73).

Again we run into Veblen's well-known *bête noir*, the hedonistic conception of man which lurks in the background of all his critical methodological writings. The first thing to be noted about his attacks against it, is that they are not merely moralizing attacks – even though he leaves no uncertainty about his personal antipathy towards that conception. In Veblen's analysis it literally is a hedonistic 'postulate', from which economists draw further methodological conclusions which he finds but weakly founded. This postulate and the theorems deduced from it, may be ordered under four different headings and discussed each in turn. In the order of importance they are: (1) the hedonistic conception of the individual, (2) the calculative conception of human rationality, (3) the atomistic conception of society and (4) the positions of causality and teleology in the analysis of individual conduct and social processes. I take up these questions from two angles, first as they are formulated by Veblen in his critical confrontation with economics, then again in the form he offers his own suggestions.

The Hedonistic Individual

In one sense, of course, the hedonism Veblen attacks is an inversion of the old pejorative term, 'asceticism', that the utilitarian philosopher Jeremy Bentham has used. Only a committed ascetic, says Bentham, would not agree with him that '*pain* and *pleasure* . . . alone point out what we ought to do, as well as determine what we shall do' (Bentham 1789, pp. 65–6; original emphasis; see also pp. 72ff.). Veblen turns the tables on Bentham and maintains that it is the latter and his followers who are committed to hedonism – not only on the ground that they highlight pleasure and pain as determinants of human behaviour, but even more on the ground that they assume *rest* to be the normal state for human beings. It is this that makes the economic conception hedonistic in Veblen's terms. After suggesting 'economic action' for the subject matter of economics, he goes on as follows:

> The psychological and anthropological preconceptions of the economists have been those which were accepted by the psychological and social sciences some generations ago. The hedonistic conception of man is that of a lightning calculator of pleasures and pains, who oscillates like a homogenous globule of desire of happiness under the impulse of stimuli that shift him about the area, but leave him intact . . . When the force of the impact is spent, he *comes to rest*, a self-contained globule of desire as before. Spiritually, the hedonistic man is not a prime mover. (Veblen 1919, pp. 73–4; emphasis added)

Veblen presents his own alternative to this conception in the clearest terms in another paper (1898), 'The Instinct of Workmanship and the Irksomeness of Labour'. There he laconically states, 'Man's life is activity; and as he acts, so he thinks and feels. This is necessarily so, since it is the agent man that does the thinking and feeling' (Veblen 1898, p. 85). To be human is to be a doer. The relation between humanity and activity is not contingent; rather, the former logically implies the latter. We do not do things 'incidentally', in addition to our other being. According to modern psychology and anthropology, it is 'the characteristic of man to do something, not simply to suffer pleasures and pains' (Veblen 1919, pp. 74–5).

'Utilitarian hedonism', we know, is no straw man of Veblen's. No lesser theorist than Talcott Parsons sets out against it, in his classic work, *The Structure of Social Action* (1937). However, there are notable differences between the priorities of these two critics of utilitarianism. Parsons is upset by its inherent social atomism, the conception of the individual as a definitive human datum, as Veblen once says (1919, p. 74; for Parsons see 1937, pp. 52, 72). The question of utilitarian atomism is on Veblen's agenda also, but not as the starting point. In his terms it comes only after the hedonistic individual and his or her rationality have been treated. Economic utilitarians have not realized that, in the first place, men always and everywhere seek to do something, as Veblen says (1919, p. 75). Parsons, for his part, might say that it is not right to criticize economics, an abstractive science, on anthropological grounds. That would be a 'fallacy of misplaced concreteness', as his favourite Whiteheadian expression goes. However, there is an anthropological presupposition in Parsons also, which he shares with the utilitarians. It is the idea that human rationality is more or less the same thing as *calculation*.

Limited Rationality in the Calculative Conception

Veblen's conception thus seems to be one of '*homo faber*', of an active human being, which he puts forth to replace the passive utilitarian notion. His idea has similarities with those eloquently presented and defended by Johann Huizinga (1956) and Hannah Arendt (1958) in their respective classic works. However, Veblen's *Menschenbild* (Herrmann-Pillath 1996) all the time has its central critical thrust: to reject the utilitarian one with all its implications, another of which is its misleading interpretation of human rationality as a purely calculative operation. According to the utilitarian–economic tradition, he avers (1919, p. 223), the gift of appraisement and calculation is 'the hypothetical hedonist's only human trait'.

In Veblen's book, the hedonistic conception represents dated anthropology and questionable ethics, we learned above. In addition to this, we now see Veblen bringing out some *logical* faults in it. In his critical analysis, the hedonistic postulate serves as a starting point for the utilitarian's further reasonings, as a premise from which the methodological procedures of economics are deduced (1919, p. 234). However, they turn out to be dubious reasonings, based as they are on a false premiss. This in itself does not yet yield them logically invalid, but renders questionable the utilitarian's claim about the universality of his reasonings. Deductive inference, namely, typically proceeds from (a) wider premise(s) to a conclusion narrower in its scope, and this is at war with the common economical presupposition, according to which rational choice and calculation are *universal* modes of action. As Veblen says, under the guidance of this tenet of hedonistic calculus, and of other psychological conceptions associated and consonant with it, 'human conduct is conceived of and interpreted as a rational response to the exigencies of the situation in which mankind is placed; as regards economic conduct it is such a rational and unprejudiced response to the stimulus of anticipated pleasure and pain' (Veblen 1919, pp. 234–5).

Now we begin to see how economic analysis from Veblen's viewpoint can lead even to those proto-behaviouristic assumptions in terms of stimulus and response, which we met above. However, even this reading would not save the utilitarian–economic interpretation of human conduct, we noted. Stimulus and response are to be considered in terms of the life-activity of the organism (or of the economic individual), not vice versa, was Veblen's conclusion (1919, p. 156). 'Such a theory can take account of conduct only in so far as it is rational conduct, guided by deliberate and exhaustively intelligent choice . . . It deals with this conduct only in so far as it may be construed in rationalistic, teleological terms of calculation and choice' (Veblen 1919, pp. 235, 239). Choice and calculation are rational phenomena, to be sure, but they are special cases rather than paradigmatic examples of human rationality.

There is, of course, one sphere of life where choice and calculative rationality have a major role to play, namely pecuniary evaluation and business action. However valid the calculative conception might be in this sphere, it falls short as a general description of human rationality. Taken as such, it means elevating a special case, an economic entrepreneur's *logica utens* (Peirce), to a normative model of rationality. It is a logic of businessmanship, not one of workmanship, we might say in Veblen's own terms. According to him and the pragmatists, to concentrate exclusively on calculative rationality is to make 'an abnormal case the standard one', as Veblen's colleague, Dewey, later came to put it (1922, p. 202).

Society as a Sum of Individuals

Again we can begin by juxtaposing Veblen with Bentham. While widening his frame of reference from the hedonistic individual to the utilitarian conception of society, Veblen once more stops at the classic of utilitarianism for a straightforward statement: 'Society, in the utilitarian philosophy, is the algebraic sum of the individuals', he says, and this is consonant with the classical utilitarians' original formulation (Veblen 1919, p. 139; compare Bentham 1789, p. 66).

Economic theory, in Veblen's opinion hardly distinguishable from utilitarianism, stands on these two legs: the hedonistic conception of the individual, and the atomistic conception of society, society as an algebraic sum of individuals. The two tenets are unseparable (1919, p. 157). Such a conception, of course, is sociologically naive, representing 'degree zero of sociological thought', as we might say together with Pierre Bourdieu (1980). But when we ask how this utilitarian condition should be improved, we again find a considerable difference between the answers given by the classical European tradition of social theory on the one hand, and Veblen and the pragmatists, on the other. Classical social theory starts from society in a straightforward manner; it sets out to show how economic valuation is a part of a wider normative social valuation. Veblen is well aware of this sociological truth and its importance. 'The economic interest does not act in isolation,' he says in his article about economics as an evolutionary science, it is but one of several interests which the individuals fulfil in and by their conduct (Veblen 1919, p. 77). However, he immediately goes on to repeat that under hedonism 'the economic interest is not conceived in terms of action' (1919, p. 78). Thus, even the critique of the utilitarian conception of society has to begin in recognition of action.

Animism and Mechanicism in Economic Analysis

Utilitarianism and its classical economic offspring have a reputation as optimistic lines of thought which go to great pains to point out that development and progress do take place in society, if only societal and economical processes are left undisturbed. Veblen recognizes this optimistic feature (1919, p. 235), but not its alleged utilitarian grounds.

Now, if movement, development, even progress take place in society, but human action nonetheless is conceived as a mechanism of commutation (Veblen 1919, p. 133), from whence comes the impetus to that development? According to Veblen's interpretation of economic utilitarianism, it comes from the way the individuals add up to make that algebraic sum which, for that viewpoint, makes up the whole society. There is something beneficial in this additive process itself, something which promotes the well-being of society. That supposition exemplifies what Veblen, in the 'Preconceptions' essays (1899–1900), sarcastically calls 'economic animism'. In his opinion, the two main canons of truth for economics are (a) 'a hedonistic-associational psychology', and (b) 'an uncritical conviction that there is a meliorative trend in the course of events, apart from the conscious ends of the individual members of the community' (Veblen 1919, p. 150).

The utilitarian economic individual is passive, but in spite of this, his or her society is somehow active, thanks to that alleged meliorative trend of events. This line of thought, Veblen contends, dates back to the physiocrats, natural rights theories, and Adam Smith's famous 'invisible hand'. Despite its age, this relic is alive and well in economics, even today, in its belief in the beneficial and self-corrective powers of the market. Here, Veblen says, economic thought *misplaces* the causal and animistic aspects in the analysis of social and economic processes. Again drawing on recent anthropology and psychology, his critique continues:

> (a) On the ground of the hedonistic or associational psychology, all spiritual continuity and any consequent teleological trend is tacitly denied so far as regards individual conduct, where the later psychology, and the sciences which build on this later psychology, insist upon and find such a teleological trend at every turn. (b) Such a spiritual or quasi-spiritual continuity and teleological trend is uncritically affirmed as regards the non-human sequence or the sequence of events in the affairs of collective life, where the modern sciences diligently assert that nothing of the kind is discernible. (Veblen 1919, p. 151)

This is one of those interesting points where Veblen's train of thought hardly makes sense without pragmatistic presuppositions as its support. Seen from that viewpoint, classical economics is an inherently individualistic body of thought – not only, nor in the first place, by treating human beings as individuals, but also by treating human actions as individuals. Each action, depending as the economists tell, on free and intelligent choice, takes place separately, as a discrete occurrence, the statisticians might say. In so thinking, economics in Veblen's words denies spiritual continuity and teleological trend from human action. Thus, this spiritual and teleological continuity is to be found elsewhere, in social processes. Veblen's sarcastic quip, 'animism', characterizes the way economists understand social processes, in teleological, purposive and – Veblen has the audacity to say – spiritual terms. But while denying spiritual continuity on the individual level, economists throw the baby out with the bathwater. To deny continuity is, or comes close to, denying rationality, according to the tenets of pragmatism. In Veblen's view, in economics 'The human nature into the motions of which hedonistic ethics and economics inquire is an intermediate term in a causal sequence, of which the initial and the terminal members are sensuous impressions and the details of conduct' (1919, p. 134). Having started out with a free rational individual, economic reason ends up with a link in the causal chain.

No deep wisdom is needed to realize that Veblen wants all this to be reversed; the whole edifice turned upside down. Causality and teleology ought to change places: more teleology for individual action; more causality for cumulative social processes.

Before hearing his detailed explanations, an interpretative comment may be in order. Pragmatism sees no necessary conflict between causality and purposiveness (as a form of 'teleology'), or between human action and brute physical happening; theirs is no either/or position. Both intentionality and habituality are to be supposed in human action, we recall. Peirce noted how 'a court cannot be imagined without a sheriff', so that thinking indeed implies existential action, that is, causal and corporeal intervention in the outer world. That intervention, however, is no discrete occurrence, but a continuous, habitual process. In the social sphere, teleology has to make room for causality. Societal processes may be described as ongoing cumulative trends, but without any explicit *telos* behind or in front of them (see also Penz 1996, p. 59).

VEBLEN'S CRITIQUE OF ECONOMIC REASON: REMEDIES

In his interesting recent article, 'Thorstein Veblen's negative Dialektik', Helge Peukert has suggested that Veblen's purpose was not to advance economic science in any positive sense. Rather, his intention was 'deconstructive'. He wanted to reduce the economic logic *ad absurdum*, to show its inherent self-contradictory assumptions, but he left the matter at that, and did not offer anything new in its place (Peukert 1996, pp. 220, 224ff.). Interestingly enough, pragmatism is Veblen's background also in Peukert's discussion.

I find the de-constructive reading refreshingly provocative, but still am hesitant about its conclusion, namely that Veblen's dialectics were *merely* negative. On the final score Veblen does have something positive to his credit, it seems to me. Is it an alternative kind of economics? That question, to repeat, is not my concern. Max Weber, for his part, never wrote a single piece of economic theory, despite being a respected professor of economics. Nonetheless, he made a lasting contribution in situating economy within society, in circumscribing the domain of economical reason. As I have suggested, Veblen's accomplishment might also be reviewed and evaluated from this viewpoint.

But if we take this viewpoint, again notable differences arise between Veblen's conception and that tradition tracing its ancestry to Max Weber. First and foremost, the difference concerns the nature of human action and human rationality. For classical thought, not only in economics but also in sociology, a singular action, based on rational calculative choice, is the paradigm case of rational action. For the pragmatists, Veblen included, the model is one of reflective habitual conduct, guided by the actor's *logica utens* or, in Veblen's own words, 'the accumulated, habitual knowledge of the ways and means involved in production and use of appliances' (1919, pp. 185–6).

The Production and Reproduction of Society in Habitual Action

Let us return to the critical points enumerated in the previous section as (1)–(4), the questions concerning the nature of the individual, his or her rationality, the nature of society, and the relation of individual and society.

As for (1), the general hedonistic presupposition, being a postulate in Veblen's terms, is freely replaceable by another, and above we have heard his grounds for choosing otherwise. The hedonistic calculus depends on the hedonistic postulate, so that this general model of action also ends up questionable, as we noted. What remains to be done, is to take a closer look at points (3) and (4).

To return to the postulated meliorative trend in the economic process, it is closely related to the hedonistic conception of human nature, Veblen says, and adds:

> [B]ut this connection is more intimate and organic than appears from what has been said above. The two are so related as to stand or fall together, for the latter is but the obverse of the former. The doctrine of a trend in events imputes purpose to the sequence of events . . . invests it . . . with a discretionary, teleological character . . . [whereas] . . . no [such] discretion resides in the intermediate terms through which the end is worked out. Therefore, man being such an intermediate term, discretion cannot be imputed to him without violating the supposition. Therefore, given an

indefeasible meliorative trend in events, man is but a mechanical intermediary in the sequence. It is as such a mechanical intermediary term that the stricter hedonism construes human nature. (Veblen 1919, p. 157)

If those two conceptions stand or fall together, to attack one necessarily is to attack the other. Veblen's final target, it seems, is the utilitarian, atomistic conception of society. This, of course, is no news; it is the tenor in his institutionalistic argument against classical and neoclassical economics. The prevailing schools of economics are not ignorant about the existence of the institutional furniture in society, Veblen says (1919, p. 236). Their fault is rather that they treat that furniture as static and given, 'tacitly . . . taken for granted as pre-existing in a finished, typical form . . . not subject to inquiry' (p. 236). Thus, Veblen says, even when professing to be a dynamic analysis of the economy, such analyses, in point of fact, proceed in a wholly static way (1919, pp. 189ff., 232). The most basic of those tacitly postulated, pre-existing conditions concern the individual and his or her immutably given human nature (1919, p. 73). Accordingly, the road to the critique of society has to go via the critique of the hedonistic individual, as we noted above.

The theoretical conception of society toward which Veblen himself is aspiring, seems to be the recognition that neither the individual nor society has conceptual primacy. Rather, they stand in a mutually supportive reciprocal relation. As a preliminary for this conception, Veblen first has to put social causation and purposive human action the right end up, in terms of point (4) above. He says that we first have to eliminate personality and teleological content from the perception of the sequence of events, so that they are available for their right use as determinants of human conduct. While we impute teleology and personality to the human agent, we tend to apprehend phenomena 'in terms of process rather than in terms of outcome, as [has been] the habit in earlier schemes of knowledge [in economics]' (1919, p. 158). Furthermore, says Veblen,

> categories of process applied to conduct, to discretionary action, are teleological categories: whereas categories of process applied in the case of sequence where the members of the sequence are not conceived to be charged with discretion, are, by the force of this conception itself, non-teleological, quantitative categories. The continuity comprised in the concept of process as applied to conduct is consequently a spiritual, teleological continuity: whereas the concept of process under the second head, the non-teleological sequence, comprises a continuity of a quantitative, causal kind. (1919, p. 158)

Non-teleological, quantitative and causal continuity characterize social processes; spiritual and teleological continuity characterize the conduct of the human individual. Causality makes room for teleology at the individual level, whereas it gains room, at the expense of teleology, at the societal level. This is how Veblen remodels society the right side up.

One more time we may take our clue from the pragmatistic tradition. Veblen speaks here about the 'category of process as applied to human conduct'. This seems to be none other than the construct of our previous acquaintance: habit. Besides being, in its pragmatistic usage, the constitutive feature of individual conduct, it is also the link that connects individual conduct with larger-scale societal processes, 'the enormous fly-wheel of society, its most precious conservative agent', as William James once put it.[17] At first sight this idea is old news for Veblen scholars, it brings to mind his definition of institution as an outcome of the habitual conduct of individuals. His well-known formulation states that 'all human culture [in] this material civilization is a scheme of institutions – institutional fabric and institutional growth. But institutions are an outgrowth of habit. The growth of culture is a cumulative sequence of habituation, and the ways and means of it are the habitual response of human nature to exigencies' (1919, p. 241). However, he goes on with a formulation which, it seems, is not so old news. Those exigencies 'vary incontinently', so that 'each new move creates a new situation which induces a further new variation in the habitual manner of response' (p. 241). This new response to a new situation, for its part, is what Dewey and Mead understood by the term 'reconstruction', and whose ultimate roots lie in Peirce's doubt/belief theory, as we have seen.

This gives further confirmation to the present interpretation that Veblen's understanding of human conduct is more or less the same as that of the pragmatists. Moreover, supposing as we have done, that he also has the pragmatistic, reflective understanding of habit, a very interesting conclusion for social theory comes out: Veblen has a more sophisticated conception of the relation between the individual and society than one might assume at first blush. It is right, but not sufficient, to say that social institutions are produced by habitual individual action. It is as important to keep in mind that they work back on individual behaviour, that habitual action takes place in the confines of the institutions and the society. The relation between these two spheres is not merely a one-way relationship of production, but a *reciprocal*, two-way relationship of production and reproduction. While human individuals produce social institutions by their habitual doings, they themselves are produced by these institutions. The institutions make up the arena of and the material for the doings of individuals. They are the inescapable framework which both constrains and *enables* individual action. In Veblen's own words,

> [I]t is out of the experience of the individuals, through the habituation of individuals, that institutions arise; and it is in this same experience that these institutions act to direct and define the aims and end of conduct. It is, of course, on individuals that the system of institutions imposes those conventional standards, ideals, and canons of conduct that make up the community's scheme of life. Scientific inquiry in this field,

therefore, must deal with individual conduct and must formulate its theoretical results in terms of individual conduct . . . [However,] . . . The postulates of marginal utility, and the hedonistic preconceptions generally, fail at this point in that they confine the attention to such bearings of economic conduct as are conceived not to be conditioned by habitual standards and ideals and to have no effect in the way of habituation. They disregard or abstract from the causal sequence of propensity and habituation in economic life and exclude from theoretical inquiry all such interest in the facts of cultural growth. (1919, p. 243)

In Veblen's terms, social institutions are an outcome of the habitual action of individuals. At the same time, those institutions also work back on individual action, by directing and defining the aims and ends of conduct.

SOME GENERAL CONCLUSIONS

'Veblen's choice of Menger and the Austrian school for attack becomes perhaps one of his greatest, although completely unintended, jokes', a mainstream critic has written (Seckler 1975, p. 145). Jocularity apart, there are points in Veblen's critique of the neoclassical theory that still have remained completely unanswered, it seems to me. Veblen's thesis in his 'The Limitations of Marginal Utility' (1909), and related writings, is that free choice and calculation, after all, are not the be-all and end-all of human rationality. It often is so, but 'it ain't *necessarily* so', Veblen reminds us. In so saying he gets solid support from the philosophers and logicians of pragmatism, Peirce and Dewey. I do not think, either, that Veblen's concept of habit is at all the same as that of the neo-classicals, Ault and Ekelund (1988) to the contrary notwithstanding. However, I promised to leave economics to its specialists.

As for social theory, Veblen seems to have adumbrated the view about the reciprocal relationship between individual and society, represented, perhaps with greater conceptual clarity, by such leading present-day theorists as Anthony Giddens and Pierre Bourdieu. Veblen understood that the individual and society make up a *duality*, not a dualistic or dichotomous relationship; that society is an accomplishment of human action, 'sustained and made to happen by the skillful action of individuals', as Giddens was wont to say (Giddens 1979, 1984).

Perhaps Veblen's accomplishment is not merely one of adumbration; he may have something to add to contemporary discussion. As for Giddens, Veblen might remark that an important concept is missing from the former's theory of structuration, namely the concept of *habit*. Without such a conception, that enormous fly-wheel of society (James, Dewey), the idea of individual action really 'making societal processes to happen', as Giddens says, might turn out to be too idealistic.

A claim like that cannot be made about Bourdieu, who, by means of his concept of *habitus*, has done a great service in re-introducing the idea of habituality to contemporary sociology. What is interesting here is that his claim about his own concept as 'as much productive and reproductive' (Bourdieu 1980) is consonant with Veblen's habit. Recently Bourdieu has said that he has enhanced his appreciation of classical pragmatism, especially of Dewey (Bourdieu and Wacquant 1992, p. 122). As a corollary of this statement he might finally acknowledge his theoretical kinship with Veblen, which he hitherto has emphatically denied (Bourdieu 1990, pp. 11, 133). That kinship is not about a similar phenomenology of social differentiation, expressed in the nuances of consumerism, as some more or less shallow comments have suggested (Elster 1983, pp. 68f.; see also Campbell 1987). It is about the quintessential, constitutive feature of human behaviour and human society.

However, if we take habit or habitus to be of such importance, a final difference arises between Veblen and pragmatism, on the one hand, and that tradition we are accustomed to call classical social theory on the other. Classical social theory has recognized the existence of habituality in human conduct, however, as a more or less residual category only (Camic 1986). The essence of the problem of action is to be searched for elsewhere, in the actor's rational choice. 'However inadequate the utilitarian model,' observes Bourricaud in his lucid exposition of Talcott Parsons, 'its virtue was that it focused attention on the importance of individual choice' (Bourricaud 1984, p. 11). For Veblen and the pragmatists, this is no virtue at all (for example, Veblen 1919, p. 235). In their terms, the question of rationality is not about how we choose our line of action, it is about how we follow that line through. We give the last word to Veblen's mentor, the logician Peirce:

> The essence of rationality lies in the fact that the rational being *will* act so as to attain certain ends. Prevent his doing so in one way, and he will act in some utterly different way which will produce the same result. Rationality is being governed by final causes. Consciousness, the feeling of the passing instant, has, as such, no room for rationality. The notion that logic is in any way concerned with it is a fallacy closely allied to hedonism in ethics. (Peirce 1902a, p. 36; original emphasis)

NOTES

1. An earlier version of this article was presented at the second conference of the International Thorstein Veblen Association, at Carleton College, Northfield, Minnesota, May 30–June 1, 1996. I thank all conference participants, especially Rick Tilman, Ralf Schimmer and Jonathan Larson. Special thanks are also due to the editors of the present volume. The research on which this article is based was made possible by a grant from the Finnish Cultural Foundation.

2. See Peukert 1996; Penz 1996; Liebhafsky 1993; Fontana, Tilman and Roe 1992; Harvey and Katovich 1992; Tilman 1990, 1992; Ross 1991; Schwartz 1990; Edgell and Tilman 1989; Waller 1988; Mirowski 1987; Jensen 1987; Dyer 1986; Griffin 1982; Dugger 1979; Diggins 1978. Daugert's pioneering study of 1950 contains still pertinent information.
3. Veblen 1919.
4. See Halton 1995 for a closer critical discussion of contemporary 'neo-pragmatism'.
5. See also the excellent volumes by Tiles 1988, Westbrook 1991 and Campbell 1995.
6. See Joas 1985 and 1996; see also Cook 1993.
7. Peirce's sem(e)iotic cannot be entered here. Social scientists will benefit from the excellent explications by Fisch 1986, Colapietro 1989 and Wiley 1994. By the concept of 'interpretant', Peirce means a new sign, brought about by a pre-existing sign, to refer to the same or a similar object, either in the mind of (a) human individual(s), or also in outer behaviour (compare Peirce 1897, p. 135).
8. As it does, for example, in mainstream economics. See Ault and Ekelund 1988, for an explicit statement to this effect.
9. Academic philosophy has tended to exaggerate the difference between Peirce's 'pragmaticism' and other kinds of pragmatism. It is true that Peirce coined the term 'pragmaticism' for his own theory of meaning to distinguish it from pragmatism in a looser sense. Nonetheless, *even here* he defines it as a sub-field of pragmatism, not as something altogether different (see Peirce 1905, pp. 275–7; 1908, p. 331).
10. Or in more psychological terms, intentionality without behavioural conditioning is empty; conditioning with intentionality is blind.
11. On this theme, see also Peukert 1996; Penz 1996; Liebhafsky 1993; Waller 1988, Mirowski 1987 and Griffin 1982.
12. Popper and other contemporary methodologists notwithstanding, they want to keep logic and imagination separate. On Peirce's theory of abduction see also Fann 1970; Sebeok and Umiker-Sebeok 1983; Hookway 1985 and Anderson 1987.
13. On this concept and conception, see Joas 1996. Anderson 1987 concentrates explicitly on creativity in Peirce's philosophy.
14. On the concept *logica utens*, see also Peirce 1898b, p. 892; 1898a, pp. 345–6; 1902a, pp. 109–11; 1903a, p. 377. In these places Peirce regularly points to the continuity between logic or rationality, and instinctive action.
15. Compare Dewey 1896, pp. 98–102. I do not insist that the whole paternity of this idea should be traced to Dewey. The term 'tropoismatic', which Veblen uses in the quoted paragraph, probably refers to Jacques Loeb's theory of physiological tropoisms. According to Loeb, Dewey's conclusions were 'commonplaces' to a physiologist (Pauly 1987, p. 120; see also Rasmussen and Tilman 1992 on Veblen's relations to Loeb). Nevertheless, for the analysis of conscious human behaviour, Dewey and Loeb's standpoints support each other. See Royce 1903 for a case of their parallel application in the pragmatistic tradition.
16. According to Veblen, economics has not advanced beyond a taxonomic state of development. 'The outcome of the [economic] method, at its best, is a body of logically consistent propositions concerning the normal relations of things, a system of economic taxonomy' (Veblen 1919, p. 67). In the preceding sentences, he has noted how the current economic method makes do with deduction and induction only, unable to handle 'abnormal cases due to disturbing causes' (p. 67). Compare Kuhn 1962, Chapter 2.
17. James 1890, pp. 121f.

REFERENCES

Anderson, Douglas (1987), *Creativity and the Philosophy of C.S. Peirce*, Dordrecht and Boston: Martinus Nijhoff.

Arendt, Hannah (1958), *On Human Condition*, Chicago: University of Chicago Press.

Ault, Richard and Robert Ekelund, Jr (1988), 'Habits in Economic Analysis: Veblen and the Neoclassicals', *History of Political Economy*, **20** (3), pp. 431–45.

Bentham, Jeremy (1789), *An Introduction to the Principles of Morals and Legislation*, abridged in A. Ryan (ed.), *John Stuart Mill and Jeremy Bentham: Utilitarianism and Other Essays*, Harmondsworth: Penguin.

Bourdieu, Pierre (1980), *Questions de sociologie*, Paris: Les Éditions de Minuit.

_____(1990), *In Other Words: Essays Towards a Reflexive Sociology*, Cambridge: Polity Press.

Bourdieu, Pierre and Loïc Wacquant (1992), *An Invitation to Reflexive Sociology*, Cambridge: Polity Press.

Bourricaud, François (1984), *The Sociology of Talcott Parsons*, Chicago: University of Chicago Press. (The French original, entitled *L'individualisme institutionnel*, 1977.)

Camic, Charles (1986), 'The Matter of Habit', *American Journal of Sociology*, **91** (5), pp. 1039–87.

Campbell, Colin (1987), *The Romantic Ethic and the Spirit of Modern Consumerism*, Oxford: Basil Blackwell.

Campbell, James (1992), *The Community Reconstructs: The Meaning of Pragmatic Social Thought*, Urbana and Chicago: University of Illinois Press.

_____(1995), *Understanding John Dewey: Nature and Cooperative Intelligence*, Chicago and La Salle: Open Court.

Colapietro, Vincent (1989), *Peirce's Approach to the Self: A Semiotic Perspective on Human Subjectivity*, Albany: SUNY Press.

Cook, Gary (1993), *George Herbert Mead: The Making of a Social Pragmatist*, Urbana and Chicago: University of Illinois Press.

Daugert, Stanley (1950), *The Philosophy of Thorstein Veblen*, New York: King's Crown Press.

Dewey, John (1896), 'The Reflex Arc Concept in Psychology', in J.A. Boydston (ed.), *John Dewey: The Early Works 1882–1898*, vol. 5, (1972), Carbondale and Edwardsville: Southern Illinois University Press, pp. 96–109.

_____(1922), *Human Nature and Conduct: An Introduction to Social Psychology*, New York: Henry Holt.

_____(1938), *Logic: The Theory of Inquiry*, New York: Henry Holt.

Diggins, John (1978), *The Bard of Savagery: Thorstein Veblen and Modern Social Theory*, New York: Seabury Press.

_____(1994), *The Promise of Pragmatism: Modernism and the Crisis of Knowledge and Authority*, Chicago: University of Chicago Press.

Dugger, William (1979), 'The Origins of Thorstein Veblen's Thought', *Social Science Quarterly*, **60** (3), pp. 424–31.

Durkheim, Émile (1964[1893]), *The Division of Labour in Society*, New York and London: The Free Press and Collier-Macmillan.

Dyer, Alan (1986), 'Veblen on Scientific Creativity: The Influence of Charles S. Peirce', *Journal of Economic Issues*, **20** (1), pp. 21–41.

Edgell, Stephen and Rick Tilman (1989), 'The Intellectual Antecedents of Thorstein Veblen: A Reappraisal', *Journal of Economic Issues*, **23** (4), pp. 1003–26.

Elster, Jon (1983), *Sour Grapes: Studies in the Subversion of Rationality*, Cambridge: Cambridge University Press.

Fann, K.T. (1970), *Peirce's Theory of Abduction*, The Hague: Martinus Nijhoff.

Feffer, Andrew (1993), *The Chicago Pragmatists and American Progressivism*, Ithaca and London: Cornell University Press.

Fisch, Max (1986), *Peirce, Semeiotic, and Pragmatism*, Bloomington: Indiana University Press.

Fontana, Andrea, Rick Tilman and Linda Roe (1992), 'Theoretical Parallels in George H. Mead and Thorstein Veblen', *The Social Science Journal*, **29** (3), pp. 241–57.

Giddens, Anthony (1979), *Central Problems in Social Theory*, London and Basingstoke: Macmillan.

_____(1984), *The Constitution of Society*, Cambridge: Polity Press.

Griffin, Robert (1982), *Thorstein Veblen: Seer of American Socialism*, Camden, NJ: The Advocate Press.

Halton, Eugene (1995), *Bereft of Reason: On the Decline of Social Thought and Prospects for Its Renewal*, Chicago: University of Chicago Press.

Harvey, John and Michael Katovich (1992), 'Symbolic Interactionism and Institutionalism: Common Roots', *Journal of Economic Issues*, **26** (3), pp. 791–812.

Herrmann-Pillath, Carsten (1996), 'Thorstein Veblen's Menschenbild: Theoretische Grundlagen und empirische Relevanz', in R. Penz and H. Wilkop (eds), *Zeit der Institutionen – Thorstein Veblens evolutorische Ökonomik*, Marburg: Metropolis-Verlag, pp. 83–131.

Hookway, Christopher (1985), *Peirce*, Arguments of the Philosophers Series, New York and London: Routledge.

Huizinga, Johann (1956), *Homo ludens: Versuch einer Bestimmung des Spielelements der Kultur*, Hamburg: Rowohlt.

James, William (1890), *The Principles of Psychology, I–II*, (1950), New York: Dover.

Jensen, Hans (1987), 'The Theory of Human Nature', *Journal of Economic Issues*, **21** (3), pp. 1039–73.

Joas, Hans (1985), *G.H. Mead: A Contemporary Re-examination of his Thought*, Cambridge, England: Polity Press; Cambridge, MA: MIT Press.

_____(1996), *The Creativity of Action*, Cambridge: Polity Press; Chicago: University of Chicago Press.

Kuhn, Thomas (1962), *The Structure of Scientific Revolutions*, Chicago: University of Chicago Press.

Liebhafsky, E.E. (1993), 'The Influence of Charles Sanders Peirce on Institutional Economics', *Journal of Economic Issues*, **27** (3), pp. 741–54.

Marshall, Alfred (1890), *Principles of Economics*, London and New York: Macmillan.

Mead, G.H. (1938), *The Philosophy of the Act*, in C.W. Morris et al. (eds), Chicago: University of Chicago Press.

Mill, John Stuart (1843), *A System of Logic, Ratiocinative and Inductive, I–II*, (1868), London: Longman's, Green, Reader and Dyer.

Mirowski, Philip (1987), 'The Philosophical Bases of Institutionalist Economics', *Journal of Economic Issues*, **21** (3), pp. 1001–37.

Norris, Christopher (1992), *Uncritical Theory*, London: Lawrence and Wishart.

Parsons, Talcott (1937), *The Structure of Social Action*, second impression, Glencoe, IL: The Free Press, 1949.

Pauly, Philip (1987), *Controlling Life: Jacques Loeb and the Engineering Ideal in Biology*, New York and Oxford: Oxford University Press.

Peirce, Charles (1868), *Collected Papers of Charles Sanders Peirce*, in C. Hartshorne and P. Weiss (eds), vol. V (1931–1935), Cambridge: Harvard University Press.

_____(1877), *Collected Papers of Charles Sanders Peirce*, in C. Hartshorne and P. Weiss (eds), vol. V (1931–1935), Cambridge: Harvard University Press.

_____(1878), *Collected Papers of Charles Sanders Peirce*, in C. Hartshorne and P. Weiss (eds), vol. V (1931–1935), Cambridge: Harvard University Press.

_____(1897), *Collected Papers of Charles Sanders Peirce*, in C. Hartshorne and P. Weiss (eds), vol. II (1931–1935), Cambridge: Harvard University Press.

_____(1898a), *Collected Papers of Charles Sanders Peirce*, in C. Hartshorne and P. Weiss (eds), vol. I (1931–1935), Cambridge: Harvard University Press.

_____(1898b), *Historical Perspectives on Peirce's Logic of Science, I–II*, in Carolyn Eisele (ed.), vol. II (1985), Cambridge: Harvard University Press.

_____(1898c), *New Elements of Mathematics, by Charles S. Peirce, I–IV*, in Carolyn Eisele (ed.), vol. IV (1976),The Hague: Mouton.

_____(1901), *Historical Perspectives on Peirce's Logic of Science, I–II*, in Carolyn Eisele (ed.), vol. II (1985), Cambridge: Harvard University Press.

_____(1902a), *Collected Papers of Charles Sanders Peirce*, in C. Hartshorne and P. Weiss (eds), vol. I (1931–1935), Cambridge: Harvard University Press.

_____(1902b), *Collected Papers of Charles Sanders Peirce*, in C. Hartshorne and P. Weiss (eds), vol. II (1931–1935), Cambridge: Harvard University Press.

_____(1902c), *New Elements of Mathematics, by Charles S. Peirce, I–IV*, in Carolyn Eisele (ed.), vol. IV (1976), The Hague: Mouton.

_____(1903a), *Collected Papers of Charles Sanders Peirce*, in C. Hartshorne and P. Weiss (eds), vol. IV (1931–1935), Cambridge: Harvard University Press.

_____(1903b), *Collected Papers of Charles Sanders Peirce*, in C. Hartshorne and P. Weiss (eds), vol. V (1931–1935), Cambridge: Harvard University Press.

_____(1905), *Collected Papers of Charles Sanders Peirce*, in C. Hartshorne and P. Weiss (eds), vol. V (1931–1935), Cambridge: Harvard University Press.

_____(1906), *Collected Papers of Charles Sanders Peirce*, in C. Hartshorne and P. Weiss (eds), vol. V (1931–1935), Cambridge: Harvard University Press.

_____(1908), *Collected Papers of Charles Sanders Peirce*, in C. Hartshorne and P. Weiss (eds), vol. VI (1931–1935), Cambridge: Harvard University Press.

_____(1909), *Collected Papers of Charles Sanders Peirce*, in C. Hartshorne and P. Weiss (eds), vol. VI (1931–1935), Cambridge: Harvard University Press.

Penz, Reinhard (1996), 'Thorstein Veblens evolutorische Methodik', in R. Penz and H. Wilkop (eds), *Zeit der Institutionen – Thorstein Veblens evolutorische Ökonomik*, Marburg: Metropolis-Verlag, pp. 51–81.

Peukert, Helge (1996), 'Thorstein Veblen's negative Dialektik: Ökonomischer Rationalismus, Empirismus und Evolutionismus – eine Kritik', in R. Penz and H. Wilkop (eds), *Zeit der Institutionen – Thorstein Veblens evolutorische Ökonomik*, Marburg: Metropolis-Verlag, pp. 219–64.

Rasmussen, Charles and Rick Tilman (1992), 'Mechanistic Physiology and Institutional Economics: Jacques Loeb and Thorstein Veblen', *International Journal of Social Economics*, **19** (10–12), pp. 235–47.

Ross, Dorothy (1991), *The Origins of American Social Science*, Cambridge: Cambridge University Press.

Royce, Josiah (1903), *Outlines of Psychology: An Elementary Treatise with Some Practical Applications*, New York: Macmillan.

Scheffler, Israel (1974), *Four Pragmatists: A Critical Introduction to Peirce, James, Mead, and Dewey*, London: Routledge and Kegan Paul.

Schwartz, Jonathan (1990), 'Tracking-down the Nordic Spirit in Thorstein Veblen's Sociology', *Acta Sociologica*, **33** (2), pp. 115–24.

Sebeok, Thomas and Umiker-Sebeok, Jean (1983), ' "You Know My Method": A Juxtaposition of Charles S. Peirce and Sherlock Holmes', in U. Eco and T. Sebeok (eds), *The Sign of Three: Dupin, Holmes, Peirce*, Bloomington: Indiana University Press.

Seckler, David (1975), *Thorstein Veblen and the Institutionalists: A Study in the Social Philosophy of Economics*, London and Basingstoke: Macmillan.

Short, T.L. (1989), 'Why we Prefer Peirce to Saussure', in T. Prewitt, J. Deely and K. Haworth (eds), *Semiotics 1988*, Lanham and New York: University Press of America, pp. 124–30.

Sleeper, R.W. (1986), *The Necessity of Pragmatism: John Dewey's Conception of Philosophy*, New Haven: Yale University Press.

Strauss, Anselm (1993), *Continual Permutations of Action*, New York: Aldine de Gruyter.

Tiles, J.E. (1988), *Dewey*, Arguments of the Philosophers Series, London and New York: Routledge.

Tilman, Rick (1990), 'New Light on John Dewey, Clarence Ayres, and the Development of Evolutionary Economics', *Journal of Economic Issues*, **24** (4), pp. 963–79.

_____(1992), *Thorstein Veblen and His Critics, 1891–1963*, Princeton: Princeton University Press.

Veblen, Thorstein (1884), 'Kant's Theory of Judgment', reprinted in the collection of Veblen's essays, *Essays in Our Changing Order*, ed. by L. Ardzrooni (1934), New York: Viking Press, pp. 175–93.

_____(1898), 'The Instinct of Workmanship and the Irksomeness of Labour', reprinted in the collection of Veblen's essays, *Essays in Our Changing Order*, ed. by L. Ardzrooni (1934), New York: Viking Press, pp. 78–96.

_____(1899), *The Theory of the Leisure Class*, New York: Dover, 1994.

_____(1899–1900), 'The Preconceptions of Economic Science', reprinted in *The Place of Science in Modern Civilization and Other Essays*, (1919), New York: Viking Press.

_____(1909), 'The Limitations of Marginal Utility', reprinted in *The Place of Science in Modern Civilization and Other Essays*, (1919), New York: Viking Press.

_____(1914), *The Instinct of Workmanship and the State of the Industrial Arts*, (1964), New York: Augustus Kelley.

_____(1919), *The Place of Science in Modern Civilization and Other Essays*, New York: Viking Press.

Waller, William, Jr (1988), 'The Concept of Habit in Economic Analysis', *Journal of Economic Issues*, **22** (1), pp. 113–26.

Westbrook, Robert (1991), *John Dewey and American Democracy*, Ithaca and London: Cornell University Press.

Wiley, Norbert (1994), *The Semiotic Self*, Cambridge: Polity Press.

3. Dichotomizing the Dichotomy: Veblen versus Ayres

Geoffrey M. Hodgson

I must start with an apology which, I hope, is instrumental as well as ceremonial.[1] Dale Bush has been a valued close friend and guide for several years. With characteristic patience and generosity he has escorted me to domains of institutionalist thought that were formerly unfamiliar to one European scholar. His own attempts to develop the Ayresian tradition of institutionalism have impressed me greatly. To some, this rebellious essay here may seem ungrateful to Dale. It is not intended to be, and such a lack of appreciation would be sorely unwarranted. My excuse, furthermore, is not merely one of anti-authoritarian Ayresian revolt against an established tradition of American institutionalist thought. More than that: it is a sincere attempt to accommodate Bush's work as an attempt to develop a broad tradition which would be best reconstructed, partly in non-Ayresian terms. But that is enough of pitiable apologies. No longer let us 'beat about the Bush' but move on, and in more scholastic mode, to the main quarry.

Clarence Ayres has had an enormous influence on postwar American institutionalism. Marc Tool (1994, p. 16) has noted: 'Ayres and his students have been among the most significant contributors to the development of institutional economics in the last half-century'. From his own personal experience, Donald Walker (1979, p. 519) described the spell Ayres had over his students:

> The room would be filled with the most unpromising human material imaginable for the sort of purposes that Ayres had – backcountry students from the small towns and ranches of Texas, rich students from Dallas and Houston. Most of them were conservative or reactionary in their social and economic views; most of them were initially supremely indifferent to the issues that agitated Ayres. Yet he would work his magic on them, and by the end of a single semester he would have them ready to leap out into the real world and to start tearing down the old institutions, ready to begin immediately with building a new society free of ceremony, superstition, and myth.

Walker (1979, p. 520) himself regarded Ayres as 'Veblen's most creative and theoretically-inclined intellectual descendant, and one of the most important advocates of institutionalism during the years since the Great Depression'.

One of the major themes of this essay is to examine the intellectual influence of Thorstein Veblen upon Ayres. The Ayresian wing of modern institutionalism lays almost exclusive claim to the Veblenian title in North America. It is argued that the extent of this influence is grossly exaggerated. As shown here, in some significant respects, Ayres's work is a departure from that of Veblen. The concluding section of this work discusses later contributions in the Ayresian tradition and briefly notes the extent that they have overcome its former problems.

THE AYRESIAN DICHOTOMIES

Educated in a Chicago with recent memories of both Veblen and Dewey, it may be expected that Ayres was their obvious, immediate and diligent synthesizer. Far from it. His first two books (1927, 1929) bear only slight traces of their influence. In *Science: The False Messiah* (1927) he dethrones science and scientists, and in *Holier Than Thou* (1929) he attacks moral absolutes. Within a few years of their publication he would reverse his position on both these issues. The point here is not to downgrade Ayres for changing his mind, for most open-minded people do so from time to time. The point is to suggest that Ayres did not build his thinking continuously upon an accumulated Veblenian bedrock.

Ayres's own theory of economic development appears tentatively in the 1930s (Ayres 1935, 1938), but receives its fullest expression in his classic *The Theory of Economic Progress* (1944). Here are laid out the foundations of an institutionalist theory of both analytical and normative dimensions that was to sustain and become central for dwindling currents of American institutionalism for more than fifty years. For Ayres, human behaviour was essentially of two types: tool-using or technological activity leading to production, on the one hand, and ceremonial behaviour reinforcing status and privilege, on the other. The former was dynamic and progressive, the latter static and conservative. He wrote:

> The history of the human race is that of a perpetual opposition of these forces, the dynamic force of technology continually making for change, and the static force of ceremony – status, mores, and legendary belief – opposing change. (Ayres 1944, p. 176)

This dichotomy between technology and ceremony was the major theme of his 1944 book. Quite late on in this work, however, he made one further step. Ceremony was identified with institutions (Ayres 1944, pp. 178–87). Two possible dichotomies, between technology and ceremony, on the one hand, and between technology and institutions, on the other, were assumed to be one. Technology was seen as dynamic and progressive: institutions as wholly backward, resistant and serving the status quo.[2] Ayres thus quietly exchanged the word 'ceremony' for 'institution', treating them as synonyms. Compare the following passage, in a later work, with the one quoted above: 'the technological process is inherently developmental, while the institutional structure of all societies is inherently static and change resistant' (Ayres 1961, p. 233). Further, under the influence of the philosopher Dewey, for Ayres science and technology also provided the normative means of valuation by which economic developments and policies can be assessed:

> It is the technological continuum which is, and has always been, the locus of value; and it has this meaning because of its continuity. (Ayres 1944, p. 220)
> We must be prepared to declare, without fear and without scorn, that nothing but science is true or meaningful. (Ayres 1949, pp. 58–9)

Nevertheless, like Ayres himself in his *Theory of Economic Progress,* we shall concentrate firstly and largely on the analytical – and downplay the normative – aspects of Ayres's dichotomies. The dichotomy between institutions and technology was central and recurrent in Ayres's writings, as was his insistence that institutions are always bars to progressive change: 'By virtue of its peculiar character, the institutional function is essentially static. In the process of social change, institutional function plays a negative part. It resists change' (Ayres 1952, p. 49).

For Ayres, technology was a transformative social force that transcended individual incentives and motivations.[3] Within Ayres's terms, some such supposition along these lines was necessary, otherwise technological innovation and adoption could be seen as themselves motivated by the very incentives and interests associated with institutions. If, for example, the institution of private property proved a stimulus for technological innovation, then institutions would be *aiding* technological progress and the Ayresian dichotomy would be undermined. Ayres explicitly eschewed such notions, writing: 'The more we examine the institutions of capitalism, the clearer it becomes that their contribution to the development of industrial society has been permissive rather than creative' (Ayres 1935, p. 189). And later, more emphatically, he wrote: 'The productive powers of industrial society have grown not because of the institutions of capitalism but in spite of them' (Ayres 1943, p. 166). In general, he argued: 'There is no such thing as an institution (or set of institutions), that is "appropriate" to a given technology in any but a negative sense' (Ayres 1944, p. 187). Institutions were always and everywhere seen to be a barrier to technological development (Ayres 1952, pp. 49–50; 1960, p. 49; 1961, pp. 30–31, 126, 134–7).

Technological Change

Casting aside any positive or dynamic role for institutions, and making technology the exclusive engine of change, for a theory of economic growth Ayres required a theory of how technology itself developed.[4] He made use of two notions. The first was mere accident. Technical innovation was seen to result from 'the serendipity of the laboratory and the machine shop . . . And what else is serendipity but idle curiosity, the free play of the enquiring mind?' (Ayres 1963, p. 58). The notion of 'idle curiosity' here is clearly borrowed from Veblen.

The second was his combinatorial principle. Great inventions are essentially new combinations of old tools and ideas:

> Thus the air plane is a combination of a kite and an internal combustion engine. An automobile is a combination of a buggy with an internal combustion engine. The internal combustion engine itself is a combination of the steam engine with a gaseous fuel which is substituted for the steam and exploded by the further combination of an electric spark . . . What is presented to the public as a 'new' invention is usually the end-product of a long series of inventions. (Ayres 1944, p. 112)

Although 'the more tools there are, the greater the number of potential combinations' (Ayres 1944, p. 119), this does not actually tell us how the basic ingredients arise in the first place. Nevertheless, his twin assertions that technological change results from accident or (re)combination have a remarkable metaphorical resemblance to the Darwinian idea of evolution through random mutation and genetic recombination. But, for Ayres, these two principles do not themselves constitute a developed theory of socio-economic change because the detailed mechanisms of technological combination and mutation are unspecified. Above all, Ayres lacked an adequate account of innovation and novelty, and this was a major lacuna in his theory (Hill 1989; Miller 1958, 1966). Even his combinatorial principle lacked detailed analysis of the (cultural) contexts and mechanisms involved. Although combinations do frequently occur, it is not the case that inventors are regularly or randomly trying to combine everything with everything else. A set of highly specific skills, resources, cues and contexts led the Wright brothers to combine the kite with the internal combustion engine, or the Stephensons to synthesize the stationary steam engine with the coalmining infrastructure of horse-drawn carts on tracks. Despite being central to his argument, Ayres gives us no detailed analysis of the general process of combination, delegating the driving forces in his theory of economic growth to unspecified mechanisms and processes.

Furthermore, terms requiring precise definition were left unclear. Crucially, Ayres 'never precisely specified the meaning and extension of the term *technology*' (Coats 1976, p. 29). Ayres repeatedly depicted technology as tool-using behaviour, but this was not enough, especially as he (Ayres 1961, p. 135) recognized the use of tools in ceremonial activity. This lack of a clear definition was another devastating omission. Clearly, for his primary dichotomy to remain untangled, his concept of technology had to be free of institutional contamination; it must not itself involve institutions.

Just as significantly, an adequate definition of an institution was also lacking in Ayres's work. True to his rejection of tradition, he shunned earlier extensive attempts at defining the key concept by fellow institutionalists.[5] He argued at some length against broad usages of the term, and for its narrower identification with status and ceremony (Ayres 1944, pp. 178–87). In one passage Ayres (1944, p. 184) described institutions as 'segments of social behaviour predominantly ceremonial in character'. The point was insistent, but the first four words here were too vague to constitute a definition. The remaining words suggested that all institutions are 'ceremonial', merely passing the burden of definition on to another inadequately defined term.

Technological Rigidity and Institutional Fluidity

However, technology is not as fluid or dynamic as Ayres asserts. Rigid lock-in can occur, and the literature on technological change brims with examples of this (Arthur 1988, 1989; David 1985; Katz and Shapiro 1985; Kindleberger 1983). For example, we are still stuck with the anachronistic and inefficient 4 feet and 8½ inches standard railway gauge, first adopted in very different circumstances in Northeast England two hundred years ago. However, in some respects, the rigidity of some technological elements is functional for technical advance. Even nature's technology depends on rigidity. For example, it is the almost total inertness and slavish reproductive fidelity of the DNA that makes the kind of evolution we observe in earthly organisms possible. In the human economy, without the stability of some established and necessary technological standards or components, investment in further innovation based upon them may be perceived as too risky and thus may be deterred (Rosenberg 1976). The Wrights probably would not have attempted to combine the kite with the piston-based internal combustion engine, and invested their scarce resources in such an uncertain project, if they had thought that the production of a viable rocket engine or anti-gravity machine was just around the corner.

Neither are institutions as rigid as Ayres suggests. Just as technology is itself conjoined with tradition, institutions can be more dynamic than Ayres recognized. Indeed, throughout his writings, Ayres argued that forms of industrial organization and property are seen to change in response to the imperatives of technology (Ayres 1944, pp. 186, 188, 198–202; 1952, pp. 58–9). To be consistent with his theoretical and normative schema, institutions must be portrayed as the laggardly respondents to the technological dynamic. However, and without any significant and evident 'technological' impetus, even some prominent 'non-instrumental' and 'ceremonial' conventions such as fashion and dress show remarkable fickleness and changeability.

And what if some institution actually helps to promote some technological advance? The development of modern patent law is a possible example. Although it was devised in part in response to self-interest, arguably, once established, it promoted further technological innovation. The Ayresian can circumvent this problem by *defining* the positive or dynamic aspects as technological. But is the denial – by definitional deployment or otherwise – of institutional innovation and progressiveness reasonable? Arguably no. But, as Walker (1979, p. 526) points out, such an admission would be fatal:

> If it is true that some institutions stem from the same sources of human inventiveness as science and technology, and are manifestations of a dynamic endogenous social process which contributes to social survival and economic growth, then it is impossible to accept the difference in function that Ayres postulated between technological activities and institutions, and the basis of his entire system collapses.

Ayres never explains why institutional development should be exempt from the same principles of accidental mutation and recombination which supposedly impel technological change. Following Veblen and many others, it is reasonable to suggest that institutions too are subject to evolutionary processes of a kind. Ayres did not deny this, nor tell us why they are not.

Ultimately, as Walker (1979, p. 535) pointed out, Ayres's 'procedure is tautological. Anything that hinders economic development is by definition an institution in Ayres's work. If a habit of thought or behavioural pattern that we would call an institution contributes efficiently to the process of production, Ayres would call it a technological activity'. Malcolm Rutherford (1994, p. 91) made a similar point concerning Ayresian institutionalism:

> there is a tendency to see evolved institutions as *entirely* backward looking, resistant to change and with no positive functions. A substantial part of this comes from Ayres's definition of an institution that seems to associate the term with 'ceremonial' functions only and to exclude any convention, law, or organizational form that is instrumentally effective . . . Such a definition, contrary to Ayres's claim, hinders rather than advances the analysis of the derivation and functioning of social rules.

The Technological as Institutional

By contrast, consider the shorthand definition of an institution provided by Veblen. Veblen (1919, pp. 239–41) saw institutions as 'settled habits of thought common to the generality of men . . . institutions are an outgrowth of habit'. Veblen repeated this definition of an institution in terms of common habits elsewhere. For example, in a later work Veblen (1923, p. 101) saw an institution as 'of the nature of a usage which has become axiomatic and indispensable by habituation and general acceptance'. But technology itself involves clusters of common habits, related to industrial know-how and technique. Nowhere does Veblen suggest that technology and institutions are mutually exclusive. *Veblen's definition of an institution embraces rather than excludes technology.* Veblen's standpoint on these issues is discussed further below.

In criticism of Ayres, Walker (1979, p. 534) made a related point: 'Technology and institutions interpenetrate each other, and the operation of tools and machines depends upon institutional habits of thought and action, and vice versa'. Indeed, Ayres (1944, p. 99; 1953, p. 283) almost went so far as to admit this point himself. But he never abandoned the wholesale identification of institutions with ceremony, and never denied the view that institutions were essentially a constraint on progress.

Technology, as understood by modern scholars, is deeply impregnated by tacit knowledge and collective habits of thought, which, in Veblen's terms, are themselves institutional in character. Richard Nelson and Sidney Winter (1982, pp. 76–82) and Giovanni Dosi (1988) have elaborated the extent to which technology involves both explicit and tacit knowledge, codified and uncodified rules, and organizational routine. The key philosophical position was elaborated by Michael Polanyi – the brother of institutional economist Karl. Polanyi (1958, 1967) pointed out that technology is often employed without explicit knowledge of its detailed operations. Hence habit, tradition and 'legendary belief' have to be relied upon in the day-to-day practice of a technology. Furthermore, the learning and acquisition of a technology cannot rely wholly on prescription; such codified knowledge is often absent. The learning of a technology typically involves the formation of habit and routine *by following the example of others.* As a result: 'To learn by example is to submit to authority. . . . A society which wants to preserve a fund of personal knowledge must submit to tradition' (Polanyi 1958, p. 53).

What can be more 'ceremonial' than the system of master and apprentice which nurtured most technological achievements of European society from the Middle Ages to the twentieth century? The modern German and Japanese systems of technological training and innovation rely in no short measure on elements of status and deference. Such institutions would draw admonition from Ayres's pen.

The Institutional as Technological

Not only is technology 'institutional' in character. Even 'ceremonial' institutions can be seen to have instrumental or 'technological' characteristics. Warren Samuels (1977b, p. 876) argued that, by a broad and reasonable definition, 'technology can include the instrumental role and value of symbols and organizations'. Further, 'institutions (ceremonial thought and behaviour) are not always irrational but may function instrumentally to organize behaviour'. Examples of such instrumental institutions include language, traffic conventions and the highway code. The English language, for example, entails a maze of perplexing rules and spellings. Yet the very rigidity and 'ceremonial' reproduction of many of these rules helps maintain the integrity and usefulness of the language, alongside its fluidity and capacity to evolve in other respects.

It has been argued above that critics of the Ayresian conception of technological drive can also raise problems such as lock-in to relatively inefficient technologies. The depiction of technology as wholly progressive, and railing against institutions, can be contradicted, for example, by the use of military technology to sustain a backward regime. An Ayresian would address these problems by separating out different aspects of the phenomena. The next step would follow: what is instrumental and progressive is, *by definition*, technology, and what is non-instrumental or ceremonial is, *by definition*, an institution. But in this case the Ayresian dichotomy becomes merely tautological: it logically follows from the definitions. To make sense of the real world we have to proceed beyond mere labelling and word-play.

Shifting Ayres

Perhaps in response to some of the problems outlined above, Ayres's own position itself shifted and evolved. He came to the view that institutions could aid as well as retard economic development. In *Towards a Reasonable Society*[6] Ayres 'attempts to show that freedom, equality, security, abundance, excellence, and democracy are all true values contained in and implied by the technological process' (Rutherford 1981, p. 661). As Ayres (1961, p. 285) himself wrote: 'the democratic process is a process of learning the truth and operating accordingly, and the unanimity towards which the process aims is that of the universitality of science and technology'. This is perilously close to an admission that democratic institutions aid rather than hinder the progress of technology and science. In itself, such an admission may seem unobjectionable, but it undermines the Ayresian dichotomy.

In fact, Ayres went further down this slippery slope of his own making. He wrote: 'much is to be said to the credit of the institution of property. Its extraordinary flexibility has suited the requirements of industrial revolution to an extraordinary degree' (Ayres 1968, p. 343). Property rights, Ayres (1967, p. 174) conceded 'and the legal system that defined them, were the institutional foundation on which the industrial economy was built. They provided the motivation that impelled common men to build the modern world'. Ayres here argues that institutions can be more than permissive – they can provide motivations for agents.

As Ayres seemed to reflect on these problems, the relationship and boundary between institutions and technology became more difficult to define.

Institutions and technology, Ayres (1953, p. 283) suggested in one passage, 'overlie each other and interpenetrate, condition, and complement each other'. Indeed, the indispensability of ceremonial functions for economic life is even hinted at in *The Theory of Economic Progress*:

> The business of 'getting a living' includes . . . activities of a technological character, and it also includes activities of a ceremonial character; and these two sets of activities not only coexist but condition each other at every point and between them define and constitute the total activity of 'getting a living'. (Ayres 1944, p. 99)

In addition, Ayres makes the important point that technology is embedded in, and not separate from, social relations:

> What most needs to be stressed in this connection is that technology – the tool-using aspect of human behaviour – is not something separate and distinct from the societal network of personal relationships. (Ayres 1961, p. 77)

By a reasonable definition of the term, 'the societal network of personal relationships' is bound up with institutions. Although these arguments did not negate the conceptual distinction between institutions and ceremonial activities on the one hand, and technology on the other, it admitted the possibility of institutions or even ceremonial activities complementing technological change. This hint was later taken up and developed by the trustees and executors of the Ayresian system, notably J. Fagg Foster, Marc R. Tool, Louis Junker and Paul Dale Bush.

With statements such as those above, it was explicitly conceded by Ayres that some institutions can promote economic growth, while others may hinder it. Walker (1979, p. 529) commented on Ayres's own revisionist words: 'Such statements amount to an abandonment of much of the sharpness of Ayres's distinction between institutional and technological behaviour'. A considerable effort was required to sustain the Ayresian heritage in the face of such problems. This effort is the subject of the third section of this chapter. The second section addresses the alleged Veblenian origins of the Ayresian dichotomy.

VEBLENIAN ORIGINS OF THE AYRESIAN DICHOTOMIES?

Ironically negating his own denials of the importance of (intellectual) tradition and pedigree, Ayres asserted repeatedly that this dichotomy between technology and ceremony was derived from the writings of Veblen. For instance, he wrote: 'Veblen made the dichotomy of technology and ceremonialism his master principle' (Ayres 1973, p. v). Ayres's treatment of institutions as largely or wholly ceremonial was also influential within American institutionalism. The so-called – and often loosely defined – 'Veblenian dichotomy' (Klein 1995; Waller, 1982, 1994) between institutions and technology was thus born. After Ayres, its Veblenian origins were generally taken for granted. As A.W. (Bob) Coats (1976, p. 25) remarked:

> Veblen's basic dichotomies – between science and ceremonialism, technology and institutions, industry and business, workmanship and waste – recur in Ayres' writings, though he was constantly reformulating, elaborating and synthesizing these elements.

Similarly, in an important analysis of the history of the dichotomy, William Waller (1982, p. 762) considered it obvious that 'Ayres's concept clearly represents an extension of Veblen's'. More recently, Rick Tilman (1993, p. xvii) has written on Veblen's alleged 'dualisms': 'A . . . dualism manifest throughout his work is that which pits technology, that is, the machine process and the industrial arts, against stagnant, change-resistant institutions that impede technology's progress'. One of the few to question such views was Floyd McFarland (1985, p. 100), who noted, in highly critical vein:

> The ostensible followers of Veblen, unanimously or very nearly so, have handled Veblen's ideas in a strikingly peculiar way: apparently by using the dichotomy conception, they define all institutions as imbecile and deleterious . . . Consequently, the central message of the Institutionalists is that institutions are bad, having been assumed or defined so; while technology is good, having been assumed or defined so.

McFarland cast some doubt on the Veblenian origins of a dichotomy between technology and institutions. He was right to do so. Veblen established many dichotomies: between waste and use, between serviceability and pecuniary gain, between pecuniary and industrial employments, between business and industry, between making goods and making money, and so on. In addition, in several passages there is a strong suggestion of a conflict between technology and ceremony. However, this is not a major theme; it is a secondary rather than a primary feature of Veblen's analysis. Furthermore, and most significantly, a general dichotomy between technology and institutions is not to be found. Indeed, it would be inconsistent with Veblen's own conception and analysis of technology and institutions, *and contrary to his own explicit pronouncements*. These controversial points will be addressed in turn.

Ayres (1944, p. 99) wrote: 'The great economic pioneer, Thorstein Veblen, was the first to see this clearly and to make this analytical distinction between technology and ceremony the point of departure of all further economic analysis'. As noted above, there is some small substance to this particular accreditation. But to see this distinction as fundamental, or as an analytical 'point of departure' is an exaggeration. Even more crucially, Veblen did not see institutions as wholly non-instrumental, nor did he define them essentially in terms of ceremony. Furthermore, Veblen saw strong institutional elements within technology itself.

Veblen, Habits and Institutions

As we have seen, Ayres conflates institutions with ceremony. In addition, he attributes to Veblen the concept and term 'ceremonialism'. Ayres (1961, p. 30) refers to 'the institutional process (or ceremonialism, as Veblen often called it)'. In fact, Veblen rarely uses that term. Words such as 'ceremonial' appear in a few passages in the *Leisure Class*, but scarcely at all elsewhere.

By contrast, the words 'habit' and 'institution' are abundant in Veblen's writings, whereas Ayres only infrequently mentioned habit, and he seemed to prefer the term 'ceremony' to 'institution'. By downplaying these concepts, and absorbing the category of 'institution' into 'ceremony', he thus lost a crucial part of the Veblenian heritage. A fundamental methodological, rather than merely terminological, issue is involved here. Unlike Veblen, Ayres abandoned the project to develop a theory of human agency to rival hedonistic or utility-maximizing, neoclassical 'economic man'. Instead, he depicted the human agent as a receptacle of culture, putting supreme explanatory emphasis on this concept. Addressing more resolutely the concept of human agency, Veblen saw institutions as both the guiding threads of individual human action and the weft and warp of any social system.

With his meaning of the word, Veblen would never have conceived of the possibility of the withering away of 'institutions' in the manner that Ayres (1944, p. 185) wrote: 'it is a matter of common observation that all institutional ties and sanctions have been progressively weakened in modern society'. Against this, the West in the last three centuries has seen an enormous growth in the legal apparatus, organization, bureaucracy, and in the diversity of routine and skill. Overall, Ayres is not so Veblenian as he is often described. In several key respects, including the definition of an institution itself, Ayres broke from the Veblenian legacy.

The Alleged Veblenian Origins of the Dichotomy

Ayres did not give a detailed analysis of the alleged origins of the 'Veblenian dichotomy' but – in making Veblenian claims – quotes Veblen's depiction of a 'triumph of imbecile institutions over life and culture' from page 25 of *The Instinct of Workmanship* (Ayres 1944, p. 176). Others claim that the idea is to be found in the first and eighth chapters of *The Theory of the Leisure Class*, or in *The Theory of Business Enterprise* (particularly pp. 322–4), or in *The Place of Science in Modern Civilization* (particularly pp. 279–323). Look here or elsewhere in Veblen's writings, however. A general dichotomy between institutions and technology is not to be found.

Unfounded too is the general evaluation that, always for Veblen: 'Institutions are static and resist change; new institutions are formed as the result of the dynamic impact of technology' (Walker 1977, p. 220). It is true that Veblen highlighted the conservative facets of institutions. An important and frequently quoted passage is the following:

> It is to be noted then, although it may be a tedious truism, that the institutions of to-day – the present accepted scheme of life – do not entirely fit the situation of to-day. At the same time, men's present habits of thought tend to persist indefinitely, except as circumstances enforce a change. These institutions which have so been handed down, these habits of thought, points of view, mental attitudes and aptitudes, or what not, are therefore themselves a conservative factor. This is the factor of social inertia, psychological inertia, conservatism. (Veblen, 1899, p. 191)

Note, first, that there is no mention of science nor technology in this quotation. In fact, these two words appear much less frequently in Veblen's writings than the Ayresians suppose. In the above passage, Veblen was simply noting a mismatch between the inherited 'institutions of to-day' and the general 'situation of to-day', and the fact that institutions may resist change. He went on immediately, however, to consider how institutions may in fact be changed:

> Social structure changes, develops, adapts itself to an altered situation, only through a change in the habits of thought of the several classes of the community; or in the last analysis, through a change in the habits of thought of the individuals which make up the community. The evolution of society is substantially a process of mental adaptation on the part of individuals under the stress of circumstances which will no longer tolerate habits of thought formed under and conforming to a different set of circumstances in the past. (ibid., p. 192)

Again there is no mention of science or technology. What causes social change is vaguely described by Veblen as an 'altered situation' or the 'stress of circumstances'. For Veblen, such 'circumstances' included other institutions as well as technological practices. Albeit elliptically, Veblen (ibid.) goes on to allude to processes by which one particular institution may adapt to the others, each institution thus interacting with the rest. This is a depiction of several jostling institutions, themselves changing and impelling change in others. Veblen's theory of institutional change is much more a process of sifting, selection and rivalry between different institutions (Edgell 1975), rather than institutions succumbing to the autonomous forces of technology.

Search throughout Veblen's works, and no dichotomy between institutions and technology will be found. Ayres's claim to find it in *The Instinct of Workmanship* turns out to be invalid. The relevant and often-quoted passage refers to the possibility that instincts such as 'the parental bent or the sense of workmanship' may overturn 'institutional elements at variance with the continued life-interests of the community' and 'the bonds of custom, prescription, principles, precedent' may be broken. 'But history records more spectacular instances of the triumph of imbecile institutions over life and culture' (Veblen, 1914, p. 25).[7]

Here Veblen simply asserted that workmanship and other instincts *can* come into conflict with some institutions, and with different possible outcomes. In some cases 'imbecile' institutions block these instinctive drives. In other cases institutions prove more accommodating. Emphatically, Veblen is *not* suggesting that *all* institutions are 'imbecile'. Hence this passage does not give us the Ayresian dichotomy.

Another, less quoted, passage in the same work seems at first sight to give Ayres's claim more support. There Veblen (1914, p. 148) wrote of changes in 'the technological scheme' and advances in 'workmanlike mastery' being potentially hindered due to 'limitations of environment'. He continued: 'The limitations may be set by the material circumstances or by circumstances of the institutional situation'. But he went on immediately to suggest that such institutional inhibitions are not universal. Clearly, Veblen asserted no general dichotomy and this passage is no ground to form the basis of one.

It should not be denied that Veblen often suggested that technology may come into conflict with specific institutions. He also considered cases where technological change led directly to institutional change. What he failed to propose, however, was a notion that technology *always and everywhere* conflicted with *all institutions*. The reason for the absence of such an idea is simple: for Veblen technology itself was also an institution. While possible *conflicts* between institutions and technology are sometimes portrayed, the principle of a general *dichotomy* between them is ruled out for this crucial reason.

A passage from *The Instinct of Workmanship* makes a decisive point. Veblen (1914, p. 176) wrote: 'the body of knowledge (facts) turned to account in workmanship, the facts made use of in devising technological processes and applications, are of the nature of habits of thought'. Recollecting Veblen's own definition of an institution in terms of habits, this is tantamount to the statement that *technology itself is a type of institution*. The fact that science and technology must themselves be seen as institutional in character can be deduced from the following passage in the same work: 'All facts of observation are necessarily seen in the light of the observer's habits of thought' (Veblen 1914, p. 53). Science and technology depend on facts, and perception of the facts depends on habits of thought. It again follows that both science and technology are, at least according to Veblen, essentially of an institutional nature. Science and technology do not simply interact with and overlay institutions, they are themselves of institutional flesh and blood.

Turning to *The Theory of Business Enterprise*, Veblen (1904, pp. 323–4) wrote of the 'ubiquitous presence of the machine in modern life' having a 'cultural effect' and a 'concomitant differentiation and specialization of occupations . . . resulting in an ever weakening sense of conviction, allegiance, or piety toward the received institutions'. Again there is no universal theory or dichotomy here. Furthermore, the immediate conflict is not between technology and institutions but between *one set* of institutions, concerning the 'differentiation and specialization of occupations', and *other* institutions of established prominence.

In his writings, Veblen devotes more attention to institutions than he does to technology. In one of the passages in which technology is mentioned – published in 1898 – he writes of the industrial community, which 'always comprises a group, large enough to contain and transmit the traditions, tools, technical knowledge, and usages without which there can be no industrial organisation and no economic relation of individuals to one another or to their environment' (Veblen 1934, p. 34). By lumping together 'traditions' with 'tools' and 'technical knowledge' in this passage, any such dichotomization between them is undermined. Traditions are clearly seen by Veblen as efficacious both for technology and for production. Other passages by Veblen make a similar point.

Veblen's Implicit Denial of the 'Veblenian Dichotomy'

Let us consider some passages in Veblen's writing that are inconsistent with the Veblenian dichotomy. For example, Veblen (1899, p. 206) considered 'the leisure class as an exponent and vehicle of conservatism or reversion in social structure. The inhibition which it exercises may be salutary or the reverse'. Here Veblen accepted the possibility that 'conservatism . . . in social structure' may be considered as 'salutary' – a formulation that would grate with Ayres. Two pages later in the same book, Veblen (1899, p. 208) addressed 'institutions of acquisition or of production . . . they are pecuniary or industrial institutions . . . institutions serving either the invidious or the non-invidious economic interest. The former category have to do with "business", the latter with industry'. While on superficial inspection it seems to give support to the Ayresian dichotomy, this passage in fact undermines it, by recognizing that some institutions are beneficial for industry and production. If we may equate 'industry' with 'technology' this would suggest that they are both served by particular institutions, thus undermining any presumed universal conflict between institutions and technology.

Again in the same work Veblen (1899, p. 266) wrote of 'the institutional structure required by the economic situation of the collectivity'. This contradicts the Ayresian dichotomy by recognizing that an 'institutional structure' could be positively 'required' and is not necessarily a drag on technology. In a similar vein, Veblen (1899, p. 363) wrote of: 'The habits of thought which are so formed under the guidance of teachers and scholastic traditions have an economic value'. Bearing in mind Veblen's own definition of an institution, this passage suggests that they may have a positive role. In the *Leisure Class* Veblen (1899, p. 193) clearly recognized that economic and technological processes are made up of and require institutions:

> Any community may be viewed as an industrial or economic mechanism, the structure of which is made up of what is called its economic institutions. These institutions are habitual methods of carrying on the life process of the community in material contact with the material environment in which it lives.

In short, institutions are a means of 'carrying on the life process'. For Veblen, institutions are instrumental. Overall, *The Theory of the Leisure Class* clearly contradicts rather than lends support to the Ayresian dichotomy. Passages in Veblen's other works support an equivalent verdict. One of the clearest and most dramatic is the following. In an amazingly prescient analysis of the Japanese socio-economic system – written in 1915 – Veblen (1934, p. 251) remarks: 'It is in this unique combination of a high-wrought spirit of feudalistic fealty and chivalric honour with the material efficiency given by the modern technology that the strength of the Japanese nation lies'. Such an observation is commonplace in the recent literature on the sources of the post-1945 Japanese economic miracle. But Veblen wrote it well before the rise of modern Japan, and nevertheless saw the root of its future strength. This strength does not lie in technology alone but in its *combination* with conservative and ceremonial institutions 'of feudalistic fealty and chivalric honour'. This assertion does not simply contradict the Ayresian dichotomy, it turns it inside out and upside down.

In sum, Ayres's notion of a conflict between institutions and technology is not only absent in Veblen's writings but it is contradicted by Veblen's own words and conceptions. Whatever its validity, its description as 'the Veblenian dichotomy' is unwarranted.

The Non-Veblenian Origins of the Dichotomy

If it is absent in Veblen, from whence did the Ayresian dichotomy originate? The most obvious influence on Ayres in this respect would be Dewey. In a typical discussion of the progress of modern science and associated methods of evaluation, Dewey (1939, pp. 61–2) remarked that:

> the difficulties that stand in the way are, in the main, practical. They are supplied by traditions, customs, and institutions which persist without being subjected to a systematic empirical investigation . . . Take, as an outstanding example, the difficulties experienced in getting a hearing for the Copernican astronomy a few

centuries ago. Traditional and customary beliefs which were sanctioned and maintained by powerful institutions regarded the new scientific ideas as a menace.

However, Dewey does not state that *all* institutions constrain scientific or technological advance. Furthermore, for Dewey, habits and institutions have a positive and enabling function. Dewey (1930, p. 31) wrote: 'Habits are conditions of intellectual efficiency'. Furthermore, redolent of William James, he remarked:

> Habit is however more than a restriction of thought. Habits become negative limits because they are first positive agencies. The more numerous our habits the wider the field of possible observation and foretelling. The more flexible they are, the more refined is perception in its discrimination and the more delicate the presentation evoked by imagination. (Dewey 1930, pp. 175–6)

From such a viewpoint it is understandable that Dewey directly criticized Ayres for his one-sided view of habit. In their letters to each other they were at loggerheads on this matter (Tilman 1990). Clearly, Ayres did not adopt all of Dewey's ideas on this area.

Perhaps strangely, another possible precursor of the Ayresian dichotomy is found in the writings of Karl Marx. Although Ayres rarely acknowledged Marx, we can read *The Theory of Economic Progress* as an Americanized version of Marx's theory of economic development, as if sanitized and expurgated so as not to offend American liberal tastes. The genesis of Ayres's mature views in the 1930s coincides with a period when – in reaction to fascism and economic depression – Marxist writings were gaining an increased visibility among American intellectuals. Marx saw technology as a motor of economic change and a prime determinant of fundamental changes of and within economic systems.[8] In his 1847 book *The Poverty of Philosophy* he wrote:

> Social relations are closely bound up with productive forces. In acquiring new productive forces men change their mode of production; and in changing their mode of production, in changing their way of earning a living, they change all their social relations. The hand-mill gives you society with the feudal lord; the steam-mill, society with the industrial capitalist . . . the mode of production, the relations in which productive forces are developed . . . correspond to a definite development of men and of their productive forces, and . . . a change in men's productive forces necessarily brings about a change in their relations of production. (Marx and Engels 1976, pp. 166–75)

In the famous 1859 Preface to his *Critique of Political Economy* Marx elaborated these ideas:

In the social production of their existence, men inevitably enter into definite relations, which are independent of their will, namely relations of production appropriate to a given stage in the development of the material forces of production. The totality of these relations of production constitutes the economic structure of society, the real foundation, on which arises a legal and political superstructure and to which correspond definite forms of social consciousness . . . At a certain stage of development, the material productive forces of society come into conflict with the existing relations of production or . . . with the property relations within the framework of which they have operated hitherto . . . The changes in the economic foundation lead sooner or later to the transformation of the whole immense superstructure. In studying such transformations it is always necessary to distinguish between the material transformation of the economic conditions of production, which can be determined with the precision of natural science, and the legal, political, religious, artistic or philosophic – in short, ideological forms in which men become conscious of this conflict and fight it out. (Marx, 1971, pp. 20–21)

If we replace 'productive forces' or 'material forces of production' by 'technology', and substitute 'institutions' for 'social relations' or 'relations of production', then we have passages that could almost have been written by Ayres. The dichotomy between institutions and technology has thus a close precursor in Marx's portrayal of the forces of production pushing up against the relations of production. Both Marx and Ayres believed that technology was a primary and driving force of history. They shared an optimism in the powers of technology and science that is traceable back to eighteenth century Enlightenment thinkers and which dominated the nineteenth and the early twentieth century.

A difference here, however, is that Ayres saw 'no institution . . . or set of institutions' as ' "appropriate" to a given technology in any but a negative sense' (Ayres, 1944, p. 187). In contrast, Marx saw institutions as being periodically brought into harmony with technological development. For Ayres, the conflict between technology and institutions was ongoing and continuous. For Marx, the conflict was now and then temporarily ameliorated by social revolution and by the subsequent recasting of the economy along new and progressive lines. Marx analysed change in revolutionary terms; Ayres brought the perspective of a gradualist.

Nevertheless, the similarities between Marx and Ayres go further. Ayres (1944, p. 307) accepted, just like Marx, 'the possibility of abundance' as a result of future technological advance. In their analytical approaches, both Marx and Ayres focused on grand, social forces, to the neglect of micro-socioeconomic processes and details. Problems of consciousness and agency were largely neglected by Ayres.[9] Likewise, in Marx's work as a whole the theory of agency remained underdeveloped, as Veblen (1919, pp. 313–14, 416, 441–2) himself critically remarked on several occasions.

In their political stances, however, there are clear differences. In his stress of the need for social revolution to transform society, Marx differed from

Ayres. Ayres was more optimistic about reformism, and less enthusiastic about the goal of common ownership. He advocated a form of 'limited capitalism'. Perhaps he was 'ceremonially' adjusting to American ways.

The last sentence is not mere jest. In both the scope and substance of his thinking, Ayres was ironically himself a prisoner of the broadly established mores of American libertarianism and technophilia. In its exposition his own vision was powerful and unique. But in broad terms it conformed to the anti-authoritarianism and scientism of the American liberal intelligentsia. In downgrading religion he placed himself in an American minority, but in the substitute worship of technology he was true to American cultural form. His creed was characteristically an expression of a deeply rooted tradition of progressive American culture, with a pedigree going back to Benjamin Franklin and Thomas Paine, and before that to the European Enlightenment, with its priests of science and technology such as the Marquis de Condorcet. Ayres (1961, p. 35) wrote: 'As we are just beginning to understand, it is all one process: science and freedom, technology and beauty'. For Ayres himself the wheel had turned full circle: science the Messiah had come.

IN CONCLUSION: DICHOTOMIES AFTER AYRES

The subsequent development of work in the Ayresian institutionalist tradition has been well discussed and documented elsewhere (Bush 1986, 1987; Dugger 1995; Foster 1981; Junker 1982; Tool 1979, 1995; Waller 1982, 1994). I do not intend to address this work in detail here, other than to focus on one or two aspects, and to consider in the light of the above discussion the important contribution by Bush.

It has been shown above that Ayres's definition of an institution is, at best, a mangled version of the one laid down by Veblen. He rebutted the classic attempt to elucidate the concept by Walton Hamilton (1932). However, in the post-Ayresian tradition the definition of an institution was one of the first things to be changed and clarified. Ayres's narrow and non-Veblenian definition was modified by J. Fagg Foster, one of Ayres's students. In turn, Foster taught Marc Tool, who attributes the following definition to his teacher: 'The term institution means any prescribed or proscribed pattern of correlated behaviour or attitude widely agreed upon among a group of persons organized to carry on some particular purpose' (Tool 1979, p. 74). This definition is much closer to that of Veblen, although it gives too much emphasis to particular institutions involving deliberation, organization and agreement, and downplays or excludes institutions that may arise spontaneously, without overall design. Furthermore, the crucial Veblenian concept of habit is omitted. This change in definition was of significance not simply because of the increase in Veblenian fidelity. It admitted the possibility that institutions may have *both* instrumental and ceremonial aspects, and eliminates a series of problems for that reason.

Having redefined the concept of an institution in a manner closer to the Veblen–Hamilton precedents, the next concept that required attention by Ayres's followers was technology. Especially after the rise of the American anti-war and green movements in the 1960s and 1970s, concern was expressed that Ayres had given a questionably positive evaluation to all technology, including militaristic and nuclear technologies. Accordingly, in the writings of Foster's followers, the emphasis shifted away from technology *per se*, towards more general processes of 'instrumental valuation' (Bush 1987, pp. 1086–90).

Nevertheless, it was still argued – along typically Ayresian lines – that the 'technological process is inherently dynamic' (Bush 1987, p. 1089). Any suggestion of technological lock-in or constraint was dealt with by identifying the constraining influence of 'ceremonial institutions'. Here lay the importance of Bush's (1986, 1987) concept of 'ceremonial encapsulation'. It was argued that dynamic technology may become entwined with and 'encapsulated' within hierarchy, status and other 'ceremonial' institutions.[10]

Overall, the work by Bush, Tool and others is more sophisticated and refined than that provided by Ayres himself. Not only is Ayres's inadequate definition of an institution replaced, but there is a more complex and illustrative taxonomy of possible relations between the instrumental and the ceremonial. To a large degree, the work in this tradition is a retreat from Ayres's strict and questionable dichotomy.

In the view of the present author, the deepest problem with this post-Ayresian approach lies in its notion of 'evidentially warranted knowledge' (Bush 1987, p. 1080). I agree with Philip Mirowski (1987) that this idea relies on an empiricist view of knowledge and science which is largely, but not wholly, traceable to Dewey. The influence also of Ayres still lingers strongly here. In fact, Ayres gave Dewey an additional empiricist twist. 'Where Dewey wanted to portray scientific enquiry as a continuous questioning procedure, Ayres tried to portray it as the accumulation of certain and final knowledge by means of the accumulation of tools and artefacts' (Mirowski 1987, p. 1029). Ayres read Dewey in curiously empiricist terms, seeing knowledge as a firm and visible construction upon the fixed bedrock of science, unencumbered by contingent habit or routine. Ayres shared Dewey's rejection of the possibility – cherished by the positivists – of a complete distinction between judgements of fact and of value. However, the shared rejection of one positivist tenet simply masked Ayres's own adoption of a thoroughly empiricist epistemology. For Ayres, problems of valuation were resolved merely by elaborations of accumulated scientific fact. Rather than interpenetrating each other, the domain of value was dissolved completely into the domain of fact. In contrast, Dewey saw science as more experimental, interacting with social institutions and norms. Means and ends interacted and reconstituted each other, but without losing the duality between the two. Nevertheless, in varying degrees, the positions of both Dewey and Ayres depended upon an exaggerated faith in scientific procedure and an untenable empiricist notion that science in general provided a direct and unambiguous source of knowledge about the world. The concept of 'evidentially warranted knowledge' reflects this questionable and empiricist legacy.

Consider Veblen's (1914, p. 53) remark that: 'All facts of observation are necessarily seen in the light of the observer's habits of thought' and Bush's (1987, p. 1078) own valid observation that: 'All inquiry involves interpretation, and interpretation requires judgement'. If we are to take these statements seriously then no knowledge is possible without prior habits of thought and without prior acts of judgement. The evidence alone cannot provide or 'warrant' these prior habits, judgements or conceptual schemata. No observation can be independent of the prior conceptual framework, language or theoretical system of the observer. That is one reason why an empiricist epistemology is now widely recognized as untenable.[11] This leaves the notion of 'evidentially warranted knowledge' as highly questionable and problematic. The problem is that evidence cannot speak for itself. On its own, evidence cannot warrant any form of knowledge.

A secondary criticism is that, despite the relative sophistication of the post-Ayresian approach, some unacceptable aspects of dichotomous thinking are retained. It is not recognized that, in some respects, technology *is* and *must be* ceremonial. Furthermore, to some degree, the ceremonial can be functional or instrumental.

A fundamental and complex methodological issue is involved here, perhaps best approached by distinguishing – following Anthony Giddens (1984) and others – between the concepts of *duality* and *dualism*. The two elements of a dualism are regarded as independently given, and mutually exclusive or separable, phenomena (Dow 1990). By contrast, crucial to the idea of a duality is the notion that the parts are interdependent: each element may actually help to constitute the other. In a dualism the two elements are atomistically separable; in a duality they are organically related. In a duality, one part is not external to, nor separable from, the other part; each typically enables as well as constrains the other. Hence Giddens rejected the dualism between agency and structure in some versions of social theory: that separable dualism allowing the false primacy of agency over structure or vice versa. Instead, Giddens saw agent and structure as a duality: where both human subjects and social institutions are jointly constituted in and through recurrent practices, and where no element has ontological or analytical priority over the other.

Ayres's dichotomies between technology and ceremony, and between technology and institutions, are examples of dualisms rather than dualities. Ayres saw each element in each dichotomy as potentially separable from the other. He thus alluded to a possible future world virtually free of institutions and ruled by the principles of technological instrumentalism. In practical terms, this neglects the importance of an appropriate mix of flexibility and inflexibility in the institutional structures of a complex economic system. Some degree of inflexibility is required to foster trust, stable expectations and social cohesion. Some degree of flexibility is necessary to accommodate innovation and change. Crucially, each depends on the other. Innovation depends on a degree of stability, just as stability is possible with a degree of innovation. Ayres did not advocate unrestrained free markets, but his one-sided conception of institutions as constraints fits well into the American libertarian tradition that sustains such policies.

Although the Bush–Junker concept of ceremonial encapsulation improved on Ayres's stark dichotomies, it involved internal dualisms of its own. That which encapsulates was still seen as separable from, rather than organically dependent upon, that which was encapsulated. The 'organic' and 'dialectical' thinking (Whitehead 1926; Georgescu-Roegen 1971) that is involved in the contrary idea of duality may make it much more difficult to draw plain and unqualified normative conclusions from the theoretical analysis. Nevertheless, it may actually lead to policy conclusions which are more sophisticated and persuasive.

There is an additional and fundamental reason why the Foster–Tool–Bush approach is worthy of further development. At root, it addresses an enduring and central problem of economic theory and policy. Over two millennia ago, Aristotle in his *Politics* established the distinction between 'use value' and 'exchange value'. The pecuniary nature of the latter term is obvious. 'Use value', however, has been interpreted by some neoclassical-inclined writers as a precursor of subjective utility. Against this, Karl Polanyi (Polanyi et al. 1957, pp. 65–7, 80–83) suggests, however, that Aristotle saw use-value as an objective quality relating to the usefulness of an item for humankind. The dichotomy between 'use value' and 'exchange value' thus corresponds to a dichotomy between the socially instrumental and the pecuniary. As well as being one of the oldest, it is one of the most important and fundamental dichotomies for economic science.

By contrast, ignoring this ancient dichotomy, modern mainstream welfare economics is founded on the concept of individual utility. Policies are judged not in relation to scientific knowledge concerning, for example, human health or the ecosystem, but exclusively in regard to their ability to increase consumer satisfaction. This utilitarian approach is so widespread that the alternative and non-utilitarian approaches to problems of welfare – found in the writings of Aristotle, Adam Smith, Karl Marx, the German historical school and the institutionalists – are generally ignored. Bush's work is in that great alternative tradition, pointing to a concept of human need that transcends utilitarianism. Whatever the problems in this alternative approach, its further development should not be neglected. Some of what is positive in the Ayresian legacy can be transformed into a theory of human need (Doyal and Gough 1991). The insurmountable problems in an empiricist view of science give us no reason to embrace subjectivism nor to abandon a scientific outlook.

NOTES

1. The author is very grateful for comments, criticisms and suggestions by Sasan Fayazmanesh and Marc Tool on an earlier draft of this essay.
2. Ayres wrote in a letter to Dewey dated 29 January 1930: 'an institution . . . is a bad thing from which we are bound to try perpetually to redeem ourselves' (quoted in Tilman 1990, p. 966). He repeats similar sentiments later, combining these with a rejection of the institutionalist label for himself and other followers of Veblen and Commons: 'As a designation of a way of thinking in economics the term "institutionalism" is singularly unfortunate, since it points only at that from which an escape is being sought' (Ayres 1944, p. 155 n.).
3. It should be noted, however, that Ayres (for example, 1961, p. 190) at least once admitted a role for human motivation in technological change. These admissions were consistent with the thrust of his theory.
4. It is sometimes overlooked that Frank Knight was both a friend of Ayres and a self-avowed institutionalist. Knight responded to Ayres (1935) by noting that Ayres's argument assumed 'some kind of inner law of progress of an absolute and inscrutable character' for technology; that 'there is some equally absolute and inscrutable type of "causality" by which technology drags behind it and "determines" other phases of social change' (Knight 1935, p. 208) 'typically, if not universally, such [technological] changes are connected with changes in the end to be achieved as well as in the means or technique, and it cannot be maintained that the change in procedure generally precedes and causes the shift in interest' (ibid., p. 210).
5. Hamilton's (1932) sophisticated attempt at an elaborated definition of an institution was described by Ayres, in a letter to Knight of 23 February 1937, as 'nine tenths piffle' (quoted in Samuels 1977a, p. 504).
6. Remarkably, this major work contains no footnotes, nor bibliographic references. It was as if Ayres wanted to escape from all bonds with the past in his academic presentation as well as its content.
7. Contrary to Bush (1986, p. 29) this passage does not lend support to a general principle 'of the dominance of ceremonial patterns of behaviour over instrumental patterns of behaviour within the culture'. Even if 'instrumental patterns of behaviour' can be equated with Veblen's 'parental bent or the sense of workmanship', Veblen clearly also considers *their* triumph and dominance *over* ceremonial behaviour, as well as the reverse possibility.
8. For an elaboration and defence of Marx's view of technology as a driving force of history see Cohen (1978).
9. Ayres's neglect of these issues is partly explained by his acceptance of the behaviourist orthodoxy in the psychology of his time (Ayres 1936).
10. In devising the concept of ceremonial encapsulation, Bush (1986, p. 25) generously acknowledges the influence and assistance of Louis Junker.
11. Although positivism greatly increased in popularity in American scientific circles in the first half of the twentieth century, the publication in 1951 of Quine's essay 'Two Dogmas of Empiricism' (reprinted in Quine 1953) helped to check and reverse the movement. Quine effectively undermined the distinction between science and non-science in logical positivism and denied that statements could be judged true or false purely on the basis of sense experience. 'The publication of this essay in 1951 was one of the key events in the collapse of logical positivism' (Hoover 1995, p. 721). In continuing to base judgmental claims upon science, and in adopting an empiricist and positivist epistemology, the Ayresian axis did not take sufficient account of the significance of this collapse.

REFERENCES

Arthur, W. Brian (1988), 'Self-Reinforcing Mechanisms in Economics', in Philip W. Anderson, Kenneth J. Arrow and David Pines (eds), *The Economy as an Evolving Complex System*, Reading, MA: Addison-Wesley, pp. 9–31.

_____(1989), 'Competing Technologies, Increasing Returns, and Lock-in by Historical Events', *Economic Journal*, **99** (1), March, pp. 116–31. Reprinted in Freeman (1990).

Ayres, Clarence E. (1927), *Science: The False Messiah*, Indianapolis: Bobbs-Merrill. Reprinted 1973, New York: Augustus Kelley.

_____(1929), *Holier Than Thou: The Way of the Righteous*, Indianapolis: Bobbs-Merrill. Reprinted 1973, New York: Augustus Kelley.

_____(1935), 'Moral Confusion in Economics', *International Journal of Ethics*, **45**, January, pp. 170–99. Reprinted in Samuels (1988), vol. 2.

_____(1936) 'Fifty Years' Developments in Ideas of Human Nature and Motivation', *American Economic Review (Papers and Proceedings)*, **26** (1), March, pp. 224–36.

_____(1938), *The Problem of Economic Order*, New York: Farrar and Rinehart.

_____(1943), 'The Twilight of the Price System', *Antioch Review*, **3**, Summer, pp. 162–81.

_____(1944), *The Theory of Economic Progress*, 1st edn, Chapel Hill, North Carolina: University of North Carolina Press.

_____(1949), 'The Value Economy', in Ray Lepley (ed.), *Value: A Cooperative Inquiry*, New York: Columbia University Press, pp. 43–63.

_____(1952), *The Industrial Economy: Its Technological Basis and Institutional Destiny*, Cambridge, MA: Houghton Mifflin.

_____(1953), 'The Role of Technology in Economic Theory', *American Economic Review (Papers and Proceedings)*, **43** (2), May, pp. 279–87.

_____(1960), 'Institutionalism and Economic Development', *Southwestern Social Science Quarterly*, **41** (2), June, pp. 45–62.

_____ (1961), *Toward a Reasonable Society: The Values of Industrial Civilization*, Austin: University of Texas Press.

_____(1963), 'The Legacy of Thorstein Veblen', in Joseph Dorfman, Clarence W. Ayres, Neil W. Chamberlain, Simon Kuznets and Robert A. Gordon (eds), *Institutional Economics: Veblen, Commons, and Mitchell Reconsidered*, Berkeley, CA: University of California Press, pp. 46–62.

_____(1967), 'Guaranteed Income: An Institutionalist View', in Robert Theobald (ed.), *The Guaranteed Income: Next Step in Socioeconomic Evolution?*, New York: Doubleday, pp. 169–82.

_____(1968), 'The Price System and Public Policy', *Journal of Economic Issues*, **2** (3), September, pp. 342–4.

_____(1973), 'Prolegomenon to Institutionalism', introduction to the combined reprint of Ayres (1927, 1929), New York: Augustus Kelley.

Blaug, Mark (ed.) (1992a), *Thorstein Veblen (1857–1929)*, Aldershot: Edward Elgar.

_____(1992b), *Wesley Mitchell (1874–1948), John Commons (1862–1945), Clarence Ayres (1891–1972)*, Aldershot: Edward Elgar.

Bush, Paul Dale (1986), 'On the Concept of Ceremonial Encapsulation', *The Review of Institutional Thought*, **3**, December, pp. 25–45.

_____(1987), 'The Theory of Institutional Change', *Journal of Economic Issues*, **21** (3), September, pp. 1075–116. Reprinted in Hodgson (1993).

Coats, A.W. (1976), 'Clarence Ayres' Place in the History of American Economics: An Interim Assessment', in William Breit and William P. Culbertson, Jr (eds), *Science and Ceremony: The Institutional Economics of C.E. Ayres*, Austin: University of Texas Press, pp. 23–48. Reprinted in A.W. Coats (1992), *On the History of Economic Thought: British and American Economic Essays*, Volume I, London: Routledge.

Cohen, Gerald A. (1978), *Karl Marx's Theory of History: A Defence*, Oxford: Oxford University Press.

David, Paul A. (1985), 'Clio and the Economics of QWERTY', *American Economic Review (Papers and Proceedings)*, **75** (2), May, pp. 332–7. Reprinted in Freeman (1990) and Ulrich Witt (ed.) (1993), *Evolutionary Economics*, Aldershot: Edward Elgar.

Dewey, John (1930), *Human Nature and Conduct: An Introduction to Social Psychology*, New York: Random House.

_____(1939), *Theory of Valuation*, Chicago: University of Chicago Press.

Dosi, Giovanni (1988), 'The Sources, Procedures, and Microeconomic Effects of Innovation', *Journal of Economic Literature*, **26** (3), September, pp. 1120–71. Reprinted in Freeman (1990).

Dow, Sheila C. (1990), 'Beyond Dualism', *Cambridge Journal of Economics*, **14** (2), June, pp. 143–57.

Doyal, Leonard and Ian Gough (1991), *A Theory of Human Need*, London: Macmillan.

Dugger, William M. (1995), 'Veblenian Institutionalism: The Changing Concepts of Inquiry', *Journal of Economic Issues*, **29** (4), December, pp. 1013–27.

Edgell, Stephen (1975), 'Thorstein Veblen's Theory of Evolutionary Change', *American Journal of Economics and Sociology*, **34**, July, pp. 267–80.

Foster, J. Fagg (1981), 'The Relation Between the Theory of Value and Economic Analysis', *Journal of Economic Issues*, **15** (4), December, pp. 899–905. Reprinted in Marc R. Tool and Warren J. Samuels (eds) (1989), *The Methodology of Economic Thought*, 2nd edn, New Brunswick, NJ: Transaction.

Freeman, Christopher (ed.) (1990), *The Economics of Innovation*, Aldershot: Edward Elgar.

Georgescu-Roegen, Nicholas (1971), *The Entropy Law and the Economic Process*, Cambridge, MA: Harvard University Press.

Giddens, Anthony (1984), *The Constitution of Society: Outline of the Theory of Structuration*, Cambridge: Polity Press.

Hamilton, Walton H. (1932), 'Institution', in Edwin R.A. Seligman and A. Johnson (eds), *Encyclopaedia of the Social Sciences*, Vol. 8, pp. 84–9. Reprinted in Hodgson (1993).

Hill, Lewis E. (1989), 'Cultural Determinism or Emergent Evolution: An Analysis of the Controversy Between Clarence Ayres and David Miller', *Journal of Economic Issues*, **23** (2), June, pp. 465–71.

Hodgson, Geoffrey M. (ed.) (1993), *The Economics of Institutions*, Aldershot: Edward Elgar.

Hodgson, Geoffrey M., Warren J. Samuels and Marc R. Tool (eds) (1994), *The Elgar Companion to Institutional and Evolutionary Economics*, 2 vols, Aldershot: Edward Elgar.

Hoover, Kevin D. (1995), 'Why Does Methodology Matter for Economics?', *Economic*

Journal, **105** (3), May, pp. 715–34.

Junker, Louis J. (1982), 'The Ceremonial–Instrumental Dichotomy in Institutional Analysis', *American Journal of Economics and Sociology*, **41** (2), pp. 141–50.

Katz, Michael L. and Carl Shapiro (1985), 'Network Externalities, Competition, and Compatibility', *American Economic Review*, **75** (3), June, pp. 424–40.

Kindleberger, Charles P. (1983), 'Standards, as Public, Collective and Private Goods', *Kyklos*, **36**, pp. 377–96.

Klein, Philip A. (1995), 'Ayres on Institutions – a Reconsideration', *Journal of Economic Issues*, **29** (4), December, pp. 1189–96.

Knight, Frank H. (1935), 'Intellectual Confusion on Morals and Economics', *International Journal of Ethics*, **45** (1), January, pp. 200–220.

Marx, Karl (1971), *A Contribution to the Critique of Political Economy*, translated from the German edition of 1859 by S.W. Ryazanskaya and edited with an introduction by Maurice Dobb, London: Lawrence and Wishart.

Marx, Karl and Frederick Engels (1976), *Karl Marx and Frederick Engels, Collected Works, Vol. 6, Marx and Engels: 1845–48*, London: Lawrence and Wishart.

McFarland, Floyd B. (1985), 'Thorstein Veblen Versus the Institutionalists', *Review of Radical Political Economics*, **17** (4), Winter, pp. 95–105.

Miller, David L. (1958), *Modern Science and Human Freedom*, Austin, Texas: University of Texas Press.

_____(1966), *Individualism*, Austin, Texas: University of Texas Press.

Mirowski, Philip (1987), 'The Philosophical Bases of Institutional Economics', *Journal of Economic Issues*, **21** (3), September, pp. 1001–38. Reprinted in Philip Mirowski (1988), *Against Mechanism: Protecting Economics from Science*, Totowa, NJ: Rowman and Littlefield.

Nelson, Richard R. and Sidney G. Winter (1982), *An Evolutionary Theory of Economic Change*, Cambridge, MA: Harvard University Press.

Polanyi, Karl, Conrad M. Arensberg and Harry W. Pearson (eds) (1957), *Trade and Market in the Early Empires*, Chicago: Henry Regnery.

Polanyi, Michael (1958), *Personal Knowledge: Towards a Post-Critical Philosophy*, London: Routledge and Kegan Paul.

_____(1967), *The Tacit Dimension*, London: Routledge and Kegan Paul.

Quine, Willard van Orman (1953), *From a Logical Point of View*, Cambridge, MA: Harvard University Press.

Rosenberg, Nathan (1976), 'On Technological Expectations', *Economic Journal*, **86** (3), September, pp. 523–35. Reprinted in Freeman (1990).

Rutherford, Malcolm C. (1981), 'Clarence Ayres and the Instrumentalist Theory of Value', *Journal of Economic Issues*, **15** (3), September, pp. 657–74. Reprinted in Samuels (1988), vol. 3.

_____(1994), *Institutions in Economics: The Old and the New Institutionalism*, Cambridge: Cambridge University Press.

Samuels, Warren J. (1977a), 'The Knight–Ayres Correspondence: The Grounds of Knowledge and Social Action', *Journal of Economic Issues*, **11** (3), September, pp. 485–525. Reprinted in Blaug (1992b).

_____(1977b), 'Technology *Vis-à-Vis* Institutions in the JEI: A Suggested Interpretation', *Journal of Economic Issues*, **11** (4), December, pp. 871–95. Reprinted in Samuels (1988) vol. 3.

_____(ed.) (1988), *Institutional Economics*, 3 vols, Aldershot: Edward Elgar.

Tilman, Rick (1990), 'New Light on John Dewey, Clarence Ayres, and the Development of Evolutionary Economics', *Journal of Economic Issues*, **24** (4), December, pp. 963–79.

Tilman, Rick (ed.) (1993), *A Veblen Treasury: From Leisure Class to War, Peace and Capitalism*, Armonk, NY: M.E. Sharpe.

Tool, Marc R. (1979), *The Discretionary Economy*, Santa Monica, CA: Goodyear.

_____(1994), 'Ayres, Clarence E.', in Hodgson et al. (1994), vol. 1, pp. 16–22.

_____(1995), *Pricing, Valuation and Systems: Essays in Neoinstitutional Economics*, Aldershot: Edward Elgar.

Veblen, Thorstein B. (1899), *The Theory of the Leisure Class: An Economic Study in the Evolution of Institutions*, New York: Macmillan. Republished 1961, New York: Random House.

_____(1904), *The Theory of Business Enterprise*, New York: Charles Scribners. Reprinted 1975 by Augustus Kelley.

_____ (1914), *The Instinct of Workmanship, and the State of the Industrial Arts*, New York: Augustus Kelley. Reprinted 1990 with a new introduction by Murray G. Murphey and a 1964 introductory note by J. Dorfman, New Brunswick, NJ: Transaction Books.

_____(1919), *The Place of Science in Modern Civilization and Other Essays*, New York: Huebsch. Reprinted 1990 with a new introduction by W.J. Samuels, New Brunswick, NJ: Transaction Books.

_____ (1923), *Absentee Ownership and Business Enterprise in Recent Times*, New York: Huebsch.

_____(1934), *Essays on Our Changing Order*, ed. Leon Ardzrooni, New York: The Viking Press.

Walker, Donald A. (1977), 'Thorstein Veblen's Economic System', *Economic Inquiry*, **15** (2), April, pp. 213–37. Reprinted in Samuels (1988), vol. 1 and in Blaug (1992a).

_____(1979), 'The Institutionalist Economic Theories of Clarence Ayres', *Economic Inquiry*, **17** (4), October, pp. 519–38. Reprinted in Samuels (1988) vol. 1and Blaug (1992b).

Waller, William J., Jr (1982), 'The Evolution of the Veblenian Dichotomy: Veblen, Hamilton, Ayres, and Foster', *Journal of Economic Issues*, **16** (3), September, pp. 757–71. Reprinted in R. Albeda, C. Gunn and W. Waller (eds) (1987), *Alternatives to Economic Orthodoxy*, Armonk, NY: M.E. Sharpe, in Blaug (1992a) and in Hodgson (1993).

_____(1994), 'The Veblenian Dichotomy and its Critics', in Hodgson et al. (1994), vol. 2, pp. 368–72.

Whitehead, Alfred N. (1926), *Science and the Modern World*, Cambridge: Cambridge University Press.

4. On Veblen's Coining of the Term 'Neoclassical'

Sasan Fayazmanesh[1]

It is an ironic twist of history that one of the most original and profound critics of the marginal utility theorists, Thorstein Veblen, is also the one who gave them the name 'neoclassical', a name that they happily embraced. We owe this finding to Tony Aspromourgos, who writes that Veblen 'coined the term in the last installment of a three-part essay on "The Preconceptions of Economic Science" published in the *Quarterly Journal of Economics* in 1899 and 1900' (Aspromourgos 1986, p. 266).[2] In these essays, Aspromourgos argues, 'Veblen conceived Marshallian economics to be "neoclassical" because it had in common with the classics a utilitarian approach and employed a hedonistic psychology' (p. 269). According to Aspromourgos, this argument is correct 'with regard to the utilitarianism' (p. 269). But he contends that Veblen's argument is flawed on two counts: 'On the one hand he sought to argue that the subjective theory of value was essentially an expression of that utilitarianism, on the other, that the Marshallian system was fundamentally the same as that of other marginalists" (p. 269). According to Aspromourgos, John Hicks has already pointed out that utilitarian assumptions are not necessary for a subjective theory of value. This 'more correct conception of marginalism employed by Hicks and Stigler', writes Aspromourgos, 'should have pre-empted a view of continuity between classical and marginalist theory', and hence, it would be best if the term 'neo-classical' were to be 'expunged' from the language of economics (p. 269).

Aspromourgos's finding was more than just a historical footnote. The expression 'neoclassical economics' implies, as we will see, continuity of thought between the classical economists and the marginal utility theorists, a continuity which has often been claimed by the marginalists themselves. Yet it has become increasingly evident in recent years that such claims are unjustified. In constructing their theories, marginalists emulated nineteenth century physics, as Philip Mirowski has forcefully pointed out (Mirowski 1984, 1989b). They gave, or attempted to give, economic meaning to concepts already existing in mathematical physics, as I have argued elsewhere (Fayazmanesh 1996, forthcoming 1998). In so doing, they drastically changed the method of analysis

74

and introduced new concepts. However, often they called these new concepts by the old terms, and this created the illusion of continuity. Aspromourgos made a significant contribution to our understanding of this illusion by pointing out the origin of the term 'neoclassical', and claiming that this concept was flawed from the very beginning. Yet his argument and plea to reconsider the use of the term 'neoclassical' seems to have fallen mostly on deaf ears. Economists, particularly marginalists, continue to use 'neoclassical', and its even less meaningful extension 'new classical'. This is not surprising. The general disdain of economists toward 'exercises in semantics', and their pragmatic attitude toward conceptual clarity, is well known (Machlup 1963, p. 3). Yet, in the interest of those who value such exercises and find their implications important, I would like to discuss Aspromourgos's contention and its implication. In particular, I hope my friend and colleague Professor Bush, whose interest in hermeneutics is well known, would find my argument interesting, even though he may disagree with my reading of Veblen.

More specifically, I would like to argue in this essay that the term 'neoclassical' is indeed flawed, and that it should be discarded from the language of economics, as Aspromourgos contends. But my argument is based on very different reasoning from that of Aspromourgos. I claim, in the second section of the essay, that Veblen's concept of 'classical economics', which forms the basis for his term 'neo-classical', is itself not a well-crafted concept. According to Veblen, the most important characteristic of 'classical economics' is 'utilitarianism'. However, I argue that Veblen's concept of 'utilitarianism' is so broad and ambiguous that it renders the term 'classical economics' unintelligible. In the third section of the essay, I will demonstrate how Veblen's problem of not clearly defining 'classical economics' spills over into defining the concept 'neoclassical'. Here, it will be argued that, as a result of not meticulously sorting out his concepts, Veblen puts forward two incongruent positions with regard to the relation between the proponents of marginal utility theory and the 'classical economists'. On the one hand, he seems to believe that the two schools are continuous. This necessitates coining the phrase 'neo-classical'. On the other, he argues that the two schools are actually identical. This makes the term 'neo-classical' unnecessary and, as a result, Veblen himself abandons the use of the term. The fourth section presents a summary of the essay and some concluding remarks. Before all of this, however, I would like to trace the root of the term 'classical economics' and discuss the difficulty in its interpretation.

MARX AND 'CLASSICAL POLITICAL ECONOMY'

On the first page of the first chapter of the *General Theory*, John Maynard Keynes (1936, p. 3) writes in a footnote:

> 'The classical economists' was a name invented by Marx to cover Ricardo and James Mill and their predecessors, that is to say for the founders of the theory which culminated in the Ricardian economics. I have become accustomed, perhaps perpetrating a solecism, to include in 'the classical school' the followers of Ricardo, those that is to say, who adopted and perfected the theory of Ricardian economics, including (for example) J.S. Mill, Marshall, Edgeworth and Prof. Pigou.

Keynes clearly recognizes that Marx was the originator of the term 'classical political economy'. He is also clearly aware that including such an economist as Marshall in the 'classical' school is an act of solecism. What is not clear, however, is if Keynes knew the extent of his solecistic act.

In the *General Theory*, Keynes himself uses the designation 'classical' in three different ways, without ever defining the term explicitly. First, the term appears to refer to all those who believe that 'supply creates its own demand', or the so-called Say's Law (Keynes 1936, p. 18). Second, it seems to refer to those who 'safely neglect the aggregate demand function' (p. 33).[3] Third, it is used to designate those 'who believe that saving and investment . . . are equal' (p. 177).[4] All of these indirect definitions may of course be identical from Keynes's perspective, but none has anything to do with Marx's definition.

'Classical political economy' is one of those terms that originated in what Keynes would call the 'under-worlds' of Karl Marx (1936, p. 32). It is defined only once in *Capital* in a very esoteric fashion and as part of a footnote on the distinction between value as a form and value as a content:

> Let me point once and for all that by classical political economy I mean all the economists, who since the time of W. Petty, have investigated the real internal framework of bourgeois relations of production, as opposed to the vulgar economists who only flounder around within the apparent framework of those relations, ceaselessly ruminate on the materials long since provided by scientific political economy, and seek there plausible explanations of the crudest phenomena for the domestic purposes of the bourgeoisie. Apart from this, the vulgar economists confine themselves to systematizing in a pedantic way, and proclaiming for everlasting truths, the banal and complacent notions held by the bourgeois agents of production about their own world, which is to them the best possible one. (Marx 1873, pp. 174–5)

To the uninitiated, such expressions as 'internal framework' and 'apparent framework' mean very little. The distinction between 'classical political economists' and 'vulgar economists' does not mean much either, except that the latter sounds pejorative. As a result, it is difficult for the casual reader to get a full sense of Marx's definition of 'classical political economy'. It is only when one investigates Marx's concept of science and scientific method of political economy and, as part of this investigation, one searches for the meanings of words, that a true sense of Marx's concept of 'classical political economy' emerges. Since I have attempted this elsewhere, I will not dwell on the issue and will confine myself to the following brief note (Fayazmanesh 1984).

One of the most distinctive aspects of Marx's economic writings, one that emerges from his investigation in *Grundrisse*, is the belief that the object of political economy, similar to the object of natural science, creates illusions and inversions. As a result, Marx comes to believe that in order to comprehend capitalist society fully, one must leave the domain of sense perception, where illusions and inversions are encountered, and enter the domain of scientific inquiry, where abstract concepts and theories are constructed. This epistemological distinction between 'scientific' investigation and sensory perception appears in many expressions in Marx's writings.[5] One such pair of expressions is what appears in the above passage in *Capital*, that is, 'internal framework' and 'apparent framework'. The first expression usually refers to highly abstract concepts or theories that have no immediate reference to reality. For example, such concepts as value, value of labour power and surplus value, are for Marx part of the 'internal framework' of capitalist society. The second expression usually refers to those concepts or theories that exist at the level of sensory perception and are known to the agents in capitalist society. Examples of such concepts would be price, wage rate and profit. A scientific discourse, in Marx's estimate, would involve a movement from the 'internal' to the 'apparent framework', a movement which would explain why things appear the way they do. According to Marx, a group of writers, whose lineage goes back to Sir William Petty in England and Pierre Le Pesant Boisguilbert in France and whose demise coincides with the disintegration of the Ricardian school, attempted such a discourse, even though unsuccessfully. To this group Marx gives the designation 'classical political economy'. A second group, such as Senior and Bastiat, however, stayed at the level of sense perception and only systematized that which was sensed by the capitalist agents. Marx calls this group the 'vulgar economists'. In other words, the 'vulgar economists', as opposed to the 'classical political economists', were sheer empiricists whose concepts and theories coincided with the interests of the bourgeoisie.[6]

In sum, Marx coined the phrase 'classical political economists' on the basis of epistemological and methodological distinctions. The term distinguishes certain groups of economists from others, depending on whether they were or were not empiricist. This fact, however, has hardly been recognized. As a result, the term has been used by various economists, such as Keynes, rather loosely and eclectically.

VEBLEN AND 'CLASSICAL ECONOMICS'

It appears that Veblen was one of those economists who did not notice the particular meaning attached by Marx to the expression 'classical political economy'. This is evident in Veblen's writings on the history of economic thought, where one can find no reference to the origin of the term. In particular, even though Veblen cites a number of passages from the first volume of *Capital*, he does not include among these citations the footnote in which Marx defines the term 'classical political economy'.

There are also other reasons to believe that Veblen was unaware of Marx's intended meaning of the term. His periodization of the classical era differs markedly from that of Marx, without any acknowledgment of such a difference. For Marx, as mentioned earlier, the founding fathers of classical political economy were Petty and Boisguilbert. Veblen, however, considers Adam Smith as 'the point of departure of the Classical School' (1919, p. 113). On the other hand, the end of the classical period, according to Marx, was the disintegration of the Ricardian school. Veblen, however, as we shall soon see, is not very clear as to when the classical era came to an end. Also, Veblen's account of the membership of the 'classical school' is often at odds with that of Marx. For Veblen, such writers as Bentham and Senior were definitely 'classical economists'. Indeed, the former, as we shall also see, is considered by Veblen to be a leading figure in the school. For Marx, on the other hand, neither of these individuals was a classical political economist. The latter, as mentioned earlier, he considered to be a 'vulgar economist'. The former, for whom Marx showed nothing but contempt, he did not even elevate to the rank of an economist.

All this leads to an important question: If Veblen was unaware of Marx's intended meaning of the term 'classical economics', and he was, therefore, not using this term in Marx's sense, then in what sense was he using it? From Veblen's writings on the history of economic theory, one can conclude that for Veblen the most distinctive characteristic of the 'classical school', putting aside their Physiocratic 'preconceptions' of 'natural rights' and 'order of nature', is that they were all 'utilitarian' or, what is often the same thing for Veblen, 'hedonistic' (1919, pp. 142–5). This poses an immediate and obvious question: What does Veblen mean by 'utilitarian' or 'hedonistic'? Unfortunately, the answer to this question is not straightforward. There is no singular way that Veblen uses the term 'utilitarian'. Indeed, he uses the word to refer to a wide range of beliefs and practices. In what follows I will examine some of these meanings and explore the logical difficulties that they entail. This will be done, in particular, in reference to Veblen's designation of Adam Smith, David Ricardo and Karl Marx as 'utilitarian'.

Adam Smith as the Founding Father of the 'Classical School'

The most predominant concept of 'utilitarian' or 'hedonistic' which appears in Veblen's writings is the following: 'The hedonistic conception of man is that of a lightning calculator of pleasures and pains, who oscillates like a homogeneous globule of desire of happiness under the impulse of stimuli that shift him about the area, but leave him intact' (1919, p. 73). The above concept is very much in accord with Bentham's concept of human nature and his definition of 'utility' as 'that property in any object, whereby it tends to produce benefit, advantage, pleasure, good, happiness' (Bentham 1780, p. 86). It is as such that Veblen considers Bentham to be one of the most prominent members of the 'classical school' and believes that Benthamism plays a crucial role in the development of this school.[7] Veblen often contrasts this Benthamite concept with his own notion of 'human nature', which he attributes to the 'later psychology, reenforced by modern anthropological research':

> According to this conception, it is the characteristic of man to do something, not simply to suffer pleasures and pains through the impact of suitable forces. He is not simply a bundle of desires that are to be saturated by being placed in the path of forces of the environment, but rather a coherent structure of propensities and habits which seeks realization and expression in an unfolding activity. (1919, p. 74)

Veblen goes so far with this conception of human nature as to argue that: 'Economic action is teleological, in the sense that men always and everywhere seek to do something' (p. 75).

The above definition of 'utilitarian' and Veblen's own concept of human nature are straightforward and unproblematic. Yet these concepts do pose a problem insofar as Veblen's account of the paternity of the 'classical school' is concerned. As pointed out earlier, Veblen considers Adam Smith to be the founding father of the 'classical school'. But if this school is identified with Benthamite 'utilitarianism', why should the point of departure of the school be Smith? Putting aside many pre-Bentham philosophers, there were a number of well-known economists prior to Smith whose concept of human nature closely resembled that of Bentham. One such writer is Ferdinando Galiani (1751, p. 22) who writes:

> Utility is the ability a thing has to provide us with happiness. Man is a mixture of passions which move him with unequal force. Pleasure consists of gratifying these passions; and happiness is the acquisition of pleasure.

This concept of 'utility' and its corresponding concept of human nature are far closer to those of Bentham than anything Adam Smith has ever written. Why not, then, consider the whole Italian school and in particular Galiani as the point of departure of the 'classical school' rather than Smith?

Indeed, one can argue that Smith never viewed human nature as a 'lightning calculator of pleasures and pains'. This is quite evident from his concept of 'utility'. As I have argued elsewhere, and as many historians of economic theory have argued before me, a close textual analysis of Smith's writings would reveal that he uses the word 'utility' or 'value in use', not in any hedonistic sense, but in the sense of 'usefulness' (Fayazmanesh forthcoming 1998). That is, for Smith a class of objects has 'utility' or 'value in use' if it has one or more uses; and the more the number of uses, the more 'utility' it has. In this sense, Smith contends, 'if we except iron', gold and silver are the 'most useful' metals since, among their various uses, 'household utensils' can be made from them (1763, p. 370). However, 'diamonds and other jewels' are for Smith not very useful, because 'one can hardly say what they serve for' (p. 333). In the same vein, Smith often writes in reference to precious stones in general that 'their use we can hardly conceive' or that 'they are of no use, but ornaments' (Smith 1763, p. 358 and Smith 1776, p. 172).

Not only do the above ideas concerning 'value in use' or 'utility' have nothing in common with Benthamite 'utilitarianism', but in many ways they resemble Veblen's own concept of 'utility'. In his discussion of the concept of 'usefulness', Bush observes that for Veblen the true test of any economic activity is its 'impersonal usefulness; that is, "usefulness as seen from the point of view of the generically human" ' (Bush 1996, p. 3). But this is very similar to Smith's concept of 'utility' or 'usefulness' as 'serving for' something. Indeed, when Veblen writes in reference to 'precious stones and metals' that apart 'from their serviceability in other respects, these objects are beautiful and have utility as such', he is in many ways repeating what Smith had to say on the same subject (Veblen 1899, p. 96). Actually Veblen himself at times admits that Smith, and the Physiocrats before him, 'rarely, if ever, lose touch with the concept of generic serviceability as the characteristic feature of production' (1919, p. 138).

If, as I contend, Smith's concept of utility was very close to that of Veblen himself, then why does Veblen consider Smith to be a 'utilitarian'? The answer is found in Veblen's other references to 'utilitarianism', which appear, for example, in the passage below:

> In hedonistic theory the substantial end of economic life is the individual gain; and for this purpose production and acquisition may be taken as fairly coincident, if not identical. Moreover, society, in a utilitarian philosophy, is the algebraic sum of the individuals; and the interest of the society is the sum of the interests of the individuals . . . Productivity or serviceability is, therefore, to be presumed of any occupation or enterprise that looks to a pecuniary gain; and so, by a roundabout path, we get back to the ancient conclusion of Adam Smith, that the remuneration of classes engaged in industry coincides with their productive contribution to the output of services and consumable goods. (1919, p. 139).

In the passage above Smith is associated with 'hedonistic theory'. However, on closer examination, it appears that what Veblen is describing is hardly the normal description of a 'hedonist', at least not in the sense of an individual being a 'lightning calculator of pleasures and pains'.

Consider, for example, the first part of the first sentence. It describes not the ususal concept of hedonism, but what is normally called the philosophy of 'individualism' or, perhaps more correctly, the philosophy of 'possessive individualism', that is, the assumption that 'the human being is essentially a striver for, and a receptacle for the acquisition of, material goods' (MacPherson 1987, p. 791). The second part of the first sentence, as well as the sentence referring to Smith, however, apparently describe one who can hardly separate the production of useful goods from monetary gains. This same concept appears in Veblen when he states: 'Hedonistic economics may be taken as an interpretation of human nature in terms of the market place' (Veblen 1919, p. 141). The second sentence, on the other hand, seems to describe a common practice in economic theorizing, reducing society to the sum of the individuals. A Benthamite hedonist may of course subscribe to all of these views; however, the opposite is not true. That is, it is quite possible for an individual to subscribe to all of the above and yet not be a Benthamite 'hedonist'. Smith is indeed a possessive individualist; he also reduces society to the sum of the individuals, and he may sometimes even have difficulty separating pecuniary gains from production of useful object, yet none of these makes him a hedonist in the proper sense of the word.

Veblen himself feels uneasy about including Smith in the utilitarian or hedonistic camp. He often tries to moderate his criticisms of Smith by the use of certain adjectives. For example, even though he argues that Smith 'normalizes' the motives and movements of human beings 'to fit the requirements of hedonistically conceived order of nature', he still refers to Smith's concept of human nature as 'somewhat hedonistic' (Veblen, 1919, p. 128). Or, after stating that there 'is no wide breach between Adam Smith and the utilitarians', either in theory or in policy conclusions, he labels Smith as only 'a moderate utilitarian' (p. 131). Or, Veblen tones down his criticism of Smith's identification of the production process with pecuniary gains by arguing that this appears in 'a less degree' in him than in his followers (p. 138).

On various occasions Veblen even tries to exclude Smith from the camp of 'utilitarians' altogether. This happens, for example, in the passage just referred to above, where Smith appears apart from the 'utilitarian' school, even though there is 'no wide breach' between him and the 'utilitarians'. It also happens when Veblen writes: 'With Adam Smith, value is discussed from the point of view of production. With the utilitarians, production is discussed from the point of view of value' (p. 132). This argument not only undermines Veblen's characterization of Smith as one who identifies production with monetary gains, but it clearly subverts Veblen's inclusion of Smith in the 'utilitarian' camp.

Veblen's uneasiness about labelling Smith as a 'utilitarian' also shows up in his inconsistent argument concerning the exact point of entry of 'utilitarianism' into economics. On the one hand, Smith is considered to be the point of departure of the classical and, therefore, the utilitarian school. On the other, Veblen argues that it was only after Adam Smith's day that 'economics fell into profane hands', and that 'undevout utilitarians' became 'spokesmen of science' (p. 130). In this vein, it is argued that utilitarian philosophy 'entered in force

and in consummate form at about the turning of the century', an argument that
again weakens the claim for Smith's being in fact a 'utilitarian' (p. 130).

In sum, I believe Veblen's account of the paternity of the classical school to
be problematic, and that this is primarily due to his broad and rather vague
definition of 'utilitarianism'. In his definition, Veblen correctly includes
Bentham's concept of human nature and perhaps some of its auxiliaries, such
as philosophy of individualism, reduction of production to pecuniary gains and
fallacy of composition. However, at times he seems to reduce 'utilitarianism'
to one or more of these auxiliaries alone. This reduction turns Smith into a
'utilitarian' and the 'point of departure of the Classical School'. But since the
fundamental concept of 'utilitarianism', namely the Benthamite concept of
human nature as a 'calculus of pain and pleasure', is missing in Smith, Veblen
frequently casts doubt on Adam Smith's being in fact a 'utilitarian' and the
founding father of 'classical economics'.

Ricardo as a 'Benthamite Utilitarian'

Veblen's definition of 'utilitarian' also poses problems for his inclusion of such
a writer as David Ricardo in the 'classical school'. Let me elaborate.

In his discussion of the relation between Smith, Malthus and Benthamism,
Veblen adds a footnote in which he mentions Ricardo for the first time. Here
he writes:

> Ricardo is here taken as a utilitarian of the Benthamite colour, although he cannot be
> classed as a disciple of Bentham. His hedonism is but the uncritically accepted
> metaphysics comprised in the common sense of his time, and his substantial
> coincidence with Bentham goes to show how well diffused the hedonist
> preconception was at the time. (Veblen 1919, p. 131)

The above passage is noteworthy in a number of ways. First, it involves, once
again, an indecision on Veblen's part. Ricardo appears to be a Benthamite
utilitarian, since he has the right 'colour' and since there is a 'substantial
coincidence' between him and Bentham. Yet Ricardo is not a Benthamite
utilitarian, since he is not a disciple of Bentham. Second, and interestingly
enough, the passage directly contradicts Ricardo's own admission, in a private
letter, that he is indeed a 'disciple of Bentham' (Ricardo 1821–23, p. 52).
Third, it is not at all clear from the passage in what sense Ricardo is a
utilitarian, except that he accepted uncritically the prevailing views of his time.
But exactly what these views were, where and how Ricardo expressed them,
and why they are utilitarian are not specified. This, once again, poses a number
of problems.

Generally, Ricardo is not known as a Benthamite utilitarian, since, despite
his lip service that he is a disciple of Bentham, there is nothing in his theoretical
system that indicates any influence of Bentham. Indeed, there is not a single

reference to Bentham in Ricardo's *Principles of Political Economy and Taxation*, even when the term 'utility' appears in this work. This is for good reasons. Ricardo uses 'utility' in two different ways, neither of which is in accord with Bentham's use of the term. The first sense appears on the first page of the first chapter, where after quoting Adam Smith on the meanings of 'value in use' and 'value in exchange', Ricardo adds: 'If a commodity were in no way useful – in other words, if it could in no way contribute to gratification – it would be destitute of exchange-value' (Ricardo 1821, p. 5). Here, Ricardo appears to have unintentionally added an entailment to Smith's concept. For Smith, a commodity has value in use or utility if it is useful or has some uses; for Ricardo, however, this seems to imply that the commodity must 'contribute to our gratification'. This is, of course, a change in the definition of the word 'utility', and one may argue that Ricardo's entailment brings the concept one step closer to that of Bentham. Yet it is still a far cry from the latter. The second sense in which Ricardo uses the term appears towards the end of the *Principles*. Here, Ricardo uses the term in the sense of physical goods or 'riches', which he wrongly understands to be Smith's meaning of the term (1821, p. 187). This meaning of the term obviously has nothing to do with Bentham either. So why does Veblen characterize Ricardo as a Benthamite utilitarian?

Once again, there is no direct and clear answer to the above question. Some passages, however, give us clues and point out certain problems with Veblen's reasoning. For example, after contending that the 'post-Bentham economics is substantially a theory of value' whereas 'Adam Smith's economics is a theory of production', Veblen writes: 'The point of departure with Adam Smith is the "productive power of labour." With Ricardo it is a pecuniary problem concerned in the distribution of ownership' (1919, pp. 132–3).[8] This argument is apparently intended to show the shift in the 'centre of gravity from production to valuation' in post-Bentham economics (Veblen 1919, p. 133). It also appears to be an argument in support of Veblen's claim that Ricardo was a Benthamite utilitarian. Yet Veblen's argument appears to be based on a rather peculiar reading of both Smith and Ricardo.

The point of departure of Adam Smith is not 'productive power of labour', but it is, as generally understood, and as the title of the first chapter clearly indicates, the 'division of labour' (Smith 1776, p. 3). This point of departure does allow Smith to discuss 'improvement in the productive power of labour', but clearly the aim here is not to discuss production as such (1776, p. 3). Rather, Smith's purpose is to move to the concept of 'value', a movement which, of course, passes through the discussion of propensity to exchange, the extent of the market, and the origin and use of money (p. 28). Ricardo's point of departure is not 'pecuniary problems concerned with the distribution of ownership' either, but rather, 'value', as the title of the first chapter indicates (Ricardo 1821, p. 5). In other words, Smith's and Ricardo's aims are substantially the same: explaining value. The former, however, sets the stage before his explanation, and the latter gets to it immediately. Neither of these writers discusses the issue of the production process any more than the other. Thus one cannot argue, as Veblen apparently tries to do, that Ricardo is more of a Benthamite utilitarian than Smith because he pays less attention to the production process. Moreover, even if Ricardo did pay less attention to the production process than did Smith, it is still not clear why this would turn him into a Benthamite utilitarian.

There is another argument in Veblen with regard to Ricardo's alleged utilitarianism. It appears as such:

> In Ricardo's theory the source and measure of value is sought in the effort and sacrifice undergone by the producer, consistently, on the whole with the Benthamite –utilitarian position to which Ricardo somewhat loosely adhered. The decisive fact about labour, that quality by virtue of which it is assumed to be the final term in the theory of production, is its irksomeness. (Veblen 1919, pp. 422–3)

These comments, concerning Ricardo seeking to explain value on the basis of 'irksomeness of labour', are repeated elsewhere in Veblen's account of the history of economic ideas as well. Indeed, Veblen at times tries to distinguish between Smith and Ricardo on this ground, tying the argument, once again, to their different conceptions of production.[9] However, Veblen does not explain, beyond what is said above, how Ricardo sought to explain value on the basis of 'irksomeness of labour' and how his concept of labour differs from that of Smith.

In fact, one can easily make the case that neither Smith nor Ricardo ever articulated a clear and explicit conception of labour. Smith actually had many implicit and confused concepts of 'labour'. Among these was the notion that 'labour was the first price, the original purchase money that was paid for all things', a concept which exemplifies how Smith viewed the production process in general from the perspective of the capitalist relations of exchange (Smith 1776, p. 30). Another concept is reflected in Smith's statement that the 'real price of everything, what everything really costs to the man who acquires it, is the toil and trouble of acquiring it' (p. 130). Here, clearly labour is reduced to 'toil and trouble', indicating the 'irksomeness of labour', to use Veblen's phrase. Ricardo, on the other hand, added nothing new to these concepts. Indeed, in the first few pages of his chapter on 'value', Ricardo approvingly quotes many of Smith's statements concerning 'labour', including the one involving 'toil and trouble' (Ricardo 1821, p. 6). Why then consider Ricardo's concept of labour any more 'irksome' than that of Smith? Veblen does not explain.

In short, Veblen's claim that Ricardo is a post-Benthamite utilitarian remains unsubstantiated for two reasons. First, Veblen unconventionally defines a Benthamite or post-Benthamite utilitarian as one who pays greater attention to the pecuniary problems concerned with distribution than to the productive power of labour, or as one who considers labour as 'irksome'. Yet nowhere does Veblen explain how these views stem from, or are even related to, Bentham's concept of human nature. Second, in attempting to turn Ricardo, as opposed to Smith, into a post-Benthamite economist, Veblen reads differences between the two authors which on closer inspection do not exist.

Marx as a Non-Member of the 'Classical School'

As mentioned earlier, in his writings Marx showed nothing but disdain for Bentham and his utilitarian philosophy. Marx's definition of 'value in use', as a 'useful object', also indicates that he had nothing whatsoever to do with the Benthamite notion of 'utility' (see Fayazmanesh 1994). Yet, curiously enough, Veblen ties Marx to Bentham and 'utilitarianism' when he writes: 'For many details and for much of his animus Marx may be indebted to the Utilitarians' (1919, p. 413). What are these 'details' and 'animus'? Veblen does not elaborate. But from his short account of Marx's economic theories one can gather two, very general and brief, arguments concerning Marx's 'utilitarian' traits. The first argument appears when Veblen discusses the concept of class struggle. Here he writes:

> A further characteristic of the doctrine of class struggle requires mention. While the concept is not Darwinian, it is also not legitimately Hegelian, whether of the Right or the Left. It is of a utilitarian origin and of English pedigree, and it belongs to Marx by the virtue of his having borrowed its elements from the system of self-interest. It is in fact a piece of hedonism, and is related to Bentham rather than to Hegel. It proceeds on the grounds of the hedonistic calculus, which is equally foreign to the Hegelian notion of an unfolding process and to the post-Darwinian notions of cumulative causation. (Veblen 1919, pp. 417–18)

It is, of course, true that the concept of class struggle is neither Darwinian nor Hegelian in origin.[10] It is also equally true that this concept is not Benthamite by any stretch of imagination. Actually, as Marx himself points out in a private letter, the concept originated with 'bourgeois historians' and 'bourgeois economists' (Marx 1975, p. 64). But then why does Veblen make it sound as if the concept somehow originated from Bentham or, at least, is related to him? The answer seems to depend on the following set of arguments: (1) the concept of class struggle involves the concept of self-interest, (2) the concept of self-interest is hedonistic, and (3) class struggle is, therefore, a Benthamite utilitarian concept.

The above set of arguments, however, involves conceptual and logical ambiguities. First, it is by no means self-evident that the concept of class struggle, particularly in Marx, involves the concept of self-interest; and Veblen makes no attempt to substantiate this contention. Second, and even if we accept the first argument, self-interestedness may be an element of Benthamite utilitarianism, but this does not mean that the two can be reduced to one another. Indeed, the concept of self-interest appeared long before Bentham's concept of human nature as a 'calculus of pain and pleasure' emerged. It therefore seems to this writer that Veblen does not make a strong case for including Marx in the utilitarian camp on the basis of the concept of 'class struggle'.

Veblen's second argument in support of his contention that Marx, for many 'details' and 'animus', is indebted to the utilitarians, appears in his discussion of Marx's preconceptions. After asserting that by 'early training' Marx is a 'neo-Hegelian', Veblen writes:

> By later experience he acquired the point of view of that Liberal–Utilitarian school which dominated English thought through the greater part of his active life. To this experience he owes (probably) the somewhat pronounced individualistic preconceptions on which the doctrine of the Full Product of Labour and the Exploitation of Labour is based. (Veblen 1919, p. 431)

A few notes are necessary here. First, in an earlier account, Veblen argues that Marx's preconceptions, besides the 'Hegelian system', include the 'system of Natural Rights and Natural Liberty' (1919, p. 411). This argument, combined with the above passage, seems to imply that Veblen is reducing that school of economic theory which believes in the 'system of the natural rights and liberty' to the 'liberal–utilitarian school'. Such a reduction seems to be at odds with Veblen's earlier argument that the former is merely a preconception of the latter. Given, however, the ambiguity in Veblen's concept of 'utilitarianism', his reduction is not surprising. Second, the use of the word 'probably' shows, once again, an element of indecision on Veblen's part. Based on the writings of Menger and Foxwell, Veblen claims that the source of Marx's theory of surplus value is in 'all probability' the 'English writers of the early nineteenth century, more particularly William Thompson' (Veblen 1919, p. 412). Yet there is no evidence for this claim. Indeed, a detailed reading of Marx's economic writings and in particular *Grundrisse* – where Marx's economic theory in general and the theory of surplus value in particular begin to coalesce – conveys the invalidity of this contention (see Fayazmanesh 1984). Third, even if one wrongly assumes that Marx did borrow his theory of surplus value from a writer such as William Thompson, it is by no means self-evident that this turns Marx into a utilitarian. In fact, one can argue that Thompson's own labour theory of value is incompatible with his utilitarianism (see Hunt 1992, pp. 190–204). In short, Veblen's argument that Marx borrows his theory from the utilitarian writers, and that this turns him into a Benthamite utilitarian, is factually unsupported and logically untenable.

Veblen's labelling of Marx as a utilitarian poses yet another problem. According to Veblen, Marx 'is of no single school of philosophy' and 'takes his place as an originator of a school of thought' (Veblen 1919, p. 410). This implies that Marx is not a member of the 'classical school'. In fact, when referring to Marx, Veblen often words his sentences in such a way that Marx is excluded from this school.[11] But this exclusion causes a logical difficulty. If Marx has all the right colours of the 'classical school', that is, if he has the preconception of natural rights and natural liberty, as well as an underlying utilitarian philosophy, why is he not included in this school? After all, are not these characteristics those which define the 'classical school' and its members?

There is, once again, no clear and explicit answer to the above question. One possible explanation, however, appears in Veblen's discussion of the major difference between Ricardo's and Marx's value theory. According to Veblen, the similarity between the two theories is only 'superficial' because Ricardo considered labour to be irksome, while for Marx 'the question of irksomeness of labour is irrelevant' (pp. 422–3). This argument is not without problems either. It is, of course, true that Marx's concept of labour as 'a process between man and nature' is very different from Smith's and Ricardo's concept of 'toil and trouble' (Marx 1873, p. 283). Yet Marx's concept of 'alienation' of labour, which is found particularly in his early writings, points out that, under certain social conditions, Marx too may consider labour as irksome, nor is this by any means irrelevant to his theory.[12] The difference here is that Marx continuously distinguishes between economic form and content, while Smith and Ricardo would eternalize the specific economic forms of their own time.

Whether Marx did or did not believe in the irksomeness of labour, of course, cannot be a sufficient reason for excluding Marx from the rank of 'classical economists'. So what else can account for the exclusion? The answer may lie partially in Veblen's aforementioned belief that the initial source of Marx's theory is Hegel. Marx, Veblen contends, 'is an adept in the Hegelian method of speculation and inoculated with the metaphysics of development underlying the Hegelian system' (Veblen 1919, p. 411). In other words, it appears that Veblen excludes Marx from the 'classical school' because of what he believes to be Marx's Hegelian methodology and epistemology. If this is correct, then once again we face certain difficulties. First, Veblen takes for granted the relation between Marx and Hegel. Yet this relation remains even to this day subject to numerous controversies. Marx himself saw his own relation to Hegel, at least insofar as *Capital* is concerned, as merely 'coquetting' here and there with 'the mode of expression peculiar to him [Hegel]' (Marx 1873, p. 103). Many writers, particularly philosophers, however, have not been content with this view and have tried to show a stronger relation between Marx and Hegel. Others, particularly those who have analysed in detail the development of certain aspects of Marx's economic theory from *Grundrisse* to *Capital*, such as this writer, have argued that the link between the two is far weaker than what is sometimes argued (see Fayazmanesh 1984). All this, of course, points to the fact that the relation between the two writers is complex, and that different readings of Marx are possible. Yet Veblen deals with none of this complexity and simply asserts, with very little analysis, that the latter borrowed his epistemology and methodology from the former.

There is, however, something more problematic with the exclusion of Marx from the camp of the classicists, a logical problem. Veblen's definition of 'classical economics', as has been argued, is based on certain belief in human nature. Issues concerning methodology and epistemology do not seem to enter this definition. Yet, when it comes to Marx, the definition of 'classical economics' seems to change. Now, it appears, epistemological and methodological issues are the single most important criterion in defining 'classical economics'. As a result of this twist in definition, Marx becomes a non-member of the 'classical school' for Veblen, even though he is assumed to share some of the same beliefs.

In sum, I believe Veblen's definition of 'classical economics' is not a carefully crafted concept. He bases this concept primarily on his notion of 'utilitarianism'. By the latter term he often means Benthamite utilitarianism, that is, the concept of human nature as a 'calculus of pain and pleasure'. Yet this is not the only meaning attached to the term by Veblen. Anyone who adheres to the philosophy of individualism, who believes in the concept of human beings as self-interested beings, who possibly views labour as irksome, or who accepts the concept of class struggle, is labelled by Veblen as 'utilitarian'. Even certain common practices in economic theorizing, such as reducing society to the sum of the individuals, may entitle one to have the same label. As a result of this broad and ambiguous definition, writers such as Smith, Ricardo and even Marx, all become utilitarian and sit side by side with Jeremy Bentham.

VEBLEN AND 'NEOCLASSICAL ECONOMICS'

Veblen's broad concept of 'utilitarianism' and his lack of precision in defining 'classical economics' permeates his attempt to establish a relationship between this school and the proponents of the marginal utility analysis. The result, as will be seen below, is that it never becomes clear whether the latter group is a continuation of the former or identical to it.

Let us begin this section by posing the following question: What did the 'classical economists' have in common with the marginalists? Veblen's answer is an expected one:

> Both the classical school in general and its specialized variant, the marginal utility school, in particular take as their common point of departure the traditional psychology of the early nineteenth century hedonists, which is accepted as a matter of course or of common notoriety and is held quite uncritically. The central and well-defined tenet so held is that of the hedonist calculus. (1919, p. 234)[13]

In other words, the marginalists are identical to the classicists insofar as they, too, are hedonistic or utilitarian, a point which is repeated on a number of occasions by Veblen.[14]

It should be noted that Veblen uses the term 'hedonistic' or 'utilitarian' in a very ambiguous way in reference to the proponents of the marginal utility theory as well. The marginalists are 'utilitarian' not only in the above sense of believing in the Benthamite concept of human nature, but also in the sense that they concentrate almost exclusively on the issue of 'distribution' at the expense of 'consumption and production', or they view labour as 'painful' and 'irksome' (Veblen 1919, pp. 182–3, 203–5 and 221–2). Indeed, it is in Veblen's discussion of the utilitarian nature of the marginal analysis that one realizes why he perceives the 'classical economists' as ignoring production or viewing labour as irksome. He seems to *read them after the marginalists* and thus perceives a common thread.

But if the two schools are identical in the sense that they are both utilitarian, what separates them as distinct schools? Veblen's argument is very brief and inconclusive. He writes that the marginal analysis is 'confined within narrower limits', and that the 'common postulates are more consistently adhered to at the same time that they are more neatly defined' (1919, p. 234). But narrowness of focus, consistency in arguments and neatness in definition cannot constitute fundamental differences between the two schools. Are there more substantial differences between the economic writers of the classical era and those of the late nineteenth century that would warrant defining them as two separate schools?

As far as I can tell, Veblen is silent on this point, and this silence leads to two ambiguous and incongruent stances. The first stance is that of continuity of thought between the 'classical school' and the proponents of marginal analysis, the second is that of identity. These two positions, combined with the lack of clarity with regard to the term 'classical', result in the rather ill-defined term 'neoclassical'.

Continuity of Economic Ideas

There are a number of statements in Veblen concerning the continuity of ideas between the classical writers and the proponents of marginal analysis. Nowhere, however, can one find a full and clear discussion of the exact nature of this continuity. In the absence of such a discussion, one can interpret Veblen's meaning in a number of ways. For example, one can argue that since these statements are often followed by what the marginalists have in common with the 'classical economists', then the two schools are continuous in the sense that they are both utilitarian.

There is, however, another possible interpretation. This one appears in Veblen's discussion of John Bates Clark's writings and their relations to the 'classical theory'. Here Veblen argues that the difference between the two is only a 'matter of detail' and that there is nothing in Clark's work 'as to suggest anything like a revolutionary trend or a breaking away from the conventional lines' (1919, p. 194). This argument seems to imply that continuity is the same thing as lack of a revolutionary trend.

Besides the above arguments, there is yet a third possible interpretation: the two schools of economic theory are continuous in the same sense that the marginalists have said they are. There is plenty of evidence for this interpretation. On a number of occasions, where Veblen discusses the issue of continuity, he refers to the same claim by the marginalists. For example, he writes that Clark 'had the insight and courage to see the continuity between the classical position and his own, even where he advocates drastic changes in the classical body of doctrines' (Veblen 1919, p. 181). Or, on another occasion, Veblen supports his statement concerning continuity by paraphrasing the following statement from Marshall's preface to the first edition of the *Principles of Economics*: 'There has been no breach of continuity in the development of science' (p. 150).

I believe none of the above interpretations presents a clear and viable argument in support of the continuity of economic ideas. The first argument appears to be faulty due to the ambiguous nature of the term 'utilitarianism'. Moreover, and ignoring this problem, one cannot establish continuity solely on the basis of the two schools being 'hedonistic or utilitarian'. If, for example, the differences between these schools are only minor, as Veblen seems to contend, then they should be conceived as identical rather than continuous. The same holds for Veblen's second argument. The third argument, however, is even less clear and less viable than the other two. Let me explain why this is so in greater detail.

As Philip Mirowski has correctly pointed out, the proponents of marginal analysis have themselves been unable to make up their minds as to whether their analysis represents a complete break or continuity with the past (Mirowski 1989a, p. 194). This is particularly true of Marshall himself. He often attempts to portray his own work as a continuation of the works of the classicists. It is in this vein that he writes the sentences that are paraphrased by Veblen. However, this is not the only argument put forward by Marshall. Almost immediately after this sentence, Marshall presents an entirely different argument by stating: 'The present treatise is an attempt to present a modern version of old doctrines with the aid of the new work' (Marshall 1936, p. v). This statement implies not continuity but rather substantial identity between the old and the new doctrines. It now appears that the 'new doctrine' differs from the old merely in the form of presentation. But this is not all; there is also a third argument in Marshall. This one appears in the preface to the eighth edition of *Principles*:

The new analysis is endeavouring gradually and tentatively to bring over into economics . . . those methods of the science of small increments (commonly called the differential calculus) to which man owes directly and indirectly the greater part of the control that he has obtained in recent times over physical nature. It is still in its infancy; it has no dogmas, and no standard of orthodoxy. It has not yet had time to obtain a perfectly settled terminology. (Marshall 1936, pp. xvi–xvii)

This seems to imply that a methodologically different theory with new terminology is being born, an argument which, as Mirowski notes, directly contradicts the earlier claim concerning continuity of ideas (Mirowski 1988, p. 28). I would also argue that it contradicts Marshall's second argument concerning substantial identity between the old and the new doctrines.

This is not, of course, the proper place to go deeply into why Marshall and his fellow travellers made contradictory claims, and which of these claims is closer to the truth. Let me, however, add a brief note here. Marshall's second and third claims, I believe, have to do with two concepts of the differential calculus. According to the first concept, the differential calculus is merely a set of 'symbols' which can help 'a person to write down quickly, shortly and exactly some of his thought' (Marshall 1936, p. x). It is this concept, as I have argued elsewhere, that leads Jevons, Marshall and many other marginalists, to claim that they are applying mathematics to the old political economy (see Fayazmanesh forthcoming 1998). It is also this concept that leads Jevons to make the outrageous claim that Adam Smith's terms 'value in use' and 'value in exchange' are identical to his own terms 'total utility' and 'terminal utility', or that leads Marshall to make the unfounded claim that David Ricardo's 'Value and Riches' mean, respectively, 'marginal and total utility' (Jevons 1871, p. 157; Marshall 1936, p. 814).

Marshall's second concept of the differential calculus, however, is very different from the first. According to this concept, the differential calculus is more than a set of symbols, it is a conceptual framework which brings into economic analysis a new 'method' and 'terminology'. This second concept of the nature of the differential calculus is, of course, much closer to what has been said lately by Mirowski concerning discontinuity in economic thought in the late nineteenth century, which resulted from the emulation of the energetics physics. It is also closer to my own observation that what appeared to the marginalists as the application of mathematics to economics was in actuality the application of political economy to the differential calculus (Fayazmanesh 1996).

But what about Marshall's first contention concerning continuity; what is the cause of this one? As Mirowski has noted, this claim is merely tactical; it is intended to tone down the 'brash revolution of a Jevons' (Mirowski 1988, p. 28). Given its tactical nature, Marshall cannot find any supporting evidence for this argument. He merely writes, after the sentence concerning continuity, that the 'new doctrines have supplemented the older, have extended, developed, and sometimes corrected them' (Marshall 1936, p. v). But how the 'new doctrines' have done all of these is never made clear.

In the final analysis, Veblen's appeal to the authority of Marshall and like-minded economists on the subject of continuity not only does not clarify and consolidate his own positions but does the exact opposite. Marshall and his fellow travellers made contradictory statements concerning the relation between their own theories and those of the classical economists. For every statement about continuity there are others about either identity or complete break with the past, something that Veblen seems to ignore completely. Moreover, their claim concerning continuity has no real substance and appears to be no more than window-dressing.

Identity of Economic Ideas

The term 'neoclassical' was coined by Veblen apparently based on the assumption that the marginalist school is a continuation of the 'classical school'. As noted earlier, the expression makes its first appearance in the last of the three-part essay on the 'Preconceptions of Economic Science'; and here it is used three times. Its first use is in reference to the Austrian economists, where Veblen states that the 'school is scarcely distinguishable from the neoclassical, unless it be in the different distribution of emphasis' (1919, p. 171). The second time that the term appears is in reference to Marshall's 'aspiration to treat economic life as a development', where Veblen writes: 'Indeed, the work of the neoclassical economics might be compared, probably without offending any of its adepts, with that of the early generation of Darwinism' (p. 175). Lastly, the term is used as part of the continuation of the previous discussion, where 'neoclassical political economy' is said to have a 'quasi-evolutionary tone' (p. 178). After this usage, the expression 'neoclassical' vanishes from Veblen's reading of the history of economic thought, even though he continues to discuss the works of the proponents of the 'marginal utility' theory. Why does the term vanish? Because Veblen does not always stick to the thesis that the marginalist school is a continuation of the 'classical school'. Very often he seems to follow a second thesis: the two schools are identical in general. If this is so, there is really no need for the expression 'neoclassical'. Let me explain this contention by providing some evidence.

In his discussion of Cairnes's work, Veblen uses the expression 'early classical writers' and 'later classical writers' (1919, p. 69). At first sight it appears that the distinction is between the writers of the mid-eighteenth century, such as Smith, and those of the early to mid-nineteenth century, such as Ricardo or Cairnes. On a closer inspection, however, it appears that Veblen is including among the 'later classical school' the 'Austrian group' as well (p. 70).

The same thing appears when Veblen discusses the 'classical failure to discriminate between capital as investment and capital as industrial appliances' (p. 141). Here, as an example of this failure, Veblen refers to Bohm-Bawerk's *Capital and Interest*, as if this is a work of a classical writer (p. 142). Also in the discussion of Marx's concept of 'class struggle' Veblen writes that this concept is 'quite out of harmony with the later results of psychological inquiry – just as is true of the use made of the hedonistic calculus by the classical (Austrian) economics' (p. 418). On the very same page, but in a footnote, Veblen once again refers to 'the classical (English and Austrian) economics'. These references seem to suggest that Veblen is somehow including the Austrian economists among the 'classical school'. This suspicion is confirmed when two pages later, in reference to the 'neo-Hegelian' scheme of the 'unfolding (material) life of man in society', Veblen writes in a footnote:

> In much the same way, and with an analogous effect on their theoretical work, in the preconceptions of the classical (including the Austrian) economists, the balance of pleasure and pain is taken to be the ultimate reality in terms of which all economic theory must be stated and to terms of which all phenomena should finally be reduced in any definitive analysis of economic life. (p. 420)

The passage above clearly indicates that Veblen considers the Austrians to be 'classical economists' on the grounds that they, too, are Benthamite utilitarians.

The Austrian economists, however, are not the only marginalists that Veblen considers to be 'classicists'. There are numerous statements in Veblen's writings that clearly indicate that he is also referring to such writers as Jevons and Clark as 'classical economists'. For example, at one point he writes that Clark 'is, by spiritual consanguinity, a representative of that classical school of thought that dominated the science through the better part of the nineteenth century' (Veblen 1919, p. 181). A few lines later he adds that 'Mr. Clark's work is at one with both the early classical and the late (Jevons–Austrian) marginal-utility school' (p. 182). A few pages later Veblen makes it clear that the 'late marginal utility school' is the same as the 'late classical' or it is, at least, included in it when he states: 'Mr. Clark's premises, and therewith the aim of his inquiry, are the standard ones of the classical English school (including the Jevons–Austrian wing)' (p. 190). This is then followed by the statement: 'The classical school, including Mr. Clark and his contemporary associates in the science, is hedonistic and utilitarian' (p. 191).

In short, in addition to the thesis that the marginalist and the 'classical school' are continuous, Veblen puts forth the thesis that the two schools of economic theory are in fact identical. This second thesis is, of course, quite natural from Veblen's perspective. The two schools of economic theory are identical insofar as they are both 'utilitarian'. But, since being 'utilitarian' is the most important criterion of judgment and, moreover, since there is really no substantial difference between the two groups, then the two schools must be actually identical. Furthermore, if the two schools are in fact identical, then there is really no need for the expression 'neoclassical'. This, I believe, is why the term 'neoclassical' vanishes in Veblen's writings subsequent to its coinage.

SUMMARY AND CONCLUSION

In the final analysis, I agree with Aspromourgos that Veblen's concept of 'neoclassical economics' is flawed. However, I cannot agree with Aspromourgos's reasoning. He argues that Veblen coined the phrase in reference to the 'utilitarian' character of the 'Marshallian version of marginalism' and on the basis of Marshall's claim concerning 'substantial continuity' of economic ideas (Aspromourgos 1986, p. 266). However, according to Aspromourgos, Veblen was wrong in assuming that the 'Marshallian system was fundamentally the same as that of other marginalists' and that 'all marginalists employed a utilitarian approach' (p. 269). In this vein, Aspromourgos refers to Hicks's argument that 'utilitarian postulates were not essential to the marginalist theory of value and distribution' developed later on by marginalists such as Hicks himself (p. 269). In other words, according to Aspromourgos, there may have been some continuity of ideas between the 'classical economists' and Marshall, but there was no such continuity between the classics and the later generation of marginalists. All this reasoning appears to be null and void in light of what I have argued in this paper. First, as I have indicated, Veblen did not see the Marshallian system as the only system with 'utilitarian' character; he saw all marginalist systems to be 'utilitarian'. Second, Veblen did not base his argument concerning continuity of economic ideas solely on Marshall's claim. As I have contended, he also referred to the same claim by such writers as John Bates Clark. But, as we have seen, all such references were actually irrelevant, since Veblen's idea of continuity was very different from that of Marshall or Clark. Third, if one looks at the rise of the marginalist school from the perspective of methodology and epistemology, rather than this or that particular technique employed, one has to conclude that the Marshallian system was fundamentally the same as that of any other marginalist. All such systems tried to give economic meanings to nineteenth century mathematical physics, and attempted to squeeze the concepts developed by the classics to fit this mould. As such, even the early marginalists did not need to refer to Bentham's 'utilitarianism' to establish their theories; all such references were merely sideshows intended to distract the audience from what was being imported into economic theory (see Fayazmanesh forthcoming 1998).

Above all, however, I believe Aspromourgos's argument is irrelevant to the whole issue at hand. The problem with Veblen's term 'neoclassical' is not whether the Marshallian system was or was not the same as that of other marginalists, but how Veblen was using the term 'utilitarian' and defining 'classical economics' to begin with. It has been my contention that Veblen employed the term 'utilitarian' so broadly and vaguely that just about any economist could be included in this camp.   As a result, it never became clear exactly what the 'classical school' was all about, when it started, when it came to end, and who its members were and why. This broadness of definition and ambiguity then spilled over into Veblen's phrase 'neoclassical'. The outcome was a term even more unclear than the term from which it originated. As a result, Veblen attached no particular significance to the term and stopped using it. I suggest that we do the same.

NOTES

1. I am grateful for critical comments and suggestions by Marc R. Tool on an earlier draft of this essay.
2. See also Aspromourgos 1996, p. 4.
3. Joan Robinson (1983, p. 70) writes that Keynes 'put into one box everyone, from Ricardo to Pigou, who neglected effective demand and overestimated Malthus because he did not'.
4. See also Aspromourgos 1986, p. 268.
5. 'Science' is of course a loaded term and is thrown around by economists frequently and loosely.   Here, however, I am using Marx's concept of science, which is relatively well defined.
6. For further discussion of Marx's concept of science, his commitment to 'realism' and his critique of empiricism see Bhaskar 1983, pp. 407–9.
7. 'The immediate point of Bentham's work,' writes Veblen, 'as affecting the habits of thought of the educated community is the substitution of hedonism (utility) in place of achievement of purpose, as a ground of legitimacy and a guide in normalization of knowledge' (1919, p. 133).
8. In supporting these contentions, Veblen adds footnotes in which he quotes from the first paragraph of Smith's 'Introduction and Plan of the Work' in *The Wealth of Nations* and from the first and the third paragraphs of Ricardo's 'Original Preface' to the *Principles*. But strictly speaking, these paragraphs are not points of departure, but merely introductory comments.
9. After asserting that for Smith 'production causes value', Veblen writes: 'The post-Bentham economics contemplates value as a measure of, or as measured by, irksomeness of effort involved in procuring the valuable goods. As Mr. E.C.K. Gonner has admirably pointed out, Ricardo – and the like holds true of classical economics generally – makes cost the foundation of value, not its cause' (1919, pp. 135–6).
10. Before this passage, Veblen tries to argue that the concept of class struggle is incompatible with Darwinism. Veblen was probably unaware that Marx had argued the exact opposite. In a letter to Lassalle, Marx writes that Darwin's *Origin of the Species* 'supports the class struggle in history from the point of view of natural sciences. One has, of course, to put up with the crude English method of discourse. Despite all deficiencies, it not only deals the death blow to "teleology" in the natural sciences for the first time but also sets forth the rational meaning in an empirical way' (Marx 1975, p. 115).
11. He writes, for example, that 'Marx traces his doctrine of labour-value to Ricardo, and through him to the classical economists' (Veblen 1919, p. 412).
12. In the 'Result of the Immediate Process of Production', which is a relatively late piece of economic writing by Marx, he still mentions the alienating process of capitalist production and refers to it as a 'process of enslavement' (Marx 1873, p. 990).
13. Note that if the point of departure of the 'classical school' is 'nineteenth century hedonism', then Adam Smith cannot belong to this school.

14. It should be pointed out that, on a few occasions, Veblen also mentions other common threads between the two schools. For example, both schools are said to be 'teleological', or neither is seen 'to admit arguments from cause to effect in the formulation of their main articles of theory' (Veblen 1919, p. 232). Yet the 'main' canon or the 'central' tenet that both schools share is 'hedonistic calculus' (Veblen 1919, pp. 150, 234).

REFERENCES

Aspromourgos, Tony (1986), 'On the Origin of the Term "Neoclassical"', *Cambridge Journal of Economics*, **10** (30), pp. 265–70.

_____(1996), *On the Origins of Classical Economics*, New York: Routledge.

Bentham, Jeremy (1780), *An Introduction to the Principles of Morals and Legislation*, New York: Pegasus, 1969.

Bhaskar, Roy (1983), 'Realism', in Tom Bottomore (ed.), *A Dictionary of Marxist Thought*, Cambridge: Harvard University Press.

Bush, Paul D. (1996), 'Veblen's "Olympian Detachment" Reconsidered', paper presented at the 1996 meetings of the Association for Institutional Thought, Reno, Nevada.

Fayazmanesh, Sasan (1984), *The Commodity as the Point of Departure of Capital: A Methodological Inquiry*, PhD Dissertation, University of California, Riverside.

_____(1994), 'Marx's Semantics and the Logic of the Derivation of Value', *Research in the History of Economic Thought and Methodology*, **12**, pp. 65–91.

_____(1996), 'On the Application of Mathematics to Economics: A Case Study of Jevons's Reading of Smith', paper presented at the 23rd Annual Meeting of the History of Economics Society, Vancouver, BC, Canada.

_____(forthcoming 1998), 'The Magical, Mystical "Paradox of Value"', *Research in the History of Economic Thought and Methodology*.

Galiani, Ferdinando (1751), *On Money*, translated by Peter R. Toscano, Ann Arbor: University Microfilms International, 1977.

Hunt, E.K. (1992), *History of Economic Thought: A Critical Perspective*, New York: Harper Collins.

Jevons, William Stanley (1871), *The Theory of Political Economy*, New York: Macmillan and Co.

Keynes, John Maynard (1936), *The General Theory of Employment, Interest, and Money*, New York: Harcourt Brace Jovanovich, 1964.

Machlup, Fritz (1963), *Essays on Economics Semantics*, Englewood Cliffs: Prentice-Hall.

MacPherson, C.B. (1987), 'Individualism', in *The New Palgrave*, vol. 2, London: Macmillan.

Marshall, Alfred (1936), *Principles of Economics*, London: Macmillan and Co.

Marx, Karl (1873), *Capital*, Volume 1, New York: Vintage Books, 1977.

_____(1975), *Marx/Engels Selected Correspondence*, Moscow: Progress Publishers.

Mirowski, Philip (1984), 'Physics and the Marginalist Revolution', *Cambridge Journal of Economics*, **8** (4), pp. 361–79.

_____(1988), *Against Mechanism*, Totowa: Rowman & Littlefield.

_____(1989a), *More Heat Than Light*, New York: Cambridge University Press.

_____(1989b), 'On Hollander's "Substantive Identity" of Classical and Neoclassical

Economics: A Reply', *Cambridge Journal of Economics*, **13**, pp. 459–70.

Ricardo, David (1821), *The Principles of Political Economy and Taxation*, New York: Dutton, 1973.

_____(1821–23), *The Works and Correspondences of David Ricardo*, Volume IX, Cambridge: Cambridge University Press, 1952.

Robinson, Joan (1983), 'Garegnani on Effective Demand,' in John Eatwell and Murray Milgate (eds), *Keynes's Economics and the Theory of Value and Distribution*, New York: Oxford University Press.

Smith, Adam (1763), *Lectures on Jurisprudence*, Oxford: Oxford University Press, 1978.

_____(1776), *The Wealth of Nations*, New York: Random House, 1965.

Veblen, Thorstein (1899), *The Theory of the Leisure Class*, New York: New American Library, 1953.

_____(1919), *The Place of Science in Modern Civilization*, New York: Huebsch.

5. Causality and Order in Economics: Foundational Contributions by G. Schmoller and W. Eucken

Kurt Dopfer[1]

The 'Historical Economics' of Gustav Schmoller (1838–1917) and the 'Thinking in Orders' of Walter Eucken (1891–1950) are discussed, highlighting their paradigmatic significance with a view to developing a 'historical' approach to institutional economics. In the author's view, Schmoller's approach was empirical, relied on surface regularities of actual events, and attempted to formulate causal models that should allow one to predict the consequences of policy action in various historical epochs. Eucken, in turn, started economic analysis from the creative power of ideas, suggesting that we should look for the universal in historical change, and that we take theoretically well-contemplated ideas as an ontic departure point for influencing actual processes in time and space. The paper suggests that there is much to learn from both authors when rethinking the ontological foundations of institutional economics along 'historical' lines.

INTENT AND ONTOLOGIES

The principal objective of economics as a science is to make valid generalizations about economic reality. Its primary analytical task is therefore to show how economic reality can be *transformed* into and *represented* by theoretical statements. The crucial validity test must refer to the accomplishment of a transformation task. There have been other criteria for assessing the quality of economic theories, such as logical consistency or predictive capacity. However, these criteria presume the validity of the transformation task and are thus subsidiary. In the logico-deductive approaches of modern economics this methodological priority is not accepted; instead, a reversal of the criteria is suggested. For instance, it is argued that assumptions are not designed to portray reality, and that the 'realism of assumptions' controversy falls short of recognizing that theories are nothing but a heuristic instrument, designed for prediction.

In contrast, 'historical' economists have never departed from such assertions, but rather recognized the significance of the *status of reality* for economic theory. The following discussion will highlight the conceptual features and ontological characteristics of the Historical School and the Freiburg ORDO-Lehre (Freiburg School), represented by Gustav Schmoller and Walter Eucken respectively. One would expect that the analytical preoccupation with this issue has led to converging viewpoints. However, as is often the case, further research may jeopardize eventually even those positions that initially were shared as a common treasure. While for some economists this may be proof of the futility of the ontological discourse, the increasing dissent makes it also easier to specify the reasons that led to different viewpoints.

Schmoller and Eucken shared the view that economic theories should serve as a basis for *policy* making. Departing from this instrumentalist (as used by American institutionalists) stance, an immanent objective of economics was to depict reality as faithfully as possible. Economic policy was meaningless unless economic theory depicted a 'realistic' picture of the course of economic events that were subject to change, and unless it thus allowed the consequences of policy action to be assessed. The realism in theory making was for Schmoller and Eucken therefore not a question that could be discussed on a methodological plane, for instance, trading methodological criteria of 'realism of assumptions' for those of formal beauty or logical rigour, but rather an immanent *practical* question that determined as a *pre-methodological* preliminary whether or not a theoretic construal entered the domain of scientific discourse at all. The economic reality and the problems it posed looked rather different for the two economists. Seemingly harmless, this statement itself accepts the premise that the acknowledgement of the *historicity* of economic contexts is relevant for theory making. Schmoller and Eucken presented different approaches when coping with the phenomenon of historicity, but they both accepted it as a premise to start with.

As for the diverse backgrounds, Schmoller was a man of the late nineteenth century; he died before World War I was over. These were the heydays of the Manchesterian-liberal world economy, British colonialism and the self-regulating mechanics of the Gold Standard. Schmoller's major contention was that it mattered whether a nation was in a developmental stage, say A or B, and that a harmony between economic interests could not be brought about by a universal principle that ignored these historic differences. Free trade and non-intervention were thus not universal but history-dependent. In an analogous vein, the social policy problems were intrinsically linked to the developmental stage of a nation. Schmoller and Eucken were united against (Marxian) determinism, and they recognized economic policy as a deliberate, willed endeavour to change economic and social reality. Schmoller published in 1864, still before he became a professor in Halle, three articles on the 'Worker's

Question' (*Arbeiterfrage*) in the 'Preussische Jahrbücher', fought against the 'socialist laws' (*Sozialistengesetze*) and actually was a city representative in Halle. As a particular instance, he founded in 1872 the 'Verein für Socialpolitik' that still today represents the professional organization of German-speaking economists.

Eucken was embedded in a different politico-economic, social and intellectual environment. He was a young man when the disaster of World War I ended, and a witness of the inter-war years. The impressing historic events were the Bolshevist October Revolution and the rule of interventionism in the Western economies. Eucken saw these historic events as being nourished by a common philosophical source that basically denied the autonomy of human beings. Marxist–Leninist determinism and interventionist 'punctualism' (as he called it) represented merely two poles – *les extrêmes se touchent* – on a scale of ill-conceived methodological, theoretical and political views. Eucken objected to their common denominator which drew on ideas of 'historical inevitability' or was inspired by ad hoc experiments ('Age of experiments'). Eucken's central theoretic intent was to demonstrate the existence and feasibility of a 'framework of order' (*Rahmenordnung*) that allowed the possibilities of autonomous human action to be revealed – at a level of individual action as well as at a higher plane of policy intervention – and to project the consequences of action. Eucken constructed various 'models of order' that were stated in terms of a specific *rule- and norm-system*. In his political economy (rather than economics) Eucken features a *constitutional* approach demanding explicitly from the economists that they elaborate on the concept of an *economic constitution* designed to inform any social and economic policy. It appears that Eucken's trust in the spontaneity not only of markets but also of the emergence of norms that enabled their functioning was less pronounced than Hayek's. Eucken was prepared to draw an analogy from physicalist determinism to some form of 'evolutionary determinism' in which spontaneity dethroned the autonomous decision maker.

It would be fascinating (yet beyond the scope of this paper) to further explore to what extent the principal methodological and ontological viewpoints of the authors under discussion were shaped by their distinct social, politico-economic and intellectual environments. We confine our analysis to the questions of what the major differences in the methodological and ontological viewpoints actually were, and how they influenced the basic understanding of what an economic theory can and should be.

CLASSICAL LEGACY

Schmoller has often demanded that economists go back to the classical roots. He divides clearly the founding fathers from later 'generations of sterile epigones' (Schmoller, in Kapp and Kapp 1949, pp. 323–4). He mentions that in England economics 'has experienced the peak of its scientific development at the time of . . . Adam Smith' (ibid.). It is tempting to ask whether the work of Adam Smith can indeed be taken as a prototype for Schmoller's research programme.

The answer will, first of all, depend on our interpretation of Smith's work itself. We accept the received view that Smith's fame is largely due to his concept of the 'invisible hand'. This notion is indeed a philosophical *coup de foudre*. Smith's concept of the 'invisible hand' is an explicit recognition that invisible ideas – in contradistinction to 'visible' matter-energy – have an ontic status *sui generis*. Does Schmoller's work reflect this profound insight of Smith's work? He mentions in the list of classical pioneers besides Smith also Hobbes, Locke and Hume. As is well known, these authors are generally considered to be the intellectual founding fathers of what has become the branch of English empiricism. John Locke, for instance, featured the idea that only sensory perception of reality allows one to convey its theoretical meaning. No particular method or language is required to transform experience into theoretical statements. Against this background, it is safe to assume that Schmoller recognized in Smith's analysis only its rich empirical contents rather than its full 'invisible' theoretical merits.

Schmoller, in fact, has a classical predecessor whose work he fails to acknowledge: David Ricardo. The 'classical question' was whether the economies of the 18th and 19th centuries will eventually converge towards a long-run subsistence state (in neoclassical parlance an equilibrium) or instead move on a long-run growth path propelled by the dynamics of the industrial system. Smith described the developmental dynamics of interrelated resources variables, such as technological change, increasing per capita income and population growth. Yet, besides the empirical account of the 'visible' that is open to the inspection by our senses and to scientific measurement, he tried to explain their existence and dynamics on the basis of explanatory principles. He demonstrated, for instance, that the technological dynamics of the industrial system relied on the principle of the division of labour. The natural (cost) prices to which all actual (market) prices 'gravitate' are therefore in Smith's analysis 'historically' explained. Ricardo saw no need for explanations of the 'invisible' in the factual world of resources. Instead, he arrived – from casual observations and empirical conjectures – at bold generalizations about regularities in the interrelated resources' magnitudes. Schmoller's Smith may well be seen as one to whom Ricardo did considerable scientific harm.

ONTOLOGICAL MODEL

We suggest at this point a simple ontological model that may provide us with an analytical exposition that eases our task of assessing the work of the two economists. It is in the spirit of the so-called process philosophy of Whitehead and Bergson, and draws from scientific insights of modern biophysics. As a basic premise, we suggest that any existent is composed of both idea and matter-energy. There is no matter-energy without idea, and no idea without matter-energy. Ideas are timeless and spaceless; matter-energy extends in time and space. In this view, actual economic phenomena unfold themselves in an ongoing process. Ideas constitute a potential that may be actualized in manifold physical manifestations. Ideas are, turning to Smith again, invisible; in contradistinction the actualization process is visible. Methodologically, ideas are always general, while matter-energy actualizations constitute always singularities. If we take a theory to represent a statement of the type 'if A, then B', the resultant B would not only constitute, in our view, a 'law' or generalization about singular actualized manifestations, but would also represent the ontic capacity of initiating an actualization process given A. This type of theory represents a 'process theory', since the *idea* not only represents a general statement about, but also constitutes an ontic prerequisite for, the *becoming* of reality. An idea does not require a generalization, because it is general *sui generis*.

Our classificatory task, then, is to designate an *idea as an ontic potential* that is capable of bringing about reality as actualized events. We may conceive the respective idea as constituting a class without members. It is an *explanatory class*; interlinked explanatory classes may be seen accordingly to constitute an *explanatory theory*. However, this theory would be one without reality, since reality requires that the ontic potential of ideas be actualized in time and space. Explanation without reference to an observable reality that it intends to explain is meaningless. Thus, we need a second class that is composed of members that are actualizations of the idea. These members may as actual events be observed, statistically measured and assessed with a view to common (for example, average) properties. We call this type of class *descriptive class*. Ricardo's resources aggregates, for instance, are descriptive classes. They derive their classificatory rationale and validity from the quality of empirical observations and statistical ingenuity only. They cannot themselves explain the *emergence* of actual processes. We may call a composite of interrelated descriptive classes a *descriptive theory*. A descriptive theory thus defined requires for its validity only that it portrays faithfully the general features of the observable world; it must portray, in Ricardo's words, the 'strong cases' of the visible reality. Following our ontic scheme, a complete theory must include a set of interrelated descriptive as well as explanatory classes; the latter contains statements about ideas that generate the actual events that are observable, statistically amenable and classified in the former.

HOW 'HISTORICAL' IS SCHMOLLER'S ECONOMIC THEORY?

Economic theory thus defined requires statements about (1) generating principles allowing the actualization of phenomena in time and space, and (2) characteristics and properties of the actualization process. The following discussion will show that Schmoller did not expect theoretical progress to well up from a discussion of generating principles. Furthermore, when discussing the actualization process, he featured analytical properties that resemble strongly those of classical mechanics. Anticipating our conclusion, we may say that Schmoller failed to recognize the ontic relevance of ideas and of the human mind, and that his analysis falls short of demonstrating the genuine evolutionary character of economics. It goes without saying that the validity of my objections depends on the acceptance of the ontic model suggested.

The first objection, that Schmoller failed to state explanatory principles, does apparently run counter to the received view which holds that Schmoller indeed advocated a holistic and evolutionary approach. Various quotations from Schmoller's work may lend support to this viewpoint. However, to use a holistic and evolutionary approach does not imply its use in the sense suggested. In fact, Schmoller did not discuss explanatory principles at all. One may conjecture that this has to do with his 'methodological stages theory' that suggests that observation must always precede theory formulation. While this itself could explain the neglect, it cannot rule out the possibility that there are further and more important reasons that account for it. The issue can be settled only by looking at what Schmoller's view on this critical aspect of theory making actually was.

Generally, he believed that the observation of actual events would theoretically convey the entirety of economic reality. This is immediately clear from his methodological postulates that propound a sequence of priorities. Scientific investigation should be confined 'as far as possible to (1) correct observations of phenomena, (2) their definition and classification, and (3) their causal explanation' (Schmoller 1894, p. 220). Though Schmoller did not mention in his list of classical writers Francis Bacon, the above catalogue of scientific tasks is a tribute to Bacon's legacy:

> For first of all we must prepare a *natural and experimental history*, sufficient and good; and this is the foundation of all; for we are not to imagine or suppose, but to discover what nature does or may be made to do. (Bacon 1878, p. 178, original emphasis)

The factual account 'must be made in the manner of history, without premature speculation or any great amount of subtlety' (Bacon 1878, p. 379). Analogously, Schmoller argues that 'it is by no means a neglect of theory, but rather a necessary base of it, if a science works predominantly descriptively for a while . . .' (Schmoller 1883, cited in Menger 1884, p. 35, transl. KD). Theory thus starts with observation and the collection of data – this being the first stage of his methodological stages. The second stage of scientific inquiry, however, is not defined by a search for explanatory principles as we would expect from our premises. Rather the task is to classify the data, to give them (in Bacon's term) a 'suitable order'. Based on this order, regularities and invariancies between the classes of economic data may be detected:

> The most appropriate and typical domain of historical science is that of critique and orderly arrangement. It is in this field that history, together with philology, has, especially during the last hundred years, developed exact methods and yielded definite results which live up to the highest standards of knowledge and equal the results of all other sciences. It is for this reason that one has come to look upon history as an exact science similar to the natural sciences. (Schmoller 1894, p. 223)

Schmoller's analysis follows in two major respects the assumptions of classical mechanics. First, he conceives causality – the explanation of the dynamics of the economic process – in terms of the concept of (following Aristotelian notions) *efficient* cause. The causality concept is applied to the observable matter-energy world; it is not related in any way to ontic factors such as human intentions, meaning or invisible principles. One may recall at this point Schmoller's emphasis on human action and social institutions stressing that these are intrinsically interconnected with the concept of final cause. However, while Schmoller portrays humans colourfully when it comes to the description of specific human traits, he falls short of demonstrating the causal significance of those traits in the systematic context of an economic theory that would provide ontic space for such factors. He observes behaviour primarily for the sake of arriving at behavioural regularities that may be integrated in his theory – hence transforming what originally was a potential final cause to an efficient one. His student Spiethoff has recognized this shortcoming and suggested that one use the concept of 'motive causality'. He wanted to 'understand' the inside of the black box of the behaviouristic stimulus–response scheme:

> Motive explanation is: to relate economic behaviour to a specific motive as its sufficient cause, where motive means: 'The entirety of all soul-mind aspects that cause human behaviour.' The motive causality (Motivkausalität) is the starting point for understanding (Verstehen). (Spiethoff 1948, p. 616, transl. KD)

Spiethoff provides an explanation of the economic dynamics in terms of motivational energy and of finality. Yet, his notion is still part of a conceptual scheme that advocates relative changes in resources rather than economic processes in an evolutionary sense.

Second, Schmoller relies on the time-symmetry assumption of classical mechanics. Clearly, he collects historical data not only to describe the past but to draw conclusions with regard to future events. Time future is theoretically portrayed in time past. The symmetry assumption is semantically represented in notions such as 'general truth' and 'universality'. His analysis resembles the mirror theory (*Abbildtheorie*) of the *Wiener Kreis*. Empirical positivism expected reality to reveal itself in an objective manner to our senses and our objective methods. Theoretical representation is a 'mirror' of reality expressed in the 'language of things'. There is a one-to-one correspondence between the ontic levels of observation and language; theory is thus a linguistic expression of our observations. This concept renders causality, as any other 'invisible' explanatory principle, superfluous. What cannot be observed, such as intentions, motivations, feelings or Smith's 'invisible hand', is bound to stay outside the confines of a scientific theory.

Schmoller's assumptions of invariancy and time–symmetry are apparent from his writings on methodology. In an article in the *Handwörterbuch der Staatswissenschaften*, which was obviously addressed to his lifelong opponent Menger, he contemplates the methodological requirements for economic theory:

> I have always emphasized that we would proceed only deductively in cases where we possessed all truth already, that all progress of induction leads eventually to deductively useful statements, and that the most developed sciences are those most deductive. Thus, if some have recently repeatedly stated that those who emphasize induction, contrary to Mill, Cairnes and Menger, wish to exclude deduction, this is true neither for myself nor for any other person who has a full grasp of the rules of logic. The much exaggerated dispute in the literature has to do only with the questions to what extent deduction is sufficient in economics, how developed our science is, what body of valid causal statements we possess already or may import from other sciences, such as psychology. Those who consider political economy as almost fully developed, such as the English epigones of A. Smith, will of course view it as a purely deductive science. (Schmoller 1894, pp. 535–6, transl. KD)

This statement suggests that Schmoller believed in the possibility that historical research and inductive inference will bring us some day close to the 'ultimate truth'. In some distant future we will have succeeded in completing the construction of the edifice of a deductive science. The ready acceptance of economics as a universal deductive system presumes the conceptual notions of invariancy and time-symmetry – the very counterposition of any 'historical' approach.

Schmoller's policy approach naturally reflects his theoretical stand. He distinguishes between various epochs that are defined by specific causal regularities. The epochs constitute stages within a broad historical sequence.

Each epoch is characterized by a specific type of economic policy. Economic policies are thus determined in their possibilities and scope by the synchronic laws of a specific epoch and by the diachronic laws of the developmental sequence. Walter Eucken, to whom we turn now, has strongly objected to what he considered was a deterministic view on Schmoller's part.

THE INVISIBLE IN ECONOMICS

Perhaps the most crucial difference between Eucken and Schmoller is that Eucken recognized explicitly the ontic relevance of ideas. His ideal types may be viewed as constituting systemic thought constructs. They do not claim to represent reality; ideas are always general and hence cannot express the singular. They do not claim to be generalizations of actual events. They are expressions of what the human mind is capable of thinking about reality.

However, ideal types are not a priori constructs but are the result of cognitive processes of humans who are embedded in an environment and as such in close touch with reality. This recognition of the empirical side opens the door for understanding Eucken's epistemic viewpoint. Eucken stresses, first of all, the invariant cognitive capacity of the human mind:

> There has never been any intellectually sane human being who would apply other forms of visualizing the world (Anschauung) and other cognitive devices than those we apply ourselves. We reach this conclusion irrespective of whether we talk about the old Sumerians or the Romans of the Republic, or the Incas of the 16th century or the English of the present times. Just imagine that we would encounter humans whose understanding of space and time is alien to us, or who were incapable of thinking in terms of unity and plurality or who would think, ignoring the laws of contradiction, something could simultaneously be and not be. We would not understand such humans. Probably, and with justification, we would reject talking here of humans at all. (Eucken 1938, p. 74, transl. KD)

This capacity of the human mind allows it cognitively to state ideal types. It enables the economist to view history in its 'essence'. Contrasting his view against those of the historical school he states:

> We should break radically with the custom to view history one-sidedly as development. Even so, it will not be necessary that historical experience exhausts simply in fragmentary images. This will not be the case if the inquiry into the historically individual case is conducted with great analytical care – thus arriving at what appears to be permanent in history. This answer seems to contain a paradox. However, it represents an answer that can rely on endorsement. The stronger the individual case is given profile in historical inquiry, the more intelligible becomes the permanent, the constant in history. (Eucken 1940, p. 487, transl. KD)

Eucken has obviously a method of inquiry superior to that of Schmoller since the latter requires libraries of historical inquiries in order to make the theoretical point. Indeed, Eucken emphasizes an 'appreciative interpretation' or 'understanding' of history. He features *introspection* rather than induction. The critical difference between Eucken's and Schmoller's methodological approaches is that Schmoller relies on the statistical inference from a mass of single actual events, while Eucken attempts to understand the 'inner' principle that allows the actualization of those events. He looks, analogous to Smith, for 'invisible principles'. Statements about the inherent characteristics of phenomena do not require that we calculate the averages of observational data, but that we deepen our observation and 'penetrate' into the phenomena in order to *understand the invisible*.

We may distinguish between two types of 'understanding' or 'reality appreciation' (*Verstehen*). One refers to the human mind; we understand the human mind because our minds as observers show the same characteristics as the minds of those observed. We may call this 'intrinsic understanding'. Following Eucken, we do not understand in the same fundamental sense what an ape thinks or feels. The method of 'intrinsic understanding' allows us not only to observe the regular aspects of human behaviour but also to grasp its *meaning*. The analytical unit of an *understanding science* of economics is in this view not 'behavioural man', but rather 'humans in action'. The notion of action presumes cognitive and emotional processes. An analytical treatment of humans as cognitive black boxes leaves economic theory meaningless.

The second type of understanding refers to the organizing principles that for humans constitute the environmental context. We may conceive this as 'extrinsic understanding'. Eucken's quest for illuminating in the single case the permanency of history represents such extrinsic understanding.

IDEAS AS POTENTIAL FOR ORDER AND EVOLUTION

Eucken argues that an evolutionary approach bears the danger of becoming blind for the 'universal order' of reality. In fact, he opposes even a *living system* approach since this would imply an evolutionary perspective. He quotes Dilthey as saying: 'Life is paramount and ubiquitous and the abstractions of our knowledge are of secondary importance relevant only to the extent they refer to life' (Eucken 1938, p. 65, transl. KD). He then objects to this view by saying:

> Since this elementary force (Grundmacht) of life changes permanently, there are no timeless categories any more for him. Reason is equally subject to historization, the truth is relativated accepting only a sole absolute aspect: the changing life. (Eucken 1938, p. 65, transl. KD)

Eucken assumes that the virtues of an idealistic approach are at stake if it is applied also to evolutionary or developmental issues. It is, however, difficult to see why this should be so. For instance, Smith's 'invisible principle' of the division of labour explains the industrial evolution in a way that is consistent with 'historical introspection'. Eucken's rejection of historical laws that rely on inductive inference from statistical data of actual events, as advocated by Schmoller, appears to be sound; but this rationale does not justify one's rejection of equally 'invisible' evolutionary principles.

How do the actual processes in Eucken's system come about? In Schmoller's construal, causality served as a device for promoting the dynamics of the system. What is the 'cause' initiating processes in an ideal-type construct? Applying our ontic scheme, we recognize that the idea itself is the first cause of an actualization process. In physicalist interpretation, ideas would represent simply *uncaused cause*. An idea, say that of planning in Eucken's morphology of economic ideas, may initiate an actual process provided certain contextual conditions are given. The concept of idea as 'generating cause' may be applied more generally. It may refer, particularly, to diachronic principles, such as the generation of novelty, path dependency, and so on, explaining the phenomenon of evolutionary change.

The ontic and epistemic characteristics of Eucken's approach make understandable his view towards economic policy. He conceives ideas in their primary capacity to bring about order. Reality results as an actualization process from ideas that humans must clearly define and politically implement. Humans are not pushed by historical events into predetermined problem solutions, nor does the implementation of an idea lead necessarily to a unique actualization process (that, for instance, would secure a welfare optimum). Against this background, Eucken stresses the importance of the *state* when implementing systemic principles:

> On the basis of clearly spelled out morphological principles . . . the state must become active in the competition law, cartel law, company law, and so on, and ensure that the self-responsible activities of the individual agents do not result in hostile and unrelated activities but that they be supported in the context of an economic order that benefits all. Starting from practical questions of economic and legal policy, it is the task of economics and of the legal sciences to provide the intellectual preparation for such economic constitutions and to be held generally responsible for thinking in terms of economic constitutions (Wirtschaftsverfassungen). (Eucken 1938, p. 80, transl. KD)

Adam Smith rejected governmental intervention on the basis of his apparently bad experience with governmental officials and politicians. The 'invisible hand' appears as a self-organizing principle that has inherent self-implementing qualities that need not be imported into the economy. However, there are several chapters in Smith's *Wealth of Nations* on monopolies, colonies and the like. Smith may not have objected to an improvement of the 'invisible hand'; he only doubted that under the historical conditions of his time systemic policies (*Ordnungspolitik*) would work.

CONCLUSION

Schmoller and Eucken shared a concern for policy. Schmoller's approach was empirical, relied on surface regularities of actual events, and attempted to formulate causal models that allowed the prediction of the consequences of policy action in various historical epochs. Eucken, in turn, started from the creative power of ideas, suggesting that we should look for the universal in historical change. He advocates an understanding both in terms of an intrinsic understanding of the human mind and an extrinsic understanding of the invisible principles that are the ontic departure points for any actual process in time and space. Eucken's construal appears to be more useful for understanding what the origins of an actual process are; Schmoller's empirical insights may provide inferential evidence useful with regard to the description of a specific historical case. There is much to learn from both.

NOTE

1. I gratefully acknowledge comments by Bob Coats, Lukas Hagen and the editors of this volume.

REFERENCES

Bacon, F. (1878), 'Novum Organum', in J. Spedding, R.L. Ellis and D.D. Heath (eds), *The Works of Francis Bacon*, New York: Hurd & Houghton.
Bush, P.D. (1987), 'The Theory of Institutional Change', *Journal of Economic Issues*, **21** (3), pp. 1075–116.
_____(1993), 'The Methodology of Institutional Economics: A Pragmatic Instrumentalist Perspective', in Marc R. Tool (ed.), *Institutional Economics: Theory, Method, Policy*, Boston: Kluwer Academic Publishers, pp. 59–107.
Coats, A.W. (1993), 'What Can We Accomplish With Historical Approaches in an Advanced Discipline such as Economics?', *History of Economic Ideas*, I/1993/3–II/1994/1, pp. 227–65.
Dopfer, K. (1988), 'How Historical is Schmoller's Economic Theory?', *Journal of Institutional and Theoretical Economics*, **144**, pp. 552–69; reprinted in M. Blaug (ed.) (1992), *Gustav Schmoller (1838–1917) and Werner Sombart (1863–1941)*, Pioneers in Economics Series, E. Elgar Collection, Aldershot: Edward Elgar, pp. 141–58.
Eisermann, G. (1993), *Max Weber und die Nationalökonomie*, Marburg: Metropolis.

Eucken, W. (1937), 'Die Leistung der deutschen Volkswirtschaftslehre', *Jahrbücher für Nationalökonomie und Statistik*, **146**, pp. 225–31.

_____(1938), 'Die Überwindung des Historismus', *Schmollers Jahrbuch*, **62**, pp. 191–214.

_____(1940), 'Wissenschaft im Stile Schmollers', *Weltwirtschaftliches Archiv*, **52** (3), pp. 468–506.

Foss, N.J. (1994), 'Realism and Evolutionary Economics', *Journal of Social and Evolutionary Systems*, **17** (1), pp. 21–40.

Hayden, F.G. (1995), 'Instrumentalist Policymaking: Policy Criteria in a Transactional Context', *Journal of Economic Issues*, **29** (2), pp. 361–82.

Herrmann-Pillath, C. (1991), 'Der Vergleich von Wirtschafts-und Gesellschaftssystemen: Wissenschaftsphilosophische und methodologische Betrachtungen zur Zukunft eines ordnungstheoretischen Forschungsprogramms', *ORDO*, **42**, pp. 15–67.

Kapp, K.W. and L. Kapp (1949), *History of Economic Thought*, New York: Barnes and Noble.

Lawson, T. (1994), 'A Realist Theory for Economics', in R.E. Backhouse (ed.), *New Directions in Economic Theory*, London: Routledge, pp. 257–85.

_____(1995), 'A Realist Perspective on Contemporary "Economic Theory"', *Journal of Economic Issues*, **29** (1), pp. 1–32.

Menger, C. (1884), *Die Irrthümer des Historismus in der deutschen Nationalökonomie*, Wien: Alfred Hölder.

Perlman, M. (1991), 'Understanding the "Old" American Institutionalism', paper, *4ème Colloque de l'Association Charles Gide pour l'Etude de la Pensée Economique*, Paris: Presses Universitaires de France.

Schefold, B. (1989), 'Schmoller als Theoretiker', in H.C. Recktenwald (ed.), *Vademecum zu einem Klassiker der historischen Methode in der ökonomischen Wissenschaft*, Düsseldorf: Wirtschaft und Finanzen, pp. 77–103.

Schmoller, G. (1883), 'Zur Methodologie der Staats- und Sozialwissenschaften', Jahrbuch für Gesetzgebung, Verwaltung und Volkswirtschaft im deutschen Reiche, pp. 239–58.

_____(1894), 'Volkswirtschaft, Volkswirtschaftslehre und ihre Methode', in I. Conrad et al. (eds), *Handwörterbuch der Staatswissenschaften*, Jena: Gustav Fischer; transl. by the Contemporary Civilisation Staff of Columbia College, Columbia University Press, 1946, reprinted in K.W. Kapp and L. Kapp (1949).

_____(1919), *Grundriss der Allgemeinen Volkswirtschaftslehre*, München/Leipzig: Duncker & Humblot.

Senn, P.R. (1989), 'What Has Happened To Gustav Schmoller In English?', *HES Bulletin*, **11** (2), pp. 252–94, reprinted in M. Blaug (ed.) (1992), *Gustav Schmoller (1838–1917) and Werner Sombart (1863–1941)*, Pioneers in Economics Series, E. Elgar Collection, Aldershot: Edward Elgar, pp. 190–232.

_____(1993), 'Gustav Schmoller in English: How Has He Fared?', *History of Economic Ideas*, I/1993/3–II/1994/1, pp. 267–329.

Spiethoff, A. (1948), 'Anschauliche und reine volkswirtschaftliche Theorie und ihr Verhältnis zueinander', *Synopsis*, Festgabe für Max Weber, Heidelberg: Lambert Schneider.

Tool, M.R. (1986), *Essays in Social Value Theory, A Neoinstitutionalist Contribution*, New York: M.E. Sharpe.

_____(1995), 'Institutional Adjustment and Instrumental Value', in M.R. Tool (ed.), *Pricing, Valuation and Systems*, Aldershot: Edward Elgar, pp. 181–218.

Veblen, T. (1901), 'Gustav Schmoller's Economics', *The Quarterly Journal of Economics*, XVI; reprinted in T. Veblen (1961), *The Place of Science in Modern Civilization and other Essays*, New York: Russel & Russel.

6. The Historical Quest for Principles of Valuation: An Interpretive Essay

Warren J. Samuels

> When reason argues about particular cases, it needs not only universal but also particular principles.
>
> *Thomas Aquinas*

> Men with definite and final formulas or issues soon become bores.
>
> *Oliver Wendell Holmes, Jr[1]*

INTRODUCTION

Society, within physical constraints, is a matter of human construction and encompasses, indeed constitutes, a valuation process. The economy, both insofar as it deals with scarcity and otherwise, is part of this process. Scarcity imposes the necessity of choice, which leads to conflict. The conflicts may be between people or between alternatives; questions of 'which' often, if not usually, are accompanied by questions of 'whose'. Decisions have to be made and these have to be made by some decision–making processes which themselves have to be made through decision making. In all these and other respects, society is a vast valuation process.

It is a characteristic of post-Enlightenment modernity that increasing numbers of people have been conscious of the policy character of social arrangements – choice, in part a function of power structure, which is itself a matter of choice. On the one hand, in the past these arrangements were legitimized as natural and/or divine and more or less accepted as such by the masses. On the other hand, following Émile Durkheim's distinction between latent and manifest function, these arrangements were the product of choices made by leaders, their manifest function being both known by the elite and the very object of their machinations, and the latent legitimation role for the masses was in part the purpose of it all. In other words, the elite practised deliberative decision making while the masses were induced – intellectually sedated – to accept the results non-deliberatively. This is now substantially, but by no means completely, changed. Utilitarian (or pragmatic or instrumental) thinking is increasingly more widespread and engaged in more self-consciously (and even, ironically, unselfconsciously).

One of the objectives of philosophers, and more recently social scientists as well, has been to construct intellectual systems which would both make sense of the situation facing society and provide foundations or criteria for the making of choices, perhaps even generate the choices themselves. These intellectual systems, including the various principles or criteria of choice (not always so perceived or designated), came to constitute the social valuation process for many people. The provision of these intellectual systems and principles, examples of which are elaborated below, was typically coupled, insofar as they were practised, by efforts at absolutist legitimation of both the system and its principles and the results of their application. At bottom was a quest for the philosopher's stone, some basis of putatively conclusive decision making, a basis itself somehow above cavil and decision making. This quest was readily pursued but also easily compromised or finessed by the evident tailoring of systems and principles to the specific objectives of the thinker involved. This could be described as either casuistry or pragmatism, but in either case the process of legitimation was muddied if not seriously marred, at least theoretically.

More analytically important, these systems and principles have had two difficulties, or at least two characteristics. First, each system or principle could be applied differently by different users. Second, in actuality the results of the valuation process were seemingly, if not conclusively, the result not of any one system or principle alone, but of the interaction and aggregation of the use of whichever of them were deployed and used and the manner of their use. Taken together, these two characteristics meant that valuation was a process in which values were worked out, not the result of a more or less mechanical application of some set of words. Individuals could seek, or could say they were seeking, particular values, but their private (or collective) quests were only so many inputs into the social valuation process. In their individual quests, they could believe they were trying to achieve particular values, values with perhaps independent and transcendent ontological status. But in practice it has seemed that the results were mixed and socially constructed. Values were perhaps the motivating ideas, the more or less perceived intellectualized expressions or meanings of social arrangements. Perhaps they were more than this, but not all have thought so.

In sum, therefore, society is a valuation process. People have sought valuational systems and principles with which to confront and pursue problems of choice. The valuational process has been one of working things out. Using again Durkheim's distinction, in seeking and employing particular, definitive valuational systems and principles, people were engaged in manifest function. All the while this activity had the latent function of participating in something more problematic and open-ended, namely, the social valuation process; the pursuit of particular values had meaning largely in terms of participation in that valuation process. Two further points: first, values are the criteria of judgement used in reasoned evaluation and decision making (even when received values are deemed to be accepted by virtue of their traditional status alone). Second, the valuational process is not solely an intellectual one, as the foregoing discussion might seem to contemplate. It is also driven by psychological and power variables and considerations.

This essay surveys, as examples of the foregoing characterizations, some of the more dramatic and interesting attempts in the history of economic thought to construct intellectual systems and principles of valuation pertinent to decision making in one way or another. It identifies the nature and content of each and the way in which each was arguably inconclusive, however otherwise useful and interesting it may have been. Some collateral topics or points will also be considered. The discussion should be recognized to be fundamentally interpretive. It is not an attempt to present a text-bookish historical account.

The reader is cautioned to remember two important distinctions – first, that between the construction and use of an intellectual system and/or principle of valuation by a particular person(s) and its participation in the total valuational process; and second, that between the proposal of a system or principle by a philosopher or social scientist and its use by ordinary people, including philosophers and scientist-analysts.

Terms like 'worked out' are used throughout this paper. The intended meaning of the term can be illustrated by an example. In organized sports, some rules must be deployed, which will be adopted – worked out – in advance of any particular game by those with the authority to do so. Given the rules, the game will be played and a result will be worked out, or reached. The term 'worked out' as used herein assumes no particular structure, mode of reasoning or decision making, or operational or performance result. The term is also used in such a way that 'not worked out' has no meaning. The fundamental principles on which 'worked out' is based are that no ontologically given basis is given by nature or otherwise, that results cannot conclusively be established in advance, that some selection must be made in one way or another, and that the effective selection probably will be the result of the juxtaposition of contended approaches within the mode of selection adopted and within which it is worked out, with the mode of selection itself having to be worked out in the same manner. The emphasis is on the process, which itself must be worked out, rather than on some result given, on the basis of some putative selection criterion/criteria, by some principle deemed to yield unequivocally self-subsistent and conclusive results, of which none seems available that lack either opportunity or necessity for further choice.

HISTORICAL SURVEY

Plato and Aristotle

Let us commence with Plato and Aristotle and their respective theories of knowledge in relation to social action. For both of them, generally speaking, knowledge comes from experience, or rather the perception of experience, and is the result of perception combined with reasoning. Both proper perception and rational reasoning are required.

Plato's emphasis is on neither the experience *per se* nor the reality presumed to underlie that experience, but rather on the ideal derived from that experience/reality. What counts is not the reality but the idea thereof and especially the ideal derived therefrom, which becomes the basis and objective of action. Plato's is a philosophy of reform or of potential reform.

This may well illustrate a deeply important, human process; the valuation process is one of articulating ideals derived from experience as a basis of action/policy. Several problems must, however, be noted. First, extant reality (for example, the existing socioeconomic system) is a given, however difficult it may be to define unequivocally. Insofar as extant reality changes, the basis of the idealization/valuation process changes. Second, the derivation of the ideal, and likewise the articulation of experience, are acts of creative imagination, and both the conduct and the content of such acts may vary. Third, because any extant reality is heterogeneous and multifaceted, it is capable of being perceived and thence idealized differently. Insofar as people approach that heterogeneous extant reality from different perspectives, the result is a multiplicity of ideals each somehow arguably derived from the same extant reality. The burden of Platonism, therefore, is one of choice: choice of the definition of extant reality and, especially, of the competing putative idealizations of that reality.

Aristotle's emphasis is on the reality itself. Existing reality exists. It is real in itself. It has a separate existence apart from our perception (and valuation) of it. The important thing is not the ideal(s) which a creative imagination may derive from extant reality but the reality itself, which, because it exists or must be presumed to exist, must be accepted as such; after all, it (already) is. Aristotle's is a philosophy of neither a denial of reform nor fatalistic acceptance. It is a caution that that which is has to be reckoned with and not changed lightly. The real thing exists itself and the mind has only an uncertain image of it; hence caution.

This too illustrates a deeply important, human process, that of paying attention to where one already is, not only to where one might be or go. The complex overriding problem here, however, is this: extant reality does not define itself. 'It' exists or may be said to exist, but what 'it' is, is the very point at issue. In the formulation of a definition of extant reality an ideational, or idealist, element inevitably enters; the specification of that reality, as a basis of action or policy, is a matter of human construction. Assuming everyone to be a realist, therefore, it is nonetheless more than likely that a multiplicity of specifications of extant reality will emerge from which a choice must be made.

The upshot is that both Platonic idealism and Aristotelian realism, while commencing from quite different initial positions, end up in the same predicament: one has to choose among constructions of the ideal and the other has to choose among alternative specifications of the real. Both involve choosing between idealized conceptualizations, called ideal by one and real by the other, in each case having been multiply created. (It will be noticed that this situation underlies both Kantian epistemology and contemporary Post Modernism.) In both cases it is a matter of hubris, ulterior motive or preconception to assume that some putatively true specification of extant reality or of its idealization exists and that one him- or herself knows it.

Insofar, therefore, as Platonic idealism and Aristotelian realism, considered as theories of knowledge in relation to social action, are both approaches to valuation and constitutive of principles of valuation, they are inconclusive. Neither is able to serve as more than a metaphysical, a priori or presumptive framework, and both are therefore unable conclusively to solve the problems to which they are addressed. That each in practice is instrumented differently (which is another problem) and that differences of presumption between frameworks are important, does not vitiate the inconclusivity of both approaches.

We need to glance at Aristotle's conception of ethics and justice. Plato initially (in the *Republic*) focused on the ideal state but came later (in the *Laws*) to treat the best practicable state. Aristotle focused in his *Ethics* on the achievement not of the absolute good but of the good practicably attainable. Virtue is the achievement of the right balance, the practical mean between the extremes. Recognizing the diversity and conflict of values and of ends, Aristotle believed the mean mediated between the extremes, and this was the highest good.

One problem here is that this philosophy of moderation will not appeal to a committed fundamentalist of any philosophical position. Another problem is that moderation may be a fine sentiment but the balancing called for by Aristotle can only be undertaken differently by different people; people, for example, with different agendas, preconceptions or perceptions; the content of 'balancing' remains an issue.

Accordingly, this approach to or principle of valuation is inconclusive; it is not self-subsistent in reaching results. The implication lies at hand that no conclusive or self-subsistent principles are available, notwithstanding beliefs and wishful thinking to the contrary.

Aristotle considered not only universal justice – the meaning of virtue considered above – but particular justice, justice dealing with interpersonal relations and thereby with the distributions of honour, wealth, military service, income, taxes, and so on; that is, with distributive justice. Aristotle's solution was to affirm equality in the sense of proportionality to some standard. Here he distinguished between arithmetic and geometric equality, illustrated by a pyramid in which individuals on the same level are equal but inequality exists between individuals on different levels. Justice is proportional to where you are situated in the social scale.

The problem with this formulation is that it describes social structures but offers no conclusive formula for either determining where a particular individual should be located or undertaking reform of social structures. It too is inconclusive.

We might further illustrate our predicament by reference to Plato's and Aristotle's respective specifications of the ideal state. While both envisioned, among other things, that the ideal state would take advantage of the division of labour, albeit on a small scale, Plato's ideal polity was a relatively self-sufficient group away from the sea in order to help prevent the lure of 'unnatural' attractions from alien cultures (though with some trading of surplus goods); whereas Aristotle's ideal state was located near the sea, to facilitate trade. Aristotle, practising Platonic idealism, created an ideal state different in structural and other details from that produced by Plato.

Roman Thought

Moving on to Roman thought, here we find the formation of Roman law. One may contemplate law – law in general or Roman law in particular – as something given. Centuries of Roman civilization exhibited enormous struggles over the distribution of land and correlative thereto the distribution of political power. Issues of what we would call economic policy were issues of both private power and control of the state. Conflicts between rich and poor and among factions of the rich continually arose. Furthermore, therefore, Roman law was a process (itself a function of conflict) of working out solutions, or giving effect to solutions otherwise (for example, militarily) reached. Reference to 'Roman law' was and is not enough. Even if one presumes that it was better to have a legal process than not to have it, the existence of that process in and of itself was manifestly insufficient to generate results; one also needed additional normative premises and conceptions of the desired state of society to be constructed through Roman law. These premises and conceptions were adopted and changed during centuries of conflict.

Mediaeval Scholastic Thought

We come next to mediaeval Scholastic thought. This was a paradigm involving the superimposition of the church's ethical or valuational system, ostensibly derived from its theology, upon economic life. Within the Judeo-Christian tradition, the church followed upon the Hebrew Bible, subsequently the Old Testament. That document, considered as an approach to human decision making and valuation, was itself heterogeneous. In Ecclesiastes one reads of the ubiquity of vanity, the futility of wisdom and the futility of human affairs. In 1 Samuel one reads of limited change or reform, with such as occurs emanating from God. In Isaiah one reads of a universalist and messianic utopianism. These different books of the Old Testament not only clearly differ among themselves but each may itself be both variably interpreted and, especially, applied. Not surprisingly, no unequivocal and conclusive policy calculus is there.

Arguably both the Old Testament and the writings of the Scholastics, subsequently the Roman Catholic church, provided reasonably clear (but different) frameworks within which problems of valuation and of policy could be considered, clarified and selected. But, as with our other examples, these were only frameworks, not self-subsistent generators of conclusive solutions. All these approaches amounted, in part, to sets of concepts or discursive (rhetorical) systems of language on the terms of each of which debate could be conducted and/or rationalization articulated.

This discursiveness and inconclusivity is illustrated by Thomism. Thomas Aquinas argued that human beings could process a problem through the hierarchical network of church principles and out of this would result by definition the best solution, a solution which, because of the exercise of right reason, could be taken as God's will. The problem, of course, is that different philosophers, theologians and policy analysts may so process a problem (however identified) but reach quite different conclusions or solutions. The church has apparently always had internal doctrinal and other schisms on issues of theology, explanation and conduct. Apropos of the epigraph from Aquinas, reason has a choice of both universal and particular principles.

Glancing for a moment at the history of Catholic and Protestant socioeconomic thought, we note that some writers have affirmed a religious basis for capitalism. Other writers, however, have argued that whereas the Christian ethos is an ethos of love, that of bourgeois civilization is one of egoism, and the two are incompatible. Christianity, it appears, offers no singular, conclusive judgement on the major question of the moral status of capitalism.

Mercantilism

Let us turn to Mercantilism. Without examining any of the multiplicity of interpretive problems raised by this complex and unsystematic corpus of theory, policy and rationalization, one key relevant point emerges. Insofar as Mercantilism involved the quest for a favourable balance of trade – and it clearly involved much more than that, and in a more or less sophisticated way – this principle of policy required application. This principle of policy involved (in Adam Smith's terminology) a system of extraordinary restrictions and extraordinary encouragements. But the principle was not self-subsistent; it did not apply itself. Mercantilism in practice was a 'system' of ad hoc arrangements, the principle of the favourable balance of trade was used to rationalize specific favouritisms rather than to determine what they were to be. Mercantilism was a system of symbiosis of power and of interest between selected mercantile and manufacturing interests on the one hand and the Crown on the other, and not the pure and simple application of mercantilist principles. Those interests which gained monarchical approval were protected, and vice versa. The principle was a framework within which specific policy decisions made on other grounds could be given a rational, legitimizing construction, but it did not determine them.

John Locke

We now come to John Locke and the entire politico-economic tradition of Western civilization, of which he was, along with Adam Smith, its premier philosopher. Several of his doctrines are important for our purposes.

One doctrine is his idea that civil government is instituted for the great and chief end of the preservation, or protection, of property. This has become a major principle of valuation applicable to questions of economic policy in Western societies. Several problems arise, however, which illustrate the incoherence and inconclusivity of the principle. First, it must be recognized that Locke was the great philosopher of middle-class society and of non-landed property. In his day, his doctrines of property and government were revolutionary. At stake was precisely what constituted the property which government was to preserve and protect. Before government can protect property it must first determine what it will protect as property, and Locke was an advocate of a major transformation of the property system, ergo of the legal foundations of the modern economy. Second, the same point applies on the level of particular property rights. The property rights which count are those of civil government (not that of the state of nature). Civil government exists not only to protect the items and elements of property but to determine them. Property is not protected because it is property, it is property because it is protected. The magnificent principle, that government is to protect property, accords (as Vilfredo Pareto would put it) with modern sentiments, but as a principle it is inconclusive and question-begging as to both the interests which are to be protected as property, and changes in the interests to which government is to give its protection. Even if one has little sympathy with government and with politicians, the idea of theoretical limits to government, or of theoretical formulae by which government can be directed, as if by a black box, is fundamentally misguided. Pragmatic judgements must always be made, on some basis, as to whose interests government will protect, as property rights or otherwise, and whose interests will not only not be given such protection but will be exposed to the power of those given such protection. Whatever interests are protected as property rights will be given thereby a legally specific domain of discretion by means of which the owners' participation in the economic decision-making process will be promoted.

A second doctrine of Locke is that the legislature, which is to represent the will of the people and constitute a check on the power of the executive (the Crown), is itself subject to certain limitations. These are that law must apply equally to all, that law must not be arbitrary and oppressive but must be designed for the good of the people, that no taxes should be levied without the consent of the people or of their representatives, and that government must not transfer its law-making power to anyone (and especially not to the Crown). Given both Locke's total system of thought and the nature and structure of modern polities, these too are admirable propositions, seemingly determinative valuational principles. But they are not self-subsistent. That law must apply equally to all fails to cope with the facts that a law equally applicable to people unequally situated necessarily treats them unequally, that the equal treatment of unequals may require treating them unequally, and that the basis of determining equality and inequality is a matter of choice and is variable, to be based on some supplementary principle, also a matter of choice. That law must not be arbitrary and oppressive is subject to selective perception as to procedure and content. Similarly, it is clear that different people have widely varying ideas as to what is necessary and/or desirable for the good of the people – and this includes the fact that different policies enhance conditions for different people, to wit, the problem of distribution. That taxes may not be levied without consent encounters the evident fact of manufacture of consent, not the giving or withholding of an independent consent; the field is latent with fictions and arguments based on fictions. And so on. These principles, for all that they accomplish relative to their alternatives – which may be their important role – are not in and of themselves conclusively dispositive of the valuational issues to which they seem to be addressed and in aid of which they are often invoked.

Bernard Mandeville

Turning to Bernard Mandeville, we find comparable difficulties. He too, like Locke before him and many others afterward, was utilitarian in the broad sense that policies should be evaluated on the basis not solely of received moral principles but with regard to material consequences. Utilitarianism is, not unlike the mediaeval Scholastic philosophy, a framework within which policies can be evaluated, rather than a principle immediately applicable to and determinative of policy. True, Scholasticism affirmed salvation in the hereafter and Mandeville's utilitarianism affirmed the benefits of material well-being in the present world, and this difference is significant. But considered as total frameworks within which policies can be evaluated, neither is unequivocally dispositive of the issues brought to them. Different users of a framework will reach different conclusions and solutions. It is pleasing to affirm singular solutions but they are produced not by the framework or principle with which they are associated but by the act (with or without conscious principle) of creative imagination of the user; indeed, the framework or principle is both a mode of discourse and a means of legitimation.

In connection with Mandeville, the so-called 'market plus framework' approach to the problem of the economic role of government was developed. It stressed that markets were a function of and operated within important legal and non-legal framing institutions. Both analytically and descriptively the market-plus-framework approach was something of an advance over certain naive formulations, generally the 'laissez faire' or 'laissez faire with exceptions' interpretation. At the very least, it permitted the incorporation of legal and non-legal social control into models which often postulate an autonomous self-adjusting economy with minimal collective action of any kind, especially that of government. But certain problems arise. One is the substantive content of the framework-filling activities of law and morals (by which I intend also to include custom, religion and education); this always remains to be determined. Another is the relative scope of or degree of reliance upon legal and non-legal social control. Still another is whether the framework is to be static, set up once for all time, or dynamic and evolutionary. All of these are underscored by the problem posed by inferring from the market-plus-framework model that specific policies can be tested by whether they are framework-filling, and thus permitted, or particularistic interventions, and not allowed. The problem is that these are not self-subsistent, self-applying, determinative categories. Are the antitrust laws, pollution control laws – a form of change of the law of property – and so on, framework-filling or particularistic interventions? The market-plus-framework approach – arguably the most widely (explicitly or implicitly) used approach in the social sciences, second overall in public discourse only to ideological non-interventionism – can serve as a framework of discourse. It will not in and of itself produce definitive, conclusively dispositive results as to either what government is and is not to do or whose interests government is or is not to protect.

In light of the foregoing, it is not surprising that different writers have interpreted Mandeville as individualist, interventionist and as transitionalist.

The Physiocrats

Next consider the vaunted naturalism of Physiocracy, whose very name means rule of nature. The problem here is simple and straightforward. The Physiocrats had (a more or less Platonic) idealization of mid-18th century French society and economy, which they then proceeded (perhaps in an analogue to the tradition of Thomism) to identify as the natural order. Inasmuch as different specifications of the natural order of things can be and indeed have been given, naturalism as an approach to policy is inconclusive. Strictly speaking, naturalism is ontological or philosophical realism: it is a mode of discourse within which advocates must somehow determine – choose – what policies to follow, which will be deemed to be those called for by the natural order.

This means that the Physiocratic call for mankind to allow the rules of the natural order to work, thereby promoting material well-being, was in effect the proposition that their programme, and no other, was to be identified as that of the natural order, a claim that was asserted only a priori and could be asserted no other way. (This does not mean that, for example, their call for a capital-intensive commercial agriculture was not sensible; only that it is a pragmatic, not an ontological, argument.) Indeed, the more or less conventional view that the Physiocrats supported the idea of laissez faire (they do not seem to have used the term in print) is simply wrong and is wrong for several reasons, even though they can be read as advocating the 'perfect freedom' of commerce. First, their idea of freedom was not for individuals to be free to choose; it was freedom for the rules of the natural order – as they understood them – to reign. Second, their agenda for government, once the metaphysical language of naturalism is deconstructed, called for: (1) government determination and redetermination of the rights of property holders in accordance with instrumental reasoning; (2) government provision of remedial relief; (3) a programme of social reconstruction favouring the creation of an agricultural kingdom (a *royaume agricole*), in which government would be no less activist than under Mercantilism, only the agenda would be different (though not entirely: some protection of agricultural markets would likely be pursued); (4) a programme of government promotion of economic development, including the promotion of favourable agricultural prices and an adequate flow of resources to agriculture and the avoidance of leakages from the spending flow; and, a result of Quesnay's identification of problems of economic instability, (5) a programme of government promotion of economic stabilization, notably with regard to the pattern and the level of spending. All this was in the name of the natural order of things. And, of course, all the details of this would still have to be worked out.

England Before Adam Smith

In England in the late 17th and early 18th centuries there were those, such as Richard Cumberland, Anthony Ashley Cooper (3rd Earl of Shaftesbury) and Joseph Butler, the first and third of whom were clergymen, who believed that natural law in the form of moral rules is imprinted upon the human psyche so as, within each human mind, to temper self-interest and render individual behaviour consonant with the principles by which the moral and physical world have been designed, thereby giving effect to the universal pattern in both the physical and moral universe. This general model, however attractive to some minds, was given significantly different specification by each of the three thinkers. These differences pall, however, in the light of a pervasive problem: If such implanting of natural law took place, then how is one to explain immoral, not to say illegal, behaviour? Moreover, how is one to identify such behaviour? The problem is parallel to another: how do arguably bad things happen in a world ruled by an omniscient and omnipotent deity? And from this problem follows the others: How to explain, as well as to identify, immoral behaviour? How much responsibility is given to mankind for its actions in such a world in which so much is assigned to God? The general model may, depending on one's state of mind, solve one problem, but it both raises and does not dispose of still other problems. No philosopher's, or prelate's, stone here.

Adam Smith

Consider Adam Smith's argument in his *Theory of Moral Sentiments* (1759). Smith may be said to argue several things: that moral rules are necessary for individuals and for groups; that moral rules are worked out through the application of the principles of approbation and disapprobation, with which we evaluate our own and others' behaviour, make comparisons and form the ever-emergent rules; and that the principles of approbation and disapprobation are given to man by the Benevolent Author of Nature. The first two propositions amount to the sociology of morality as to its function and its operation; the third, a manifestation of either a Deistic belief system or a mode of discourse. Patently absent from Smith's analysis is any pretence that the principles of approbation and disapprobation would or could lead to specific moral rules or that such rules awaited discovery. Rather, he was describing and explaining how moral rules were formed, the process of their derivation and evolution. Both his model and his analysis are different from the other models we have been examining, different precisely in these respects.

Jeremy Bentham

We come next to Jeremy Bentham. Bentham proposed two principles, the principle of utility and the principle of the greatest happiness for the greatest number. The former principle, as we saw above, was both a descriptive (positive) and a normative proposition. On the one hand, Bentham was arguing that even the application of received moral rules was undertaken with regard to consequences (casuistry or pragmatism); in other words, the world is actually a world of utilitarian practice, whatever other name or belief system is attached to it. On the other hand, Bentham was arguing that this situation was right and proper, as well as inevitable.

As for the second principle, the greatest happiness of the greatest number, this was Bentham's answer to the question of whose interests should count, those of one person (together with the favoured few that person allowed gratification), the few or the many. But this answer, assuming one did not question the principle of the greatest happiness of the greatest number, raised but did not unequivocally and dispositively answer another question, that of whether the greatest happiness of the greatest number was to be maximized along the intensive or the extensive margins, that is, by increasing the happiness of those already very happy or by increasing the number of those made happy. The answer to this question would have to be worked out – and much subsequent history is the story of the ideas and policies of the Benthamite right versus the Benthamite left, each providing a different answer to the question Bentham's answer raised but did not answer.

Utopist Literature

Next to be considered is the vast literature of utopianism. This literature has been an important part of the human valuational process. It has constituted the erection and the critique of values. It has offered criticisms of various societies either as they were received or as they were developing, at least as the authors perceived them. It has been an important vehicle for the quest and expression of values. It has been an important instrument for the production of views for and against socio-politico-economic change. It has been Platonism in action.

And it has shared the limitations of Platonism. Utopian writings are typically an extension, providing affirmation or critique, of the author's own society. Different writers have reacted differently to their society, and different utopias and dystopias have been created accordingly. The same society has given rise to different utopian writings. And the fact of multiple utopias creates the necessity of choice among these idealized conceptual, typically fictional, reconstructions of their authors' society(ies).

The utopian literature provides another insight into the problem treated here. One fundamental criticism of this literature is that almost no utopian writing has anything but a static construction. This literature typically has no provision for endogenous change; they are 'once and for all time' reconstructions. The real utopian character of this literature is not its putative unrealism as to how much change is possible. It lies in the authors' neglect of the problem of change within the context of their system. In a utopia there are no problems, at least of any importance, left to perplex and to solve. Each author has a principal organization with which to establish the right system, which system is then to be left to run on its own. However much this is a solid, and perhaps substantially unavoidable, fictional strategy, it is too simplistic and too disengaging a view of the complexity of the world in which we live and its problems. What is true, therefore, of the utopist literature is also true of all models, lines of reasoning and principles of valuation.

The Economists' Theory of Value

I come next to the economists' theory of value, whether it be the labour or marginal utility or any other theory of 'value'. Such is not a theory of price. It is a theory of the ultimate and invariable basis of price, of the metaphysical principle governing price, as that toward which price necessarily gravitates. The history of economic thought evidences the substantial eclipse of value theory in favour of price theory. Except for unreconstructed Marxists and Austrians, economists no longer seek, or seek to apply, some singular absolute metaphysical principle (which does not preclude the operation of valuational principles in all policy-relevant analysis). In the former Soviet Union, efforts to apply the labour theory of value involved convoluted measurements which, at least with regard to military spending, were not allowed to interfere with the planned allocation of resources for that purpose. The quest for the economists' holy grail was to no avail. In retrospect it would appear that what counted was not some absolute and transcendent principle of value, such as labour or marginal utility, but determinations by those whose interests counted, by way of both power structure and price mechanism, of the allocation of resources.

Pareto Optimality

Still other efforts to construct definitive principles of valuation have been forthcoming. One of them is Pareto optimality. This has the virtue of providing for and giving effect to individual consent in exchange. But it has its limits as a determinative principle of valuation. It is, within neoclassical economics, enmeshed in a programme and a technique of generating ostensibly unique determinate optimal equilibrium solutions. To this end highly restrictive assumptions (for example, as to the identification and assignment of rights) need to be made in order to generate single optimal solutions. In actuality, there are no unique optimal solutions, only solutions specific to, inter alia, particular power structures and patterns of learned preferences. Power structures, in particular, determine whose preferences are to count in the working out of Pareto optimal solutions. The concept of Pareto optimality alone is insufficient to serve as a principle of valuation, in either an explanatory or normative sense. As explanation, it ignores the formation and operation of power structure; as normative proposition, it ignores the problems of the criteria by which power is to be structured and therefore of whose interests ought to count.

Neoinstitutionalism

Still another is the neoinstitutionalist effort to provide a value principle by which 'to choose among value premises' (Tool 1995, p. 160). I have written extensively on this question (Samuels 1995 and forthcoming). The principal problems are those which have been observed with similar efforts: That the social value principle requires specification and particular application and can be specified and applied differently by different people. That in a process of infinite regression any value principle with which to choose among other value premises is itself subject to the same problem of choice. That any value principle, and application of any value principle, is but a contributor to the valuational *process*, a valued contributor but only a contributor and not a principle conclusively dispositive of the issues to which any value principle is addressed.

This emphasis on *process* was recognized by Thorstein Veblen and John R. Commons, the founders of institutional economics. Veblen discussed the problem of valuation in terms of what contributed to the 'life process', and Commons did likewise in regard to the judgements of 'reasonable value' which became ensconced in the working rules of law (and custom, and so on) which governed access to and use of power in economic affairs. For neither of them did recognition of these processes, of the life process and of reasonable value, provide anything but a mode of discourse, certainly not a calculus by which unique or proper or best solutions of problems of valuation could be conclusively reached. For both of them, valuation and solutions to problems of policy would have to be worked out. For Veblen, this working out would have to be abetted by recognition of the need to distinguish between pecuniary and industrial employments, between making money and making goods, perhaps (in the tradition of Clarence Ayres and Fagg Foster) between institutional inhibitions and technological advancement; but it would still have to be worked out, no black box or strict formula was available to do the job. For Commons, this working out would have to be abetted by recognizing the need to choose between the customs and ambitions of different, competing groups. He had his own objectives for policy (such as promoting the inclusion of groups – notably workers and consumers – whose interests had hitherto been largely excluded) but his analysis stressed the importance of the process of choosing between customs and between objectives. And so on. In both cases, results would have to be worked out and would always be tentative and subject to revision. Neither had a touchstone with which to choose among value premises.

CONCLUSION

There is no question but that we work out more or less tentative solutions to problems of valuation. These are worked out, not mechanically determined by valuational theories or principles. The putative fact of the matter is the inexorable necessity of choice. Human beings often have a need or desire for, or to believe they have, conclusively dispositive determinate solutions to valuational problems, such as those advocated by the writers surveyed above. But no theory and no principle will preclude the real problems of the necessary exercise of choice both among principles and in their instrumentation as well as in the determination of who makes those choices.

Some principles of valuation are arguably 'better' than others. But that does not warrant the erection of those principles, or the theory or lines of reasoning by which they are deemed 'better', into ontological absolutes. It is all something to be worked out, without an unequivocal basis on which to do so; the meaning of 'better' is what is worked out. And one does not require ontologically absolute principles of value in order to reach decisions as to good and bad, better or worse, or, for that matter, 'evil' in either a theological or non-theological sense.

One objection to the argument of this essay is that it normatively supports 'anything goes'. On the contrary, the argument is, first, that the selection of any particular valuational principle permits 'anything goes' at the levels of both choice of principle and application of principle; and second, that, as a matter of putative fact, choices are made and have to be made, that we make them willy nilly. No subjective preference or principle will suffice to eliminate the fact and necessity of choice. We choose the principle and its application. Under the aegis of most if not all principles, the principle itself seems to govern. Whereas the fact of the matter is that such is illusion, choices continue to be made. Finally, we are left with the problem of choosing who is to choose the principle and then who is to apply the principle chosen. Choice is inexorable.

In one of his charming and often irascible essays, on Thomas Carlyle, Lytton Strachey wrote,

> Morality, curiously enough, seems to belong to that class of things which are of the highest value, which perform a necessary function, which are, in fact, an essential part of the human mechanism, but which should only be referred to with the greatest circumspection. Carlyle had no notion that this was the case, and the result was disastrous. In his history, especially, it is impossible to escape from the devastating effects of his reckless moral sense. (Strachey 1931, pp. 183–4)

I have no particular view of Carlyle in these matters. I also think that I understand that neither any individual nor any society can at every junction make a fetish of raising questions of value – though I do appreciate that everything done, or not done, through individual and collective action involves taking at least implicit valuational positions. Strachey acknowledges that morality – for us, valuation – is 'an essential part of the human mechanism' (I would have selected a different word here). I concur that circumspection, even the 'greatest circumspection', is called for from time to time, perhaps often. But Strachey's position should obscure neither the fact nor the necessity of valuation.

Nor should the attractiveness of any particular valuational formula or principle. For no such principle banishes the inexorable necessity of choice. Making choices compels recourse to some criteria of choice, which itself involves choice. Morris Cohen, the eminent philosopher, once referred to 'the great scandal of traditional philosophy – the claim of absolutely certain results in fields where there is the greatest conflict of opinion' (Cohen 1923, p. xxiv). Much the same could be said of efforts, however otherwise laudable, which finesse problems of values as if valuation were not the case. Humankind seeks values but in doing so participates in valuation; it is the process that counts.

The human mind seeks solace and balm and readily proposes, projects and adopts formulas for bliss. Although they do provide insights into problems and issues, these principles and formulas do not produce unequivocally dispositive solutions to the problems to which they are addressed, although they are often believed to do so. Despite the fundamentally antinomian nature of their positions, these formulas reify and hypostatize what are arguably, for example, either subjective judgements or wishful thinking or more or less pragmatic exercises of social control. These latter phenomena are both derivations of and contributions to the problematic, instrumental, on-going process of valuation. Our laudable individual entitlement to our own positions on valuational issues is correlative to the inevitable socializing impact of culturally dominant moral rules. But both are aspects of and contributions to the total valuational process. Moreover, our own individually perceived principles or ultimates are not necessarily cosmic ultimates, if any should exist; and quite different principles and applications of principles are perceived by different individuals and peoples. The quest for valuational principles is the modus vivendi of the valuational process. It needs to be taken, and participated in, seriously. But no principle will either substitute for or obviate the necessity of human choice.

NOTE

1. The epigraphs are from St Thomas Aquinas, Summa Theologica, I.II.q.58.a.5; and Peabody 1964, p. 70 (Holmes to Lewis Einstein, 2 September 1912).

REFERENCES

Cohen, Morris R. (1923), 'Introduction' to Charles S. Peirce, *Chance, Love, and Logic: Philosophical Essays*, New York: Harcourt, Brace. Reprinted, New York: George Braziller, 1956.

Peabody, James Bishop (1964), *The Holmes–Einstein Letters*, New York: St Martin's Press.

Samuels, Warren J. (1995), 'The Instrumental Value Principle and its Role', in C.M.A. Clark (ed.), *Institutional Economics and the Theory of Social Value: Essays in Honor of Marc R. Tool*, Boston, MA: Kluwer, pp. 97–112.

_____(forthcoming), 'Instrumental Valuation', in Warren J. Samuels, Steven G. Medema and A. Allan Schmid (eds), *Essays on the Economy as a Process of Valuation*, Brookfield, VT: Edward Elgar.

Smith, Adam (1759), *Theory of Moral Sentiments*, New York: Oxford University Press, 1976.

Strachey, Lytton (1931), *Portraits in Miniature and Other Essays*, New York: Harcourt, Brace.

Tool, Marc R. (1995), *Pricing, Valuation and Systems: Essays in Neoinstitutional Economics*, Brookfield, VT: Edward Elgar.

7. Institutional Economics and Eternal Verities: A Contribution to the Discussion

Edythe S. Miller[1]

The role of values has been a matter of unremitting controversy within the economics discipline. It certainly has been a disputed issue within institutional economics almost from the time of its inception as a school. The debate continues to this day. In recent years, the pages of the institutionalist journal, the *Journal of Economic Issues*, have been abundantly enlivened by periodic exchanges on the topic. The discussion involves some of the most illustrious contemporary institutional economists, including Marc R. Tool, Wendell Gordon, Warren J. Samuels, Paul D. Bush, Anne Mayhew and numerous others. Matters at issue involve questions of whether economics is a positive or normative science, and whether institutional economics employs a criterion of relative or, alternatively, of absolute value. Thus, the controversy explicitly and unavoidably centres upon such core questions as whether the rejection of a value neutral and/or a relativist position necessarily involves the embrace of absolutism, including the acceptance of one or more 'eternal verities'. The conflict also entails, at least implicitly, fundamental questions of the nature of truth and knowledge, and the significance and purpose of theory itself.

For an institutional economist, the charge that a position entails an adherence to eternal verities constitutes fighting words. From the start, institutional economics has been an anti-essentialist, anti-foundational philosophy and methodology. Consistently, it has denied that knowledge and truth are matters of discovering underlying antecedent realities, and has contested the assertion that conclusions must precisely and meticulously track first principles. Indeed, institutional economics rejects the very applicability of first principles to the subject matter of economics. Without exception, institutionalism has rejected the animism and teleology inherent in a view of history comprising forces that incline affairs toward specific, benign ends; ends that at bottom do not vary, or vary only negligibly, from a contemporaneous common-sense of the community.

Institutionalism maintains, to the contrary, that we are where we are in history because of the choices that people have made. It sees humans as active participants in their societies, making real choices, and not choices that are determined exogenously. Persons are perceived as acting as members of collectivities, with their behaviour both shaped by and shaping communal norms and standards. Institutionalism thus rejects the view of humans as passive and atomistic automata following pre-specified paths. Unfailingly, institutional economists call for experimentation to formulate and test proposed solutions, rather than for the imposition of specific preconceived models for problem resolution, irrespective of the nature and reach of the problem at hand.

Imagine with me, then, the collective gasp of dismay that followed from Wendell Gordon's critical appraisal in various issues of the *Journal of Economic Issues* of Marc Tool's formulation of social value principle. Gordon asserted that the promulgation of the social value principle was akin to acceptance of an 'eternal verity' (Gordon 1984, p. 377), that is, that it 'sometimes' seemed to him that Tool's social value principle consists of 'a definitive or eternal verity or truth' (Gordon 1990, p. 881). Gordon's comments are directed to Tool's statement of an institutional social value principle; to wit, 'the continuity of human life and the noninvidious re-creation of community through the instrumental use of knowledge' (for example, Tool 1979, p. 293; 1986, pp. 55–6; 1993b, p. 121).

THE QUESTION OF VALUE

It is Gordon's contention that Tool's social value principle may entail, in effect, an inappropriate commitment to a specific criterion of value. Gordon maintains, in contrast, that institutional economics is value free and uncommitted to any particular value. The appropriate stance for economics as Gordon perceives it is not to formulate specific value criteria, but to explain the origin of the values held by individuals and to recognize that value judgments matter.

A value, according to Gordon, is a judgment by an individual of desirable ends, a judgment 'not coming out of a black box but being a result of the individual's biological heredity and social background (institutionalized behavior norms)' (Gordon 1990, p. 880). Thus, in Gordon's view a judgment of value is an individual matter. Individual values are relative and subjective, matters of taste and opinion, and not open to dispute or evaluation. Value, that is, is in the psyche of the beholder. It follows therefrom that economics is a positive, and not a normative, science, and is based in descriptive analysis, rather than prescription.

Most economists who advocate a position of ethical relativism do so in the name of scholarly neutrality, detachment and objectivity. Because we are all creatures of our culture, it is contended, we are not capable of objective judgment. Perceptions are filtered through a culturally obscured individual prism. The purpose of scholarship is descriptive analysis (assumed, somewhat ambiguously, to be free of such cultural biases), and not assessment of particular conditions, nor advancement or endorsement of specific positions or policies.

These economists maintain that policy advocacy evidences an inappropriate hubris on the part of the advocate (Samuels 1993, p. 237). Moreover, they contend that espousal of particular values inappropriately denigrates differing viewpoints, evidencing an intolerance and even, under certain circumstances, xenophobia on the part of the proponent (Mayhew 1987, p. 602; Neale 1990, p. 342). They assert additionally that '[p]articular value judgments remain always tentative and subject to reappraisal' (Gordon 1984, p. 378).

Tool, in contrast, contends that social value theory necessarily is an integral part of economic inquiry and that all inquiry is 'purposive in the normative sense'. In his view the very definition of a problem involves a distinction between 'what is' and 'what ought to be' (Tool 1993b, p. 119). It is his belief that all inquiry is purposive, and '[i]f inquiry is purposive, it is value laden' (Tool 1986, p. 33). Bush notes the normative dimension present in all stages of inquiry, including the very selection of problems as subjects of inquiry and the choice of facts included as explanatory and illustrative factors (Bush 1993, pp. 91–2). He points out that '[t]he methodological stricture that economic inquiry must be *wertfrei* is itself a normative stricture of considerable significance. The notion that it is improper for the investigator to make valuations in the course of inquiry is itself a valuation' (Bush 1991, p. 335).

I take the position in this essay, while agreeing with Gordon that 'particular value judgments remain always tentative and subject to reappraisal', that acceptance of a relativist position is in effect a denial of the tangibility of external reality, an affirmation of a belief that facts exist only in the mind, and therefore a reduction of the material world to ideas. I maintain, in contrast, that institutional economics is, rather, grounded in realism. I further allege that the rejection of relativism does not imply, much less dictate, an acceptance of an absolutist position; that is, that absolutism is not the only, nor the preferred, alternative to relativism. I contend, in addition, precisely because of its basis in realism, that economics is value infused and that a normative perspective is, in fact, the only perspective consistent with institutionalism.

A realist perspective interprets ideas as both subjective and objective in that ideas have reference to objects and states of being that are independent of opinion about them. That is, opinion about reality takes as referent an objective world that has an independent existence. Analysis of real world facts implies valuing. Facts and values are unavoidably and inescapably intertwined. A view of individuals as purposive performers in the economic realm implies that they are deliberative, valuing participants. Value judgments cannot be eluded. That is, whether admitted or denied, explicitly or implicitly, out in the open or lurking somewhere in the background, values are an essential part of all economic analysis.

SOME ATTEMPTS AT RECONCILIATION

For most contributors to the discussion, there seems little in the way of a middle ground. There have been a few attempts, in my view largely unsuccessful, to limit, smooth over or reconcile the differences. For example, William Waller and Linda Robertson attempt to harmonize the contrasting views on this issue by means of a 'discourse' and 'stages of development' analysis.

To the extent that I understand the Waller and Robertson position, they contend that discussion of differences and similarities and agreed upon social mechanisms are required within communities for resolution of disputes. While knowledge is culturally constructed and the processes of inquiry and valuation culture specific (Waller and Robertson 1991, pp. 1033–4), communities share values, and intra- and inter-communal values and beliefs are distinguishable. More values are shared within than between communities. The more homogeneous the community, the more shared values there will be. Discussion will reveal the nature of differences and the means of their resolution.

Waller and Robertson allege that the Gordon–Mayhew approach is relevant to an early stage of development characterized by the discovery of differences and similarities; that of Tool to a later stage of development, when more values are shared and decisions to address problems may be mutually achieved (Waller and Robertson 1991, pp. 1035–6). A reconciliation of these seemingly disparate approaches thus is permitted, in the view of Waller and Robertson, by application of discourse analysis within a stages of development framework (ibid., p. 1047).

Charles Wilber also offers an alternative perspective that, at the same time, adds another dimension to the discussion. In his review (Wilber 1994) of a recent volume of essays edited by and including a contribution by Tool (Tool 1993a), he concludes that the collection confirms a view that institutional economics may be many things, but that it is not a body of theory. That is, he sees the existence of an institutional 'standpoint, orientation and method', and the potential for institutionalism to make a 'real contribution to policymaking'. He does not, however, see in the institutional framework the formulation of 'an operational institutionalist economic theory'; that is, 'a body of theory to carry out problem solving for policy purposes' (Wilber 1994, pp. 1289–91).

Significant questions about the structure, nature and purpose of theory inhere in these alternative treatments. For example, is there – and, indeed, does the possibility exist for there to be – a body of knowledge (that is, a theory) that contains an approach to the value question that is trans-cultural and trans-temporal, valid across cultures and through time? This is clearly the role that

Tool envisions for the social value principle, the possibility of which is challenged in the article by Waller and Robertson.

Additionally, the question follows from the position taken in the Wilber review of how, exactly, an 'operational theory' is defined, and how, if at all, it differs from simple, unadorned 'theory' and/or from 'standpoint, orientation and method'. If institutional thought does not constitute a theory, but only an 'approach' or 'standpoint', of what *is* theory constituted? Specifically, does it consist solely of mathematical models? Moreover, is predictability an essential component of theory? And if so, is the formulation of theory dependent on the existence in the economic world of sufficient order and symmetry to provide a basis for predictability? That is, has institutionalism accepted the position of the mainstream on these points, points that are often posited as central to the definition of theory?

We know how an important, if not indeed the dominant, branch of orthodoxy defines theory. Theory is identified as a set of logical propositions derived from first principles gleaned from a small number of axioms and relying upon hypothetico-deductive, that is, a priori models. Much of orthodoxy thus is indisputably absolutist. Moreover, in this component of orthodox theory validity is divorced from reality of assumptions and empty of empirical content. Because theory is perceived as comprising event uniformities, it is associated with predictive ability. Micro-economic, or price theory, is viewed as an optimization problem, preferably expressed in formal, mathematical terms, yielding precise solutions and unequivocal outcomes. And thus, as John Dewey observed, is the quest for certainty substituted for the pursuit of understanding.

In recent years, it has been the fashion within orthodox economics to advance models that relax one or a few of the neoclassical assumptions (for example, perfect certainty or complete rationality), but retain the core postulates (for example, individualism, optimization, equilibrium, the existence of 'natural' regularities), and maintain adherence to the laissez-faire policy prescriptions that follow from the central premises.

If, as Wilber here contends, institutional analysis does not constitute an operational theory, exactly how is theory to be defined? Wilber, while disputing the contention that institutional economics contains an operational theory, does not specify what are the requirements for an operational theory (admittedly, difficult to do in a short review article). Wilber does not, to be sure, specifically identify theory with mathematical modelling. However, nor does he offer, in this statement at any rate,[2] an alternative definition of theory, leaving us in something of a quandary.

There is little doubt that in recent years mainstream economics has achieved perceptible success nationally, and to an extent internationally, in setting the agenda and establishing the terms of the debate for the profession and the polity. Has the influence of orthodoxy so insinuated itself that the neoclassical definition of the questions, and its specification of the form and composition that the answers must take, have reached even to institutionalism? I do not suggest that Wilber accepts the mainstream definition of theory. But if there has not been an identification of 'theory' with formal modelling, capable of yielding precise answers, or of predictability, capable of yielding certain ones, the manner in which institutional thought diverges from theory requires specification. The contention that institutional economics is anti-theoretical is a widely held one within the profession, and is based upon the rejection by institutionalism of the assumptions, models and techniques of orthodoxy. As institutional economists it is difficult for us to deny the influence of such cultural norms. Have even institutionalists been persuaded by this reasoning?

Despite the consistent identification of neoclassical economics with principles of limited government and governmental nonintervention, and its unflagging advocacy of these principles, economic orthodoxy proceeds under a banner of positivism; that is, a flag coloured neutral and objective, a self-description applicable to positive economics in general. Neoclassical economists, it would seem, rival most parents as strong advocates of a 'Do as I say, and not as I do' position. In my view, the attribution to institutional economics of a positivist, relativist stance misstates and misconstrues institutional theory and methodology. Appraisal of this contention requires consideration of the role of theory in economics in general and more specifically in institutional thought.

Fagg Foster consistently defined theory as explanation in causal terms. If this definition of theory is accepted, consideration of the facts of specific cases, that is, inquiry into cause and effect real world relationships, clearly is required to formulate theory and thereby to advance understanding.

THE REALIST BASIS OF INSTITUTIONAL ECONOMICS

I have elsewhere suggested that realism is the only ontological position consistent with institutional economics (for example, Miller 1991, p. 1000, 1992, p. 118, 1995, p. 122; Klein and Miller 1996, p. 268). A comprehension of causal relationships requires acknowledgment and recognition of real world facts, not as a string of isolated incidents but as connected and contextual.

Tony Lawson (following R. Bhaskar),[3] in an important series of articles, makes an additional valuable distinction not explicitly specified in my previous discussions. Lawson distinguishes between the concept of empirical realism, identified as the consciousness of reality as actual events and states of being and our perception of them, and a concept he designates 'transcendental realism'. Transcendental realism, unlike empirical realism, includes as a component of reality not only actual phenomena and our perception of them, but also the underlying structures, mechanisms and tendencies that give rise to the phenomena, whether or not amenable to direct observation and correlation

(Lawson 1994a, pp. 512–14). That is, the category of reality, in the transcendental realist view, is not exhausted by empirical facts and our cognition or perception of reality.

Transcendental realism thus identifies three ontologically distinguishable realms of reality: the empirical, that is, the experience and impression of reality; the actual, or the tangible objects of reality that are experienced; and the structures and mechanisms that produce particular states and conditions (Lawson 1994b, pp. 262–3).[4] As one example of these structures or mechanisms, Lawson cites the phenomenon of the economic performance of Great Britain in recent years and, as a mechanism that helps to produce it, England's traditional system of industrial labour relations (Lawson 1994a, p. 513). Closer to home, we might select the overall incidence of poverty at a given time as manifest condition, and discrimination and other barriers to participation as underlying structure. Lawson emphasizes that the events and the mechanisms that govern and produce them are not necessarily synchronized, because events are influenced also by a host of additional, and possibly countervailing, mechanisms and tendencies.

Unlike orthodox economics, then, in which knowledge is comprehended as a matter of searching for regularities of an 'if X, then Y' pattern, and theory is perceived as deduction based upon such event regularities,[5] Lawson discerns science as moving by means of a process of abduction, retroduction or hypothesis from manifest condition to a comprehension of the deeper structures that produce it (Lawson 1994c, p. 70). That is, Lawson does not apprehend knowledge as capable of achievement solely through sensory observation. Intercession and direct involvement are required to recognize and understand underlying tendencies and structures that often are not immediately apparent. The acquisition of knowledge requires action and experimentation; learning is a function of and an inseverable aspect of doing. That is, understanding requires intervention in and manipulation of the facts of experience on the basis of hypotheses about outcomes, an intervention that results in a transformation of reality.

Knowledge thus is comprehended as contextual. This comprehension should be contrasted with an apprehension of knowledge as comprising the perception of singular objects and events, of reality as atomistic occurrences and accompanying regularities, and of theory as inductive or deductive inference from that conceptualization of actuality (Lawson 1994b, p. 261). Events and conditions, to be understood, cannot be viewed in isolation from other events and conditions and from the forces of which they are the outcome. Moreover, they cannot simply be observed. To be fully understood, they must also be acted upon, because underlying structures and forces are not always immediately observable. The appropriate mode of inquiry is one of the search for causal explanation, that is, of 'abduction' or 'retroduction' (Lawson 1994b, p. 264), and of manipulation and intervention to achieve understanding and the consequent ability to transform underlying structure.

In the social realm, according to Lawson, social structure is developed, survives and is changed through human agency. Humans do not create social systems; at any time, they confront an existing social structure. Individuals, although not creators of social structure, do transform or reproduce it. Individuals and social structure are interdependent and interactive. Individuals emerge initially within and function continually within and upon existing social structure (Lawson 1994a, pp. 519–20). 'Structure and human agency . . . each presuppose, although neither can be reduced to, identified with, or explained completely in terms of the other' (Lawson 1994a, p. 520). The primary task of economics is to understand and modulate the underlying forces that govern the conditions of economic life.

Significant empirical regularities do not exist as a fact of economic life – the world is open, choice is real. The aim of economics is identification of the structures that condition events (Lawson 1994d, p. 224) – that is, explanation. Ultimately, the purpose of analysis is the accretion of knowledge and understanding that permits structures to be changed so as to enhance human possibilities (Lawson 1995, p. 29).

THE PRAGMATIC REALISM OF C.S. PEIRCE

Most institutionalists would agree that the pragmatic philosophy of Charles S. Peirce[6] is an important foundation of institutional economics. Peirce's pragmatic thought, as I have noted elsewhere (Miller 1992, p. 116, 1995, p. 120) is rooted in realism. The similarity between the pragmatic realism developed by Peirce and that portrayed by Lawson is unmistakable.

Peirce defines as the real 'that whose characters are independent of what anybody may think them to be' (Peirce 1878, p. 130). He elaborates that reality consists of 'the peculiar, sensible effects' that 'things partaking of it produce. The only effect which real things have is to cause belief. . . . The question, therefore, is how is true belief (or belief in the real) distinguished from false belief (or belief in fiction)' (Peirce 1878, p. 130).

Peirce's concept of cognition is illuminated in his theory of signs. Peirce distinguishes the objective (the 'something represented') and the subjective elements of cognition. Cognition is an intuition of an immediate object (Peirce 1868a, p. 30). Peirce maintains that all thought constitutes a representation that serves as a sign. Signs have three references: a sign to some thought, which interprets it; a sign for some object, with which it is held to be equivalent; and a sign in regard to some quality which connects it with its object.

A sign, in his view, is not identical with the object with which it is associated. Moreover, no thought-sign is singular. It is part of a continuum, a train; it must be viewed within its context. All present understandings are influenced by those of the past (Peirce 1868b, pp. 51–3). There is no first cognition of any object; cognition is a matter of continuous process (Peirce 1868b, p. 41). 'From the proposition that every thought is a sign, it follows that every thought must address itself to some other, must determine some other. . .' (Peirce 1868a, p. 30). Peirce sees no beginning or end to thought and ideas. He perceives no fact as isolated – all facts are unsevered, unitary aspects of experience (Peirce 1905b, p. 219). To be correctly understood, they must be viewed within their context. All knowledge is contextual and part of a continuum.

Thus, in Peirce's view every cognition contains objective, subjective and causal elements. Every thought addresses itself to others, and determines others. In other words, Peirce perceives cognition as a process, that occurs continuously and interactively. Every cognition is logically determined by previous cognitions, and these by still earlier cognitions. Knowledge is derived through hypothetical reasoning from cognition of external facts. To be set against any cognition is an unknown but potentially knowable reality. The truth of hypothetical propositions cannot be known with certainty, but may be known with probability (Peirce 1868a, pp. 30–38, 1868b, pp. 39–42).[7]

According to Peirce, the doctrine of realism on which pragmatism is based includes the acknowledgment of real possibilities, that is, it involves the denial of the logic of necessity (Peirce 1905b, p. 215). In other words, individuals are choosing entities, choice is real, determinism is denied. Common to all humans, in this view, is the quality of self-control, of deliberative purposive action.

Peirce points out that all valid reasoning is either deductive, inductive, hypothetical or some combination of these. A system of a priori or deductive reasoning, he observes, does not rest upon observed facts, but is adopted because its propositions seem 'agreeable to reason', that is, they conform to that which we are 'inclined to believe' (Peirce 1877, p. 106). He points out, in criticism, that others might be otherwise 'inclined', and notes that, in effect, the a priori method does not differ substantially as a means of inquiry from the method of authority, that is, the basing of belief upon a doctrine of command (ibid., p. 107). In his view, a valid method of establishing belief must rather be based upon 'nothing human, but . . . some external permanency . . . something upon which our thinking has no effect' (ibid., p. 107). He finds this in the method of reality (ibid., 108).

Peirce describes the method of induction, that is, of empirical observation, as the belief that what is true of a random sampling of the members of a class must be true of an entire category (1868b, pp. 45–6). It follows that the method of induction yields probabilities rather than necessities. Moreover, the method of induction ignores the possibility of chance, spontaneity and novelty in development (Peirce 1892, pp. 160–70, 176–9). That is, reliance upon random sampling encompasses, if only by implication, a presumption of event regularity.

At any time, Peirce observes, we hold particular information or cognition that logically has been derived by induction and hypotheses from prior cognitions, that is, by an infinite series of inductions and hypotheses, as a continuous process with no beginning in time. These cognitions are either true or false – that is, they are cognitions whose objects are real or unreal. It is possible to know external things as they are, and there is little question that we do know them in a great many cases, although we never can be certain in any one case that our knowledge is accurate (Peirce 1868b, pp. 68–9). Knowledge is derived from hypothetical reasoning from external facts (ibid., p. 41), but all knowledge is tentative and corrigible.

When it comes to the contributions of the various types of reasoning to scientific understanding, Peirce observes that neither deduction nor induction contributes to new understanding. 'They render the indefinite definite; Deduction explicates; Induction evaluates; that is all.' When it comes to deduction or induction, then, 'neither . . . contributes a single new concept'. For an understanding of how scientific advance occurs we must look rather to retroduction (or abduction), that is, to the 'spontaneous conjectures of instinctive reason' (Peirce 1908, pp. 370–71).

Peirce equates the terms abduction and retroduction. He describes this process as the first stage of inquiry, a conjecture or hypothesis stemming from a search for an explanation of a phenomenon that is not understood. That is, he uses the terms abduction and retroduction to designate the series of mental operations undertaken between the time when the phenomenon initially is noticed and the hypothesis is accepted, a process of reasoning from consequent to antecedent; that is, from effect to cause. The hypothesis must then be tested.

Testing involves deduction (the second stage of inquiry) and induction (the third stage of inquiry). Deduction involves the assembling of the variety of experiential consequences that would follow from truth of the hypothesis; induction looks to the correspondence of the consequents of the hypothesis with the facts of experience (Peirce 1908, pp. 367–9).

Peirce's realistic philosophy, in sum, takes knowledge as contextual. It views thought and experience as part of a continuum; that is, as evolutionary and processual. At any given time, conditions are the result of past human choice; humans are choosing beings. His concept of realism acknowledges the existence of real possibility and denies the doctrine of necessity. Learning and knowledge occur through a process of hypothetical analysis (abduction or retroduction) from the facts of experience, and require a basis in causal reasoning (reasoning from consequent to antecedent, or from effect to cause). Reality is not necessarily known, but is potentially knowable; that is, we can never be certain of the accuracy of any given cognition. All knowledge, in other words, is provisional and corrigible or, to use Wendell Gordon's expression, 'tentative and subject to reappraisal'.

SUMMARY AND CONCLUSIONS

The pragmatic realism of Charles Peirce and the transcendental or critical realism of Tony Lawson are compatible, if not, indeed, in full accord. It is a perspective that is central to institutional economics.

Significantly, if realism is accepted as the ontological foundation of institutionalism, relativism must be rejected as its epistemological basis. The rejection of relativism, however, does not imply acceptance of absolute Truth. To pose the issue in such 'either–or' terms involves us in a miasma of a 'missing middle'. Pragmatic realism substitutes abduction for either relativistic or absolute knowledge. The contention that knowledge is fact based and processual, that it involves reasoning from consequent to antecedent, implies the rejection both of the idealism of deductivism and the supremacy of the atomistic event which inductivism posits as the basis of understanding.

In substituting abduction for deduction or induction as the basis of knowledge, pragmatic realism stresses the importance of hypothesis in seeking truth and knowledge. Lawson emphasizes the need to look beyond current circumstance to underlying structure and mechanism. Peirce stresses the importance of metaphor and analogy, and of 'as if' reasoning, of reasoning from consequent to antecedent, for comprehending reality. In both interpretations, knowledge is distinguished as tentative, fallible and corrigible. Knowledge is taken, to use Dewey's apt phrase, as the 'warrantably assertable' rather than as eternal verity.

On this basis, then, institutionalism denies the possibility of certainty, but not of knowledge or truth. Assuredly, it denies the 'timelessness' of truth. Facts, circumstances and underlying structures and mechanisms change with time. Facts cannot be understood in isolation; to be understood, they must be viewed within their social and temporal settings. That is, facts take on different meanings under different circumstances; the meaning of facts is contextual. Knowledge is not apolitical, ahistorical, asocial. The human condition is processual, evolutionary and organic, a matter of cumulative causation, and not of equilibration, of oscillation between poles, of stasis.

Heraclitus noted that the same person cannot step twice into the same river. This is so because both the person and the river are changed by the act itself; that is, the person and the river each will have been transformed as a consequence of that act and of subsequent experiences. The interaction of individuals and their physical and social surroundings transforms each. This, in addition to other essential elements of the human condition such as novelty, spontaneity, ordinary chance, to say nothing of sheer animal spirits, all help to explain why existence is not characterized by event norms and regularities of an 'if x, then y' variety.

If both the individual and the environment are changed by engagement, then response modes, habits and mores, and customary behaviour patterns unavoidably will be altered as well, resulting in a lack of predictability. The future – life itself – is uncertain and unforeseeable rather than certain and predictable. If, in the economic and social realm, event regularity is rarely, if ever, encountered, prediction will seldom be even approximately accurate. To define theory as prediction, then, makes the development of theory an unattainable objective. It is important to understand theory, instead, for what it is – causal explanation and explication, a quest for understanding.

Similarly, institutionalism is inescapably normative. It views valuing as implicit to all descriptive analysis; humans are perceived as valuing beings. Institutional economics recognizes judgment as an inherent aspect of all inquiry. Explicit to the transcendental or critical realism of Lawson, and at least implicit to the pragmatic realism of Peirce, is the belief that the identification of underlying mechanisms and causes of social conditions, and their transformation in a human purpose, cannot be separated from the pursuit of knowledge. It follows that experimentation – trial and error – is an essential factor in both philosophic pragmatism and institutional economics. That learning occurs as a corollary of doing is central to these systems of thought. The identification of learning and doing is fundamental to Fagg Foster's definition of theory as explanation in causal terms. Foster often observed that if theory does not work in practice – well then – it is, quite simply, bad theory. Theory informs practice, and practice authenticates and augments theory. Indeed, it always has seemed to me that the belief that the purpose of theory is causal explanation in the interest of beneficial practice is at least implicit to the pattern modelling and storytelling persuasively depicted by Wilber as methods of institutional analysis (Wilber with Harrison 1978). Learning and doing converge and are inherently joined.

The widespread identification of theory with mathematical modelling and prediction in contemporary economics is an attempt to 'scientize' the discipline in the mistaken belief that science is associated with the precision, certainty and 'elegance' of abstract models. Science cannot be equated with techniques or models. It must rather be understood as a mode of inquiry and a means of understanding, explanation and interpretation. Its purpose is to solve human problems.

Tool's social value principle: that is, 'the continuity of human life and the noninvidious re-creation of community through the instrumental use of knowledge' is an attempt to delineate this process and to formulate a standard consistent with it. The reference to 'the instrumental use of knowledge' is a statement of the processual aspect of institutionalism. Indeed, if institutional thought contains any eternal verity, it is specified in this processual component;

that is, in this means of inquiry and discovery, this manner of learning and doing. The 'instrumental use of knowledge' signifies that analysis entails a specific mode of inquiry: that is, that it employs methods of experimentation, trial and error, openness to mistake and failure, respect for diverse viewpoints, deference for the opinions of others, respect for dissent, and rejection both of authority and the fashion of the moment; in short, that it accepts the patterns of democracy.

The component of the social value principle referencing 'the continuity of human life and the noninvidious re-creation of community' is the substantive aspect of the principle, a specification of a design for a maxim centred upon problem solving for the enhancement of human life. It is indicative of a direction for policy and a standard by which to assess it. It should be noted that the phrase does not specify or certify particular policies. Specific policies are hypothetical and probabilistic – to be tested by experience and experimentation.

The claim that economics is a positive science, lacking in responsibility for valuing, makes of it a sterile exercise. It also constitutes a denial of much of the history of the discipline. The pursuit of knowledge cannot but be purposive. Purposive inquiry is, by definition, inquiry that is value infused. For institutional economics, purposive inquiry necessarily entails the goal of enhancing and improving the human condition.

NOTES

1. An earlier version of this essay was presented at the annual meeting of the Association for Institutional Thought, April 1994, Oakland, California. The author wishes to thank Linda Shaffer, California State University, Fresno, for helpful suggestions.
2. It should be noted, however, that an earlier article of which Wilber was lead author deals with some of these questions extensively and insightfully (see Wilber with Harrison 1978).
3. References to the work of Bhaskar may be found in the articles by Lawson cited herein.
4. Although the distinction is both relevant and important, I am not much taken with the descriptive term employed, despite my general sympathy with 'critiques of pure reason'. The term 'transcendental' evokes for me the Kantian body of philosophic thought which, along with its critique of pure reason, also includes the concept of a 'categorical imperative' and implications of a distinction between science and ethics. It is evocative also of the romantic idealism of Ralph Waldo Emerson, complete with associated notions of an 'over-soul'. A contrast between empirical and either simple, unadorned realism or, for reasons that will become clear, 'pragmatic realism' appears to me to be more apt.
5. Lawson points out that, with the exception of astronomy, most event regularities of the 'if x, then y' variety that are interpreted as scientific laws obtain only under conditions of controlled experimentation – that is, they do not occur spontaneously, but only under certain restricted conditions. Thus, they cannot properly be specified as 'if x, then y' laws, but should more appropriately be identified as 'if x, then y, under conditions z' laws, where conditions z involve the imposition of controlled experimental situations, that is, require human intervention. They cannot therefore be described as 'natural laws' in the accepted sense of the term; they are characterized not by universality, but rather 'are effectively fenced off from most of the goings on in the world' (Lawson 1994b, p. 267).
6. Peirce is generally acknowledged as the founder of the philosophic school of pragmatism. As

with other originators of systems of thought, however, he was not always happy with its treatment in the hands of his followers, so much so that he was moved to change its name. He sought to substitute for the designation pragmatism, the term pragmaticism. In Peirce's words: '... the writer, finding his bantling "pragmatism" so promoted, feels that it is time to kiss his child good-by and relinquish it to its higher destiny; while to serve the precise purpose of expressing the original definition, he begs to announce the birth of the word "pragmaticism", which is ugly enough to be safe from kidnappers' (Peirce 1905a, p. 186). Founders of other systems of thought have been known to suffer similar pangs. (Compare, for example, Karl Marx's widely quoted: 'I am not a Marxist'.) Unfortunately (or fortunately, depending upon historical, aesthetic and linguistic sensibilities), Peirce's later characterization has not survived.

7. On this point, compare Dewey's 'warrantable assertability'.

REFERENCES

Bush, Paul D. (1991), 'Reflections on the Twenty-fifth Anniversary of AFEE: Philosophical and Methodological Issues in Institutional Economics', *Journal of Economic Issues*, **2** (25), June, pp. 321–46.

_____(1993), 'The Methodology of Institutional Economics: A Pragmatic Institutionalist Perspective' in Marc R. Tool (ed.), *Institutional Economics: Theory, Method, Policy*, Boston, Dordrecht, London: Kluwer Academic Publishers, pp. 59–107.

Gordon, Wendell (1984), 'The Role of Institutional Economics', *Journal of Economic Issues*, **2** (18), June, pp. 369–81.

_____(1990), 'The Role of Tool's Social Value Principle', *Journal of Economic Issues*, **3** (24), September, pp. 879–86.

Klein, Philip A. and Edythe S. Miller (1996), 'Concepts of Value, Efficiency, and Democracy', *Journal of Economic Issues*, **1** (30), March, pp. 267–77.

Lawson, Tony (1994a), 'The Nature of Post Keynesianism and its Links to Other Traditions: A Realist Perspective', *Journal of Post Keynesian Economics*, **4** (16), Summer, pp. 503–38.

_____(1994b), 'A Realist Theory for Economics' in Roger E. Backhouse (ed.), *New Directions in Economic Methodology*, London, New York: Routledge, pp. 257–85.

_____(1994c), 'Methodology' in Geoffrey M. Hodgson, Warren J. Samuels and Marc R. Tool (eds), *The Elgar Companion to Institutional and Evolutionary Economics*, Aldershot, England and Brookfield, Vermont: Edward Elgar Publishing, Ltd., pp. 67–72.

_____(1994d), 'Philosophical Realism' in Geoffrey M. Hodgson, Warren J. Samuels and Marc R. Tool (eds), *The Elgar Companion to Institutional and Evolutionary Economics*, Aldershot, England and Brookfield, Vermont: Edward Elgar Publishing, Ltd., pp. 219–25.

_____(1995), 'Realist Perspective on "Economic Theory"', *Journal of Economic Issues*, **1** (29), March, pp. 1–32.

Mayhew, Anne (1987), 'Culture: Core Concept Under Attack', *Journal of Economic Issues*, **2** (21), June, pp. 587–603.

Miller, Edythe S. (1991), 'Of Economic Paradigms, Puzzles, Problems, and Policies; Or, is the Economy too Important to be Entrusted to the Economists?', *Journal of Economic Issues*, **4** (25), December, pp. 993–1004.

144   *Institutionalist Method and Value*

_____(1992), 'The Economics of Progress', *Journal of Economic Issues*, **1** (26), March, pp. 115–24.
_____(1995), 'The Instrumental Efficiency of Social Value Theory' in Charles M.A. Clark (ed.), *Institutional Economics and the Theory of Social Value: Essays in Honor of Marc R. Tool*, Boston, Dordrecht, London: Kluwer Academic Publishers, pp. 113–28.
Neale, Walter C. (1990), 'Absolute Cultural Relativism: Firm Foundation for Valuing and Policy', *Journal of Economic Issues*, **2** (24), June, pp. 333–44.
Peirce, Charles S. (1868a), 'Questions Concerning Certain Faculties Claimed for Man' in Philip P. Wiener (ed.), *Values in a Universe of Chance*, 1958, Garden City, New York: Doubleday Anchor Books.
_____(1868b), 'Some Consequences of Four Incapacities' in Philip P. Wiener (ed.), *Values in a Universe of Chance*, 1958, Garden City, New York: Doubleday Anchor Books.
_____(1877), 'The Fixation of Belief' in Philip P. Wiener (ed.), *Values in a Universe of Chance*, 1958, Garden City, New York: Doubleday Anchor Books.
_____(1878), 'How to Make Our Ideas Clear' in Philip P. Wiener (ed.), *Values in a Universe of Chance*, 1958, Garden City, New York: Doubleday Anchor Books.
_____(1892), 'The Doctrine of Necessity' in Philip P. Wiener (ed.), *Values in a Universe of Chance*, 1958, Garden City, New York: Doubleday Anchor Books.
_____(1905a), 'What Pragmatism Is' in Philip P. Wiener (ed.), *Values in a Universe of Chance*, 1958, Garden City, New York: Doubleday Anchor Books.
_____(1905b), 'Issues of Pragmaticism' in Philip P. Wiener (ed.), *Values in a Universe of Chance*, 1958, Garden City, New York: Doubleday Anchor Books.
_____(1908), 'A Neglected Argument for the Reality of God' in Philip P. Wiener (ed.), *Values in a Universe of Chance*, 1958, Garden City, New York: Doubleday Anchor Books.
Samuels, Warren J. (1993), 'In (Limited but Affirmative) Defence of Nihilism', *Review of Political Economy*, **5**, April, pp. 236–44.
Tool, Marc R. (1979), *The Discretionary Economy: A Normative Theory of Political Economy*, Santa Monica, CA: Goodyear Publishing Company, Inc.
_____(1986), *Essays in Social Value Theory: A Neoinstitutionalist Contribution*, Armonk, NY: M.E. Sharpe.
_____(ed.) (1993a), *Institutional Economics: Theory, Method, Policy*, Boston, Dordrecht, London: Kluwer Academic Publishers.
_____(1993b), 'The Theory of Instrumental Value: Extensions, Clarifications' in Marc R. Tool (ed.), *Institutional Economics: Theory, Method, Policy*, Boston, Dordrecht, London: Kluwer Academic Publishers.
Waller, William T. and Linda R. Robertson (1991), 'Valuation as Discourse and Process: Or, How We Got out of a Methodological Quagmire on Our Way to Purposeful Institutional Analysis', *Journal of Economic Issues*, **4** (25), December, pp. 1029–48.
Wilber, Charles K. (1994), 'Review', *Journal of Economic Issues*, **4** (28), December, pp. 1289–91.
_____with Robert S. Harrison (1978), 'The Methodological Basis of Institutional Economics: Pattern Model, Storytelling and Holism', *Journal of Economic Issues*, **1** (12), March, pp. 61–89.

8.   Institutions and Social Valuation

Ann L. Jennings and William Waller

Over its history, value theory in economics has been dominated by presumptions of a single valuational process in society. Or, if that is too harsh, additional valuational criteria operating outside 'the economy' or 'the market' are left unmentioned, unexplored and untheorized. It takes little reflection to realize, however, that valuational processes – the identification or attribution of qualities and the assessment, measurement or ranking of the presence or absence of those qualities – are unlikely to be singular or uniform activities in any culture. Moreover, once society is understood from a cultural perspective, as a multidimensional, interconnected complex of social relations integrated through a shared system of symbolic meanings and language, it is also unlikely that a society's valuational processes will be as neatly separable as conventional economics seems to hold.

Traditional ways of discussing value in economics are inherently reductionistic, often totalizing and inconsistent with a cultural approach to economic theorizing. Our claim here is not that economists wish to construct reductionistic, universalistic, totalizing, monolithic (and thus chauvinistic) value theories but, instead, lapse into such frameworks because of their training and their almost exclusive concern with compartmentalized 'economic' processes. For many orthodox economists, a concept of society itself is also virtually absent so that value is not seen as a social process, much less processes. By contrast, reasonable value, as constructed in the Commons tradition of institutionalism, locates value in particular social, political contexts and discourses and avoids reductionism. This implies the possibility of multiple social value systems and the need to negotiate conflicts. Our earlier work on evolutionary cultural hermeneutics similarly left room to argue that cultures have several valuational processes operating simultaneously and interactively.

This essay examines social institutions as valuational systems in order to illuminate the cultural conditions for multiple valuational systems, rankings over systems, conflicts among them and modes of reconciliation. In our earlier work on evolutionary cultural hermeneutics (Jennings and Waller 1994), on which the present argument rests, we maintained that meanings result from the complex interrelationships of terms and concepts that are inherently ambiguous and flexible because of their interdependence. Terms or words are not the raw

145

materials of meanings (as would be held in nominalist, essentialist or 'objectivist' views) but are themselves hermeneutically defined by connective orderings. Value criteria are similarly products of systems of cultural orderings.

Such an argument necessarily implies self-reflexive circularity; but a hermeneutic circle, particularly one conceived at the level of culture, is very large and, thus, rich. Moreover, such a cultural hermeneutic circle will not exhibit linearly logical coherence or non-contradiction in contrast to, say, well-behaved systems of simultaneous equations in mathematics. Cultures are not conscious constructions in the manner of mathematical systems; flexible ambiguity, individual volition and location and social compartmentalizations imply nondeterministically ordered variations in beliefs and behaviours that, along with conflicts, unintended consequences, imagination and problem-solving are the 'stuff' of cultural evolution. The concept of 'institutions', meanwhile, implies that beliefs and behaviours can be categorized and partially disconnected from one another; institutions exhibit patterns of internal coherence and external distinctiveness.

Values reflect the mode of ordering and coherence within a particular institutional context. But multiple modes of valuation imply both the likelihood of value conflict and the need for 'disjunctive orderings' (or other means, such as courts) that address such conflicts across valuational frameworks in any reasonably coherent cultural order. In this essay we will suggest that cultural dualisms are one such mode of disjunctive ordering, again relying on our previous work (Jennings and Waller 1990; Jennings 1992, 1993; Jennings and Champlin 1993; Waller and Jennings 1990). Following Commons (1924), legal systems are seen here as alternative, formal organizations for conflict resolution.

We will also draw heavily on two other main sources: George Lakoff's (1987) studies of cognitive theory in linguistic psychology will provide the entry point and some conceptual tools for our discussions of institutions as categories (contexts or frameworks) and also help to make the conceptual foundations of our hermeneutical framework more explicit. Philip Mirowski's (1990, 1991a, 1991b) accounts of social value theory will permit us to employ symmetry concepts in our discussions of value, apply our arguments to economic processes, and consider myths and social fictions as additional ways of reconciling valuational incoherences.

INSTITUTIONS AS COGNITIVE CATEGORIES

Institutions can be understood as prescribed patterns of correlated human behaviour. As such, the concept remains quite vague, however. Nelson (1995) has recently noted that the term is used in so many ways, and can denote so many things, that its usefulness as an analytical tool can be questioned. Yet he finds it equally unimaginable that so important a concept could be discarded: institutions are vital to any explanation of variations, from society to society, over time, or from different vantage points within society, in the ways that social processes are carried out. Nelson is not wrong to ask such questions. Institutions *are* part of nearly everything: *culture is an instituted process*. But this has not stopped anthropological studies of cultures nor has it compromised studies of meaning in cognitive linguistics, where meaning has many settings and levels of abstraction and, ultimately, encompasses everything meaningful.[1] What is needed is an appropriate point of entry into the hermeneutic circles.

Lakoff's (1987) summary discussions of developments in cognitive linguistics offer useful tools for disentangling some of the confusion in institutional analysis that Nelson notes. Lakoff's arguments can be sketched only very briefly and selectively here; we borrow three main points. He argues, first of all, that human thought exists by virtue of categories of thought. He holds that the capacity to construct such categories, and systems of categories, is probably inherent – that is, biologically innate – in human beings but that the content, nature and actual patterns of systemic thought are socially and historically determined and self-contextual (our self-reflexive hermeneutics).[2] Second, categories tend to exhibit (though they are not grounded in or caused by) some common imagery, features or relationships; the commonalities are themselves relative to the interpretations represented through the categories, however. Third, Lakoff suggests that the entry point for studying cognitive categories should be at an 'intermediate' or 'basic' level of abstraction because categories seem most 'naturally' (perhaps for biological reasons) apprehended by human beings at that level. Thus the category 'dog' is easier to acquire and use than the category 'terrier' or 'mammal'. The intermediate, basic level is perhaps best grasped as the level at which the category is usually *visualized*.[3]

As applied to 'institutions' – a very abstract category, as indeed most terms in social analysis are, since physical referents are elusive – we could identify 'the market', 'the family', 'the state', 'the church' and so on as basic categories. They are far more readily understood than more abstract categories such as 'institutions' (a metacategory that includes the basic institutional categories) or more specific subcategories such as 'nuclear family' or 'separation of powers' and were present (in the West, anyway) before the more abstract and the more specific categories were. Basic institutional categories seem 'natural' to us – because we first learn to 'see' categories at that level – though alternative basic categories probably seem more natural in other social orders or historical periods.[4]

If institutions are defined as correlated patterns of human behaviour, there must be some basis for the correlation. The classical linguistic, 'objectivist' view of commonality was the definitional 'common features' view that terms were sorted into categories according to their characteristics. For example, Malinowski's definition of 'the family' specified

> a universal function, the nurturance of young children, mapped onto (1) a bounded set of people who recognized one another and who were distinguishable from other like groups; (2) a definite physical space, a hearth and home; and (3) a particular set of emotions, family love. (Collier, Rosaldo and Yanagisako 1982, p. 27; paraphrasing Malinowski 1913)

By contrast, Lakoff offers a 'gestalt' model of commonality, often centred by 'prototypes' or by stereotypes that metonymically stand for a category as a whole and serve 'the purpose of defining cultural expectations' (Lakoff 1987, p. 82). These are 'standard' examples. Collier et al.'s critique of Malinowski implicitly follows Lakoff's critique of objectivist positions: Malinowski's 'common features' argument cannot adequately differentiate 'families' from 'nonfamilies' and, instead, projects a prior set of modern Western cultural expectations (standards and norms) about proper families. 'The family' is a cultural category centred by a prototype (consisting of clustered concepts that are standardized)[5] and radially graded according to deviations from the proper prescribed form (see Moynihan (1986) for further prescriptive examples and Jennings and Champlin (1993) for a critique of his prescriptions).

Lakoff also employs a 'container' metaphor to represent some kinds of categories. 'Containers' imply an in/out criterion of some kind, a boundary principle or process. 'The market', for example, is not governed or contained by 'the family' and does not manifest 'familial' relationships – though it has sometimes been implied (namely by Becker 1981) that the family is contained by the market; it has been said to exhibit quasi-market relationships, though it deviates from strict market rationality insofar as individual rationality in the market is replaced by the dominant, altruistic utility function of the head of household. Arguments about the family as a quasi-market have been considered offensive, even ridiculous by some, in part because they violate the boundary principles in more conventional views of market and family categories (Jennings and Waller 1990). If 'the market' (or 'the family') does not encompass all social phenomena, there must be in/out criteria, however.

SYMMETRY

The concept of symmetry frequently arises in economics as a characteristic of a matrix or as a relationship between sets. The concept of asymmetry is most frequently encountered in the context of information asymmetry. Akerloff's (1970) market for 'lemons', where the supplier of automobiles has more information than the buyers of automobiles and the acquisition of information about the qualities of automobiles is costly, is the most cited case.

For our purposes it is useful to be a bit more precise about what symmetry means. Specifically we want to be clear about what characteristics of the mathematical concept of symmetry we are importing when we employ the concept metaphorically in an economic context. Bas C. Van Fraassen's description of symmetries is extremely useful for that purpose:

> Symmetries are transformations (technically one-to-one functions which map onto their range) that leave all relevant structure intact – the result is always exactly like the original, in all *relevant* respects. What the *relevant* respects are will differ from context to context. So settle on some respect you like: colour or height or cardinality or charm or some combination thereof. You have now partitioned your domain of discourse into *equivalence classes*. The little square in which individual x is located represents its equivalence class S(x): the class of those individuals which are exactly alike x in all the respects you designated as relevant. These equivalence classes form a *partition*: that is, their sum is the whole domain and they are disjoint from one another . . .
> To sum up, S is like this:
> 1. (a) everything bears S to itself (S is *reflexive*)
>   (b) if a bears S to b, then so does b to a (S is *symmetric*)
>   (c) if a bears S to b, and b bears S to c, then a bears S to c (S is *transitive*)
> This terminology is that of logic, and in logic any relation which satisfies (a)–(c) is called an *equivalence relation*. (1989, p. 243, original emphasis)

Van Fraassen's characterization of symmetry brings its two most important aspects into sharper focus than most economic uses of this term do. First, this is a logical relationship that groups things on the basis of identical qualities. Second, the qualities are not intrinsic to the things but are constructed by whoever is doing the grouping. The very meaning of the concept of symmetry implies the presence or absence, or possibly the measurement, of some quality. More pointedly, symmetry presupposes valuation processes and the establishment of value criteria. But additionally Van Fraassen refers to a transformation that leaves the essential characters intact – there is therefore the conservation of that quality that is symmetric.

The usefulness of this definition of symmetry does not end with mathematical systems or their applications in various fields such as economics. At the heart of symmetry lie constructions of 'sameness' – likeness in all designated relevant respects – that correspond to the common features attributed to a category in thought. Lakoff employs a 'gestalt' model of categories, however, so 'common features' must be viewed as symmetries apprehended by means of the category, as prototypical clusters of concepts and standards or metonymic stereotypes that later represent a category in some manner, rather than as the terms that originally define it. That is, defining characteristics are subsequent attributions, possible only when the basic category is already apprehended. The category itself is prior to and necessary for constructions and/or attributions of symmetry.

Common features and symmetries are aspects of the manner in which categories are manipulated or projected, rather than building blocks for such categories. Malinowski undoubtedly began with a modern Western category (vision) of 'the family' rather than one created out of perceived common features. Symmetries are constructed, not given (or 'found'). Many symmetries, constructed to solve particular problems, may be poor representations or descriptions of the category's content, especially for other purposes. This might be especially true in the messy world of self-reflexive social theory and evolving social processes.

MIROWSKI'S SOCIAL VALUE THEORY

Philip Mirowski's recent work on social value theory is quite useful in making the concept of symmetry explicit in the context of valuational processes. Its significance is not yet clear to most economists, however, nor have its institutionalist moorings been explicated. We thus embark on a quite lengthy presentation of Mirowski's views[6] and an account of how his symmetry arguments might be generalized for use beyond the market context he emphasizes.

Mirowski sees all systems of value as social constructions. A quality or value is identified as being present in diverse objects, activities or other things. This common quality, whether real or imputed, becomes the value to be assessed. In economics the theory of market price has been the dominant orientation of value theory. In classical economics the quality/value that centred price was a substance, labour, that was imputed to all things that were bought and sold as commodities. The various versions of the labour theory of value were all different ways of imputing this quality to commodities. The price system, understood as markets, was the valuational process by which this quality/value was measured in monetary terms by price.

Mirowski notes that the neoclassical economists sought to banish value altogether (1990, pp. 692–3). But the mathematical formalisms that neoclassical economists borrowed for constituting the utility framework, from proto-energetics physics, carried with it a field theory of value. There are two consequences of this change that are important for our purposes. First, the tautological relationship between utility and price, often noted by institutionalists, is a consequence of this formalism. In the field formulation of value '. . . money and utility are effectively ontologically identical' (Mirowski 1989, p. 231). Second, the formalization of economic theory using a field metaphor for value requires that symmetry be imposed upon the field in order for the problem to be tractable. This means the quality/value is conserved over the field. Utility and money become interchangeable and are value in this framework.

Mirowski does turn his attention to institutionalism, wherein the structure of value is rooted in contingent social institutions and processes (Mirowski 1991a, p. 556). Within institutionalism the quality/value of interest is determined in the course of a particular social problem to be solved. An active process of valuation is imagined, rather than the passive representations of value as either labour or utility in substance and field theories of value. To avoid relativism, different institutionalists have developed different forms or categories of social valuational processes in which to situate determinations of value. In the tradition of John R. Commons, reasonable value concerns how important qualities/values emerge through political processes designed to resolve social problems. In the Veblen–Ayres tradition instrumental valuation identifies technological social processes as the locus of value. 'Technological' refers to the pragmatic problem-solving processes associated with organized scientific, technological and educational activities, where the social protocols of (provisional, fallible but corrigible) science are used to identify, measure and assess the particular qualities/values for a particular problem. Both these traditions within institutionalism offer frameworks of valuational *processes* rather than a universal quality/value that is hegemonic in economic matters.[7]

Mirowski's contribution retains the processual emphasis; it is really an archeology of market processes that explicates implicit social valuational processes involved in coordinating markets as a social institution. Thus his work takes him into the market terrain of price theory usually occupied by mainstream economists. His is an institutionalist theory of price as a social valuational process in market economies, however, and his system is neither 'natural' nor individualistic. Value is regarded as socially and historically constructed.

Mirowski's purpose is to construct a social theory of valuation in market transactions that makes the underlying social beliefs about market valuation more apparent and thereby partially explains why it is self-sustaining and self-legitimizing. He also addresses the disjunction between idealized social beliefs and the behaviour in actual markets, and how this disjunction is managed within the structure of social beliefs.

Mirowski proposes four separable, but related issues that must be addressed in a theory of market valuation: the constitution of the identity of the commodity; the conceptualization of trade as a network of permitted and blocked exchanges of idealized classes of goods between individual human beings; the description of the institution of 'value' as distinct from, yet predicated upon, the previous issues; and the expression of the contingent character of value. He expresses these with four types of mathematical formalism suited to his purpose (Mirowski 1991a, pp. 566–7),[8] though the formalisms need not concern us here.

In an earlier article Mirowski writes that value theory historically has addressed three questions:

(1) What is it about a market system that renders commodities commensurate, and hence susceptible to valuation?

(2) What conservation principles embody the tenets posited in the answer to (1), thus permitting quantitative causal analysis?

(3) How are the conservation principles identified in (2) linked to the larger metaphorical structures in the culture for purposes of justification and legitimation, given that all conservation principles are ultimately unjustifiable? We here use the terminology of 'conservation principles' in much the same way that it is used in physics: namely, as invariants or symmetries imposed upon a problem in order to simplify its solution. (Mirowski 1990, p. 693)

Again, Mirowski is attempting to explain market exchange by identifying cultural conventions that address the four prior issues and thus legitimate and sustain the market as a valuational process in society. He is not describing a natural process, but the historical construction and interpretation of a cultural process.

In Mirowski's treatment of social value in market exchange, money becomes the value invariant, the socially constructed value standard employed to express the value of commodities ('commoditiness' being a socially imputed quality/value) by a commonly accepted measure of that quality/value: price. Markets become a consistent and coherent system of value only if the value of money is held to be invariant by the participants, even though many of them understand that the value of money is changing all the time – albeit within socially acceptable limits. For markets to work people must also accept that the quality/value of imputed commoditiness – a cultural fiction imputing a common quality to all items exchanged – is accurately measured through market competition resulting in a price, which is expressed in terms of a conventional metric, money, whose value is deemed invariant.

In Mirowski's framework and most others, value theories must identify that which is to be valued.[9] The value quality must be identified and rendered measurable. This can be done through the construction of a fixed value standard, as when adopting a measurement standard such as the metre for measuring height; or alternately by accepting inexact conventions of tall, average and short for measuring height. The need for a numerical value metric is a historical development in the case of market transactions arising from the need for a price system to make the market exchanges coherent for its participants. But it is not a requirement of value standards in general.

In classical substance theories of value, the quality that made the commodity valuable (labour) was conserved in exchange; in later neoclassical field theories of value, individual exchanges did not conserve value (utility), but the field metaphor implied other conservation principles (namely, the sum of utility and money) that were not apparent to many of the economists developing the metaphor (Mirowski 1989, p. 231). Mirowski employs the concept of arbitrage as a mechanism through which the invariant character of money can be asserted and the conservation principle (value in the system of exchange, 'commoditiness' or, more simply, price) can be maintained. Arbitrage, which in the formal theoretical characterization of market transactions eliminates price differences for the same good and thereby eliminates profit opportunities, allows market economies to be modelled (by providing a mechanism that reconciles actual market transactions with the symmetry required by the idealized version in the model). Simultaneously the arbitrage concept provides an ideological justification and legitimation for the outcomes of market processes and for treating money as invariant; thereby supporting a strong cultural acquiescence to the functioning of the market as a distributional mechanism (Mirowski 1991a, pp. 574–9; Ellerman 1984).

Mirowski replaces conceptions of value premised on a natural order with a socially constructed theory of value for markets. Of interest for us are the notion of symmetry in markets and the notion of a value invariant (a standard metric of value). Classical, neoclassical and Mirowski's social value theories posit symmetry in market exchange, albeit of different kinds. The power of symmetry is the feeling of coherence – the belief that the system works[10] and is fair, the absence of unearned profits and the belief that no one gets something for nothing. All of these characteristics of the model, imputed to the functioning of the actual economy, contribute to legitimacy and justification for the market system and for the theories that purport to describe and explain its workings. This is the purpose of a social value theory after all. The socially valued quality is distributed, not dissipated, in a credible, culturally prescribed way.

But just as profit does occur in market economies and the value of the money does change, so it is the case that the messiness and complexity of real human behaviour disturbs the well-ordered world of the formal model. Both regular profits and arbitrage profits violate the symmetry of the model. Mainstream economics assumes that price arbitrage has already occurred and thereby assumes away problems of actual human behaviour, such as failures to conserve value in exchange that would open the possibility of unequal and exploitative exchanges. The model remains an idealized version of the exchange system, useful for legitimizing the system and its outcomes, but very poorly describing, representing or explaining it.

Mirowski (1994b) explores the cultural character of arbitrage processes using the history of measurement as an example of particular social arbitrage processes. The occurrence of measurement error means that the results of measuring the same term or terms in differing contexts may not be quite commensurate. Things that 'should' be equivalent, are not. Put simply, error arbitrage processes reconcile incommensurabilities so that a value for constants can be socially agreed upon for further inquiry. Mirowski notes that actual groups of scientists have created social structures whose purpose is to reconcile the differences in the measured value of these scientific terms – a form of error arbitrage. This is similar to John R. Commons's notion of reasonable value.

This leads to the following general observations about social value theories:

1. Identification – Social value theories require that some quality be identified or imputed to a socially significant group of people or things that are taken to be similar because of the presence of this quality. This quality is the value.
2. Constructing a value invariant – People must be able to ascertain the presence or absence of the quality/value (present or imputed) in the things or people in the group. The ability to measure the amount of the quality/value is even better. While the process of identification and the construction of a value invariant or metric can be conceptually separated, the two elements are almost always collapsed into a single social phenomenon (Kula 1986). The quality that can be measured is likely to become the valued characteristic; and simultaneously, its measurability will determine the value metric. The tautological character of utility, price and value, all measured in terms of money in neoclassical economics – or alternately, price, value and money becoming simultaneously the expression and measure of the value of commodities in exchange in Mirowski's formulation – is actually typical (Mirowski 1991a, pp. 566–7).
3. Symmetry or conservation principle – There must be some socially prescribed relationship among the members of the group of people or things for the group to be meaningful. The relationship could be one of equality, proportionality or the presence of the quality rather than the absence of the quality. The character of the particular metric constructed for the particular value/quality will influence the character of the relationship – but not determine it. As mentioned earlier we can measure height continuously (in inches or metres), but often measure by a looser interval metric (short/tall).
4. Arbitrage process – There must be some mechanism for reconciling conflict between the prescribed relationship and the perceived occurrence of the quality/value within the group.

Mirowski's attempt to construct a social value theory represents values, value metrics and value criteria as entirely cultural constructs, eschewing inferences of them from principles of natural law and even the use of natural metaphors (from physics or biology, for example) as analogues for social values and valuational processes. He intends his theory to provide the basis for an empirical research programme situated 'within a social process of *comprehending* the economy: no more treating people like inert unselfconscious atoms' (1991b, p. 37; emphasis added). It holds that markets 'work' by virtue of historically instituted arbitrage processes (see endnote 5) such as double-entry bookkeeping, the banking system and the rise of monetary authorities to keep the conventional value invariant at least relatively invariant and permit reasonably accurate calculations of 'the possible implications of our activities in the present and in the future' (1991b, pp. 34–5).

Mirowski's demonstration that market exchange can be expressed formally as a system of culturally accepted social conventions and not as a manifestation of any natural order (or by necessarily importing any naturalistic metaphors) is ingenious. It also shows the fragility of this social valuational framework. We will now use some of Mirowski's insights and language in combination with Lakoff's arguments (and our own previous work) to move beyond market exchange and into the system of institutionally organized and categorized social valuation processes that we see as constituting culture.

INSTITUTIONS AND SOCIAL VALUATION

The processes by which values are rendered commensurable all involve the historical construction of social meaning, though such processes are not always sufficiently self-conscious to warrant the term 'arbitrage' (see endnote 5). How are Mirowski's arguments about market values and arbitrage related to valuation processes in other institutional settings, such as the family? Becker and Malinowski offer two readily accessible cases to examine in this light. Both of them will be found lacking, though for different reasons, and the reasons suggest two different aspects of institutional valuational processes – namely valuation as the expression of prescriptive norms within institutional categories and as asymmetrical, dualistic disjunctures that order relationships across institutional contexts of valuation. A third aspect, the emergence of values from formal arbitrage processes that adjudicate value conflicts in society, will be described as well.

Becker (1981) treats the family as a quasi-market; using (fairly) standard Marshallian rational choice theory, Becker then finds the patterns of household division of labour, and consequent human capital investments and wages, just as desirable to all participants (that is, to both men and women) and just as fair as economists think that market outcomes are. Male–female wage differentials in markets cannot then be explained in terms of social and familial norms and/or gender roles, as many feminists would have it (such prior norms are expunged by rational choice within the family), nor does the wage gap appear discriminatory. It is held by many of Becker's critics that he misrepresents the family.[11] It is not a site of individualistic decision making as he supposes, nor is it as fair as he concludes that it is, nor can social norms be dismissed from the choices of men and women. Such criticisms are reasonable, but Mirowski's work makes more fundamental criticisms possible.

Mirowski's analysis implies a more basic critique of Becker that starts earlier, with Becker's initial view of 'the market'. In Mirowski's approach (see also Jennings 1994), the simple barter imagery that has been commonplace in standard economics since Adam Smith is simply inadmissible. 'Practical' economists, such as those assisting in the market reforms of Eastern Europe and the former Soviet Union (whatever their other faults), all know this and have made the establishment of a proper monetary framework for new markets their first order of business. But once it is clear that an adequate view of markets demands an adequate view of monetary and other conventionally instituted social arrangements, Becker's extensions of market principles to families lose their foundations. Standard neoclassical microeconomic barter models bear no resemblance to actual historical markets, which do require institutionalized monetary arrangements (nor does stylized neoclassical barter resemble the forms of actual barter that anthropologists have studied in nonmarket societies). But without these stylized barter assumptions Becker could never map from market to familial processes. Instead, asymmetries and disjunctures appear in consequence of recognizing the role of money in markets. Considering money greatly complicates understandings of families. They do not possess the same kinds of value invariance, are not 'exchange' and certainly have no means of generating arbitrage-free 'prices'. Markets and families involve quite different institutional processes of valuation.

Money matters in families, too, of course (see Zelizer 1994).[12] The importance of markets in modern society and the commodification of most consumer goods assures this. Families both need money and have budgets and financial plans denominated in money. That is only to say that families need access to markets, however, not that the two are structured as similar institutional categories. Instead, we should seek an analysis of the structuring symmetries and social arbitrage mechanisms that have contributed to the institutional stability of families over time. Again, the analysis must be historical, but we should not expect the kind of stability that Mirowski depicts for markets by means of mathematical formalisms. Commodification – which, as Mirowski shows, rests on money and quantitative commensurability – is not a central feature of modern family life, so value invariance will appear quite differently.

Mirowski's view that value invariants and arbitrage mechanisms permit orderly human comprehension of and action within markets puts the discussion of institutions into terms compatible with Lakoff's gestalt approach to cognitive categories. It is the history of social constructions that have, partly by trial and error over relatively long periods of time, yielded a coherent configuration – but that does not require any particular participant to comprehend all that is involved in market processes. Lakoff holds that ordinary human comprehension rests on the social acquisition of simpler categorical gestalts. Knowledge of the underlying intricacy of the structured processes to which ordinary people contribute (or of scholarly analytical representations of them) is not the source of the working gestalts.[13] They are a kind of 'gloss' that helps to maintain the intricacies of the integrated social processes, in part by cloaking their prescriptive nature in the guise of eternal verities.

We could analyse Malinowski's Victorian prescriptions for the family, many of which are still with us in only somewhat modified form (think of the 'family values' debates), within Lakoff's framework. 'The family' would appear as a category cluster (a list of features, ordered by their perceived importance) identifying the value criteria by which a particular family would be seen as either a 'good' or 'poor' example (or prototype) of the category 'family' (see Lakoff 1987, pp. 74ff.). This would illustrate how the family functions as an instituted system of social prescriptions and valuations. Interestingly, the prescriptions also proved capable of defining class aspirations and motivating important, historically observable emulatory processes in Victorian society.

Malinowski's timeless, pancultural prototype projected specifically Victorian, and specifically middle class, prescriptions for families and gender roles. The prescriptions were not adequate as descriptions or explanations of even Victorian families. As an implicit valuation system for grading and ranking families, however, they became a central goal of working class men's struggles for 'family wages' in the nineteenth century. The prescriptions simultaneously delegitimated working class women's struggles for better wages and working conditions in the same period. 'Proper' women were supposed to be home nurturing, and it was thought that paying them a living wage would only encourage impropriety. In fact, 'a woman's wage' was almost oxymoronic; they earned only 'their keep' or, often, something less (Kessler-Harris 1990). Thus the value system of the family has affected market valuations of both men's and women's labour. Alternately, consider Veblen's view that families were socially ranked by the pecuniary criteria of markets.

The value systems of market and family have interacted. We have analysed some of the patterns of their interrelationship and traced the history of their social differentiation elsewhere (Jennings 1992, 1993). Their interaction is governed partly by the manner of their differentiation, or boundary conditions. Boundary conditions between market and family emerged in more or less their present form with nineteenth century industrialization and are structured (that is, the disjuncture is *ordered*) in the form of classical Cartesian dualisms. Or, as Collier, Rosaldo and Yanagisako (1982, p. 34) express it, 'what gives shape to much of our conception of the family is its symbolic opposition to work and business . . . to the market relations of capitalism'.

The dualistic structure of market and family valuational oppositions is itself a ranking system; Cartesian dualisms such as mind/body, reason/emotion, man/woman prioritize and generalize one term in each pairing while devaluing and particularizing the other.[14] Market/family dualisms are a second kind of valuational process, operating at a higher level of abstraction than the market or family processes themselves (since they order the family's disjuncture from the market); they govern familial norms by prescribing appropriate interactions between 'family' and 'market'. Dualisms bridge – not *a*bridge, as Becker's approach does – the disparate social valuational systems and institutional gestalts, but do so asymmetrically (see Jennings 1992, 1993).[15]

There is also a third aspect of institutional valuation processes, namely formal arbitrage processes in valuation and social change. Markets, for entirely historical and social reasons, have a (more or less) invariant standard of value, money, which is necessary for arbitrage-free coherence in markets. Arbitrage mechanisms are systematically constructed social processes for reconciling deviations, incommensurabilities and conflicts within the uncertainty and flux of social systems. They introduce greater stability. Such mechanisms also exist beyond the market. Judicial decisions, for example, concern the formal establishment of social norms. 'The state' itself exists partly for purposes of social arbitrage and conflict resolution. Interestingly, however, the courts – or legislatures, or even regulatory processes in the executive branch of government – do not address all variations, disjunctures or conflicts that may disturb normal prior practices. Conflict resolution is more or less 'privatized' when official bodies do not deign to accept public, formal arbitrage roles in those cases.

Formal arbitrage processes have done far less to 'standardize' the family than has been the case for markets. Instead, we are socialized to conventional familial gestalts that prescribe, but do not formally enforce, 'proper' family forms, roles and behaviours save by invidious distinctions (that is, informal social pressures of reputation and personal worthiness). Many laws (the existing Social Security system, for example) do formally reward traditional or penalize nontraditional family forms, but they do not prevent the proliferation of new family forms (and sometimes even inadvertently promote them). Advocates of 'family values' may attempt to reverse such informal trends, through measures such as the 1996 Defense of Marriage Act in the US. DOMA is an effort to stave off eventual social recognition for the new forms (such as same-sex marriage). As Commons (1924) noted, however, many judicial and legislative actions are simply *de jure* acknowledgements of current *de facto* practices; DOMA represents a refusal to formally recognize informal social and valuational changes that are already occurring.

CONCLUDING REMARKS

We think these arguments are capable of considerable further extension and application. In addition to historical questions concerning the social evolution and institutionalization of value standards and arbitrage processes, and the valuational analysis of cognitive institutional clusters such as 'the family', many other more specific topics can also be suggested. Social distinctions between paid and unpaid labour, for example, are probably grounded in the dualistic disjunctive ordering that distinguishes the family from the market and cannot be analysed with the current tools of economics; the same is true of women's relative invisibility in national income accounts. Symmetry and asymmetry concepts probably also have applications to theories of social change over time, as do analyses of cognitive categories. Social change is nothing but a process of changing social categories, practices, settings and values that is constrained but not determined by past or present orderings.

Value theory in economics has traditionally been represented as 'price theory' and value is often merely identified with prices. This makes economic discussions of value hopelessly narrow, static, one-dimensional and trivial for most purposes. Even the instrumental valuation advocated by some institutionalists has tended to lack substance or method; we suggest here that it should be understood in terms of Commons's view of reasonable value and analysed as an aspect of the evolution of institutions, cultural dualisms, historical arbitrage processes and less formal means of conflict resolution such as social movements expressing group aspirations. If economics is to be useful for understanding and assessing social processes and well-being, better studies of actual valuational processes in the market and in other areas of society are sorely needed.

NOTES

1. Our lived experience is a seamless whole. We conceptualize and build systems for understanding that experience employing categories. The categories are abstractions constructed from actual events. The categories, in turn, are relationally organized, usually hierarchically, based on some conceptual scheme. The particular conceptual scheme selects the metaphorical relationship between different levels of hierarchical ordering. The ontological status of different hierarchical classifications schemes is highly controversial; see for example the essays in Douglas and Hull (1992). We use the term 'levels of abstraction' or levels of analysis to refer to different points of entry within a particular hierarchical conceptual scheme. Leslie White (1969) used chemical, physical, organic and super-organic (culture) to distinguish different levels at which human behaviour could be understood. Tony Lawson (1994) distinguishes among the actual event, the empirical experience of the event and the possibly unobservable deep causal structures of events in his analysis of social phenomena. Whether a particular entry point in the analysis of cultural behaviour is higher or lower, more general or specific, and so on, depends on the particular organization of each conceptual scheme. Similarly the 'level' that seems most 'natural' will be a result of a combination of factors including how the things in a category are experienced by people, and how the category's name fits into the grammatical structure of their language and the overall symbolic system of the culture.
2. Lakoff's discussion of the innate human capacity to categorize runs remarkably parallel to Veblen's discussions of human instincts as hereditary traits whose substance is thoroughly conditioned by social evolution. See Jennings and Waller 1998 (forthcoming).

3. 'Furniture', for example, is not a basic category. If you try to form a mental image of 'furniture', the image will most likely be of something that is a basic level category: a table or chair, a bed, a sofa. The specific features in the image will tend to be vague, however; the imagined chair will probably not be detailed enough to identify it as a Queen Anne chair but will tend to be more 'generic'. It may be this 'visualizing' aspect of basic categories that makes textual examples so telling for most readers or that makes reification so common in abstract arguments. Categories and associated concepts are most readily learned as gestalts (figures, images of the whole).

4. See Polanyi (1957), for example, on 'Aristotle Discovers the Economy', for an account of social orders that have not traditionally distinguished a category of economic activity from among other activities. Mirowski's (1985) descriptions of early business accounts, in which household silverware, for example, was sometimes included as a business asset, are also interesting; households and businesses were not fully distinguished as family and market institutions, even in Western society, until the nineteenth century. Jennings (1992) explores the historical development of market–family distinctions during the nineteenth century in Britain and the US.

5. Ian Hacking (1995) also uses the term 'prototype' (pp. 33–5) to describe the social process whereby clusters of symptoms of uncertain aetiology (causality) are placed together by the medical community to describe some disorders. He analyses the social process by which a disorder (his example is that of multiple personalities) is defined, identified, redefined, disputed and made an official part of the medical lexicon which, in turn, is widely used by medical practitioners, hospitals, insurance companies and the legal community. The creation, by members of these relevant communities, of a prototype and protocols of diagnosis is an explicit case of a social arbitrage process (discussed below). The conscious and explicit character of the construction of a disorder, its definition, boundaries, and the groupings and interconnections involved is different from the way that many social prototypes operate, insofar as the latter are often unconscious or will be only 'privately' arbitraged or negotiated by more inchoate social discourse – though they may define aspirations and objectives in historical social struggles (see below).

6. We are grateful for the benefit of extended conversations with Mirowski about his social value theory and our interpretations of his work. Although we believe what follows is an accurate rendering of his positions we take full responsibility for any misrepresentations that may remain.

7. But see Mayhew (1987), who expresses concern that Ayresian formulations of instrumental valuation may require a pan-cultural view of warranted knowledge that may be inconsistent with institutionalism's reliance on cultural analysis.

8. The issues are addressed employing measurement theory, graph theory, abstract algebra and probability theory respectively (Mirowski 1991a, pp. 566–7).

9. Explicitly religious theories of value do not always identify that which is to be valued.

10. The purpose of symmetry in mathematics is to make a problem solvable. In some simple sense then, when applied to social valuation, symmetry imposes a kind of equality on the problem, or at least, an algebra of value emerges. Ultimately some sort of equational justice is implied in the valuation system. The authors thank Marc Tool for bringing this to our attention.

11. Becker does, however, quite properly recognize the economic significance of many family activities. At issue is how he recognizes it (see Jennings 1994).

12. It is also clear, however, that the family does not systematically 'commodify' its resources or products and, partly for this reason, is not 'monetized' in the same sense as markets are. The fact that money does play a role in families, however, means that, to understand the family, some bridge across monetized and non-monetized interactions is needed. This raises very difficult issues since commodities and familial sharing (gifts?) are not concepts in similar social categories (see Mirowski 1994a and forthcoming).

13. Acquiring such gestalts usually occurs by socialization and immersion. Witness the present difficulties in the former Soviet Union, where 'socialization' to market gestalts is not an option.

14. Gallaway (1994) suggests another way that boundary conditions might be structured in his discussion of 'the edge', a concept borrowed from ecology to describe the very special conditions existing where distinct ecosystems meet.
15. The asymmetry involves not only the prioritization of markets over families in social desiderata of well-being, or of market over familial roles in social rankings, but also an asymmetry concerning which domain must accommodate the other in cases of conflict. 'The market' is not expected to accommodate 'the family' or thereby introduce 'personal', particularized criteria into market calculations; instead, the difficult work of navigating such conflicts is privatized as 'individual responsibility'. The substantially mythical content of such asymmetrical prescriptions, especially as they involve women's relationships to markets, is noted in Jennings (1992). Dualistic constructions, like Mirowski's value invariants, need not be 'realistic' – that is, adequate or accurate descriptions of reality – to function in social valuation.

REFERENCES

Akerloff, George (1970), 'The Market for Lemons', *Quarterly Journal of Economics*, **84**, pp. 488–500.
Becker, Gary (1981), *A Treatise on the Family*, Cambridge, MA: Harvard University Press.
Collier, Jane, Michele Rosaldo and Sylvia Yanagisako (1982), 'Is there a Family?', in B. Thorne and M. Yalom (eds), *Rethinking the Family*, New York: Longman.
Commons, John R. (1924), *The Legal Foundations of Capitalism*, New York: Macmillan.
Douglas, Mary and David Hull (eds) (1992), *How Classification Works: Nelson Goodman Among the Social Sciences*, Edinburgh: Edinburgh University Press.
Ellerman, David (1984), 'Arbitrage Theory', *SIAM Review*, **26**, pp. 241–61.
Gallaway, Terrell (1994), 'A Look at Cost Shifting and Externalities', Department of Economics, Colorado State University.
Hacking, Ian (1995), *Rewriting the Soul*, Princeton: Princeton University Press.
Jennings, Ann (1992), 'Not the Economy', in W. Dugger and W. Waller (eds), *The Stratified State*, Armonk, NY: M.E. Sharpe.
_____(1993), 'Public or Private?', in M. Ferber and J. Nelson (eds), *Beyond Economic Man*, Chicago: University of Chicago Press.
_____(1994), 'Towards a Feminist Macroeconomics', *Journal of Economic Issues*, **28**, June, pp. 555–65.
_____ and Dell Champlin (1993), 'The Cultural Contours of Race, Gender and Class Distinctions', in D. Brown and J. Peterson (eds), *The Economic Status of Women Under Capitalism*, Cheltenham: Edward Elgar.
_____ and William Waller (1990), 'Constructions of Social Hierarchy', *Journal of Economic Issues*, **24**, June, pp. 623–31.
_____ and _____(1994), 'Evolutionary Economics and Cultural Hermeneutics', *Journal of Economic Issues*, **28**, December, pp. 997–1030.
_____(1998), 'The Place of Biological Science in Veblen's Economics', *History of Political Economy*, forthcoming.
Kessler-Harris, Alice (1990), *A Woman's Wage*, Lexington: University Press of Kentucky.
Kula, Witold (1986), *Measures and Men*, Princeton, NJ: Princeton University Press.

162 *Institutionalist Method and Value*

Lakoff, George (1987), *Women, Fire, and other Dangerous Things*, Chicago: University of Chicago Press.

Lawson, Tony (1994), 'A Realist Theory for Economics', in R. Backhouse (ed.), *New Directions in Economic Methodology*, New York: Routledge, pp. 257–85.

Malinowski, Bronislaw (1913), *The Family among the Australian Aborigines*, London: University of London Press.

Mayhew, Anne (1987), 'Culture: Core Concept under Attack', *Journal of Economic Issues*, **21**, June, pp. 587–603.

Mirowski, Philip (1985), *The Birth of the Business Cycle*, New York: Garland Publishers.

_____(1989), *More Heat than Light*, New York: Cambridge University Press.

_____(1990), 'Learning the Meaning of a Dollar: Conservation Principles and the Social Theory of Value in Economic Theory', *Social Research*, **57**, pp. 689–717.

_____(1991a), 'Postmodernism and the Social Theory of Value', *Journal of Post Keynesian Economics*, **13**, pp. 565–82.

_____(1991b), 'Arbitrage, Symmetries, and the Social Theory of Value', Department of Economics, University of Notre Dame, Notre Dame, Indiana.

_____(1994a), 'Tit for Tat: Concepts of Exchange, Higgling, and Barter in Two Episodes in the History of Economic Anthropology', in N. de Marchi and M. Morgan (eds), *Higgling: Transactors and their Markets in the History of Economics*, *History of Political Economy*, **26**, suppl. Durham: Duke University Press.

_____(1994b), 'A Visible Hand in the Marketplace of Ideas', *Science in Context*, **7**, Autumn, pp. 563–89.

_____(forthcoming), 'Refusing the Gift', in Steve Cullenberg (ed.), *Postmodernism and Economics*, London: Routledge.

Moynihan, Daniel Patrick (1986), *Family and Nation*, New York: Harcourt Brace Jovanovich.

Nelson, Richard (1995), 'Recent Evolutionary Theorizing about Economic Change', *Journal of Economic Literature*, **33**, March, pp. 48–90.

Polanyi, Karl (1957), 'Aristotle Discovers the Economy', in K. Polanyi, C. Arensberg and H. Pearson (eds), *Trade and Markets in the Early Empires*, Glencoe: The Free Press.

Van Fraassen, Bas C. (1989), *Laws and Symmetry*, Oxford: Clarendon Press.

Waller, William and Ann Jennings (1990), 'On the Possibility of a Feminist Economics', *Journal of Economic Issues*, **24**, June, pp. 613–22.

White, Leslie (1969), *The Science of Culture*, New York: Farrar, Strauss & Giroux.

Zelizer, Viviana (1994), *The Social Meaning of Money*, New York: Basic Books.

Index